Hildegard Mary Ryan, OSB

OBSCULTA
LISTEN CAREFULLY

A Study of Benedictine Continuity of Charism and Tradition with a focus on the Benedictine nuns of *Subiaco*, Rydalmere, New South Wales, Australia

Studies in
Australian Colonial History
— 7 —

Hildegard Mary Ryan, OSB
OBSCULTA
LISTEN CAREFULLY

A Study of Benedictine Continuity of Charism and Tradition with a focus on the Benedictine nuns of *Subiaco*, Rydalmere, New South Wales, Australia

BOLT PUBLISHING

Obsculta. Listen Carefully: A Study of Benedictine Continuity of Charism and Tradition with a focus on the Benedictine nuns of Subiaco, Rydalmere, New South Wales, Australia.
Studies in Australian Colonial History (ISSN 1834-6936) No. 7
© Hildegard Mary Ryan 2024

Bolt Publishing Services Pty.Ltd.
ACN 123024920

Cover pictures:
Front: *Subiaco* front drive, *ca.* 1910
Rear: View of *Vineyard*, Parramatta, *ca.* 1851–1858.

ISBN Paperback   978-0-9946349-4-8
ISBN e-version   978-0-9946349-5-5

A catalogue record for this book is available from the National Library of Australia

Cover design and layout by Lankshear Design.
Printed by Ingram Spark Lightning Source.

PUBLISHER'S PREFACE

Many are content to live life as it is. Others are inspired by a grander vision of what life ought to be. Their 'faith, hope, and love' play out within the plans and purposes of the living God, who has revealed himself in the Lord Jesus Christ. This long vision fills everyday existence with great significance. The key human need becomes to listen. Despite the clamour of the world. For the world's sake.

Obsculta is not *obscuritas*. For the outside 'observer' without any concern to understand, the beliefs and practices of others are overlooked, dismissed, or even condemned. They become obscure by the 'observer' not observing at all. Because second-century Christians didn't worship the Roman pantheon of gods, they were accused of being 'atheists'. Because they loved 'brother and sister', they were 'incestuous'. Remembering the death of Jesus Christ by 'eating' his body and 'drinking' his blood: 'cannibals'. For those having eyes, but never seeing, everything remains in *obscuritas*. Even the light is turned into darkness.

Such *obscuritas* is overcome by *obsculta*, listening carefully. In all the sheer brilliance of his humanity, Jesus of Nazareth clarified human complexity from the depths of his divinity. One of his pithiest sayings points the pathway to understanding: 'see how you hear' (Mark 4:24). Mixing his metaphors of sense experience, he declared that proper sight only comes through proper hearing. Since the coming of Christ into this world, the light is now shining into the darkness, and the darkness is not able to overcome it (John 1:5). The darkness is overcome by the light. *Obscuritas* is overcome by *obsculta*. Insight only comes through listening carefully.

In the third decade of the twenty-first century, listening is no longer easy. The 'cancel culture' arising from human ideology shouts down alternative voices. Conversation is replaced by conflict. It is no longer fashionable to listen to anybody whose lifestyle may disturb the prejudices of the current political status quo. Since the eternal gospel travels on human lips through human conversations, when such unwillingness to listen is applied to the people of God it stifles the opportunity to hear his word and experience its transformative power (1 Thessalonians 2:13). That is a risk best run by nobody.

In the previous century, Karl Barth was not a stranger to ideologically-caused turmoil himself, nor to the contrasting and calming message of the gospel of Jesus of Nazareth. Seeing such turmoil as evidence that the idol was shaking, he counselled:

> Those who do not want to be afraid must be people who have decided to see with their own eyes, to hear with their own ears, and to think with their own heads. They must not let themselves be turned into a mass product through public opinion or propaganda. Peace is in danger because there are so few free people.[1]

Sitting on the edge of Australian society from colonial times through to today, a small group of Benedictine nuns has quietly gone about their daily business, driven by their commitment to listen carefully to the living God—always for the sake of the world they serve by their seclusion. Those who have chosen the pathway of *obsculta*, deserve such *obsculta* from others. Now, for the very first time, the story of these women has been told from within.

Peter Bolt, March 2024

---

1   Barth, 'Fearless', 12.

STUDIES IN AUSTRALIAN COLONIAL HISTORY
ISSN 1834-6936

1. Peter G. Bolt, *Thomas Moore of Liverpool (1762–1840): One of Our Oldest Colonists. Essays & Addresses to Celebrate 150 Years of Moore College* (2007).
2. Peter G. Bolt, *William Cowper (1778–1858). The Indispensable Parson. The Life and Influence of Australia's First Parish Clergyman* (2009).
   – Full-text Edition
   – Commemorative Pictorial Edition produced for Cowper200.
3. Peter G. Bolt, *A Portrait in his Actions. Thomas Moore of Liverpool (1762–1840). Part 1: Lesbury to Liverpool* (2010)
4. Peter G. Bolt, *A Portrait in his Actions. Thomas Moore of Liverpool (1762–1840). Part 2: Liverpool to Legacy* (forthcoming)
5. David B. Pettett, *Samuel Marsden. Preacher, Pastor, Magistrate and Missionary* (2016)
6. Peter G. Bolt & Malcolm Falloon (Eds.), *Freedom to Libel? Samuel Marsden v Philo Free: Australia's First Libel Case* (2017)
7. Hildegard Mary Ryan OSB, *Obsculta. Listen Carefully: A Study of Benedictine Continuity of Charism and Tradition with a focus on the Benedictine nuns of Subiaco, Rydalmere, New South Wales, Australia* (2024)

PROLOGUE

*O*bsculta is the first word of the Benedictine Rule written for monasteries by Benedict of Nursia in the Sixth Century AD. *Obsculta* translates into English as 'listen carefully', with the expectation of making a response.

Literally, as part of verse 1 of the Prologue to the Rule of Benedict, it is a call to: *Obsculta [...] et inclina aurem cordis tui*—'listen carefully [...] and incline the ear of your heart' to the precepts of the Benedictine Rule.[1]

Secondly, and more broadly, as interpreted in the last two hundred years, it has come to mean a listening to the voice of Christ in the poor, the dispossessed, victims of violence, and in the case of the community which is the focus of this book, to the needs of Australian society in general. It is the challenging, prophetic call to which Benedictines are attuned on a daily basis, first in Liturgical Prayer and *lectio divina*, and secondly in their ministry to those who come to the monastery seeking God.

In the present day, with the Abbey now situated in the Jamberoo valley, on the beautiful south coast of New South Wales,[2] this Benedictine community provides retreats, spiritual direction, financial support for refugee families, a safe environment for the victims of the Stolen Generations, and hospitality to victims of sexual abuse by Catholic

---

[1] This call echoes 'that to be found in the wisdom literature of the Old Testament'; Fry, *RB 1980*, 411.
[2] See https://www.jamberooabbey.org.au.

clerics. These are the fruits of Benedictine monasticism, which takes 'the gospel for its guide'.³

Obsculta, in its magnanimous understanding, is a spiritual force which impels Benedictine women and men across the world to witness to the love of Christ for his people on earth.

---

3   Fry, *RB 1980*, Prologue, v.21.

CONTENTS

Publisher's Preface	vii
Prologue	xi
Tables of Figures and Illustrations	2
Author's Preface	3
Introduction	5
1. Foundresses for the Australian Benedictine Women's Community	35
2. Beginnings	59
3. Obsculta: the *Labora* (work) of the Benedictine Rule	77
4. A Window into the Subiaco Community (1856–1864): Tradition as tyranny	87
5. The Subiaco School (1851–1854)	109
6. The First Elected Prioress Walburge (Ruth Woods) Wallis (1864–1889)	129
7. Continuing the Wallis Years (1889–1902)	155
8. Prioress Ignatius (Louisa) Harnett (1902–1915)	203
9. Prioress Mary Joseph (Hilda) Brady (1916–1945)	217
10. Prioress Mildred (Gladys) Potts (1945–1957): Leaving Subiaco	265
Conclusion	277
Bibliography	281
Acknowledgements	307
Index	313

TABLE OF FIGURES

FIGURE	DESCRIPTION	PAGE
1	Catholic Emancipation in England	7
2	Timeline for the Order of Saint Benedict from Europe to the Australian Mission, AD 480–1847	32–33
3	The Early History of 'The Vineyard'	61
4	The daily Horarium at Subiaco	68
5	Deaths at Subiaco from Tuberculosis 1850 to 1900	83
6	Liturgical Classification of Feasts	166–167

AUTHOR'S PREFACE

This book is a study of one monastery of Benedictine nuns, who came from England to the Colony of New South Wales in 1848–49. Their story revolves on the first word of their Rule: *Obsculta* (listen). Their lived *obsculta* embraced the Benedictine values of: prayer (*lectio Divina* and the Liturgy of the Hours), work, peace and justice, zeal for the gospel of Christ, and preference for Christ above all. Until now, their history has, for the most part, been hidden behind the history of a male-dominated Roman Catholic Church. The fact that they have survived in Australia for over 170 years, while remaining obedient to the Roman Catholic Church, is a statement of the strength of these monastic women who allowed the flame of their courage, determination and faith, to shine brightly within this ancient land.

This book has been written through the academic support of the Sydney College of Divinity. Both Professor James Harrison and Professor Peter Bolt have encouraged me in the writing and publication of this story. I also acknowledge the encouragement of Fr. Michael Casey, OCSO, a prolific author, whose monastic theology and spirituality has enlightened my community for over fifty years. Three scholars who guided me and fine-tuned this history were: Dr Stefano Girola, Dr Mary O'Connell and Dr Shé Mackenzie-Hawke. Mrs Verity Chianea assisted me with the archaic style of French, found in a set of Monastic Constitutions of the 18th Century.

The two archivists who preceded me, Sr Marie Therese Malone, and Sr Marie Gregory Forster left a legacy of material waiting for someone to come along and pull it all together. I hope I have done that. Without their research this book wouldn't be possible.

Finally, I owe gratitude to our Abbess Emerita Mary Barnes, for appointing me to this work. In the present, Abbess Hilda Scott and my community have given me support and encouragement. This book is a gift to my community—past, present and future.

Today, the community at the centre of this book dwells in a monastery which nestles under the Illawarra Escarpment, on a portion of the land of the Dharawal Nation. They respectfully acknowledge the people of the Dharawal Nation, who trod this land before them.

Sr Hildegard Mary Ryan
February 2024

INTRODUCTION

This is a study in Benedictine continuity of charism and tradition. It will look at the history of the Benedictine nuns who came to New South Wales at the instigation of John Bede Polding (1794–1877), the First Catholic Archbishop of Sydney, and who, in the spirit of Benedictine *obsculta*, responded to the 'susceptive and responsive' quality which shaped their story within the story of Australia. To understand the beauty and value of the mission, it begins with a brief introduction to the Rule of St Benedict (hereafter RB80), and a general timeline. Subsequent chapters will then detail the specificity of each aspect of the Benedictine history, and in particular the Benedictine women who shared in the shaping of Catholic Australia.

Continuity of charism

While the meaning of charism is essentially 'gift', it is, in the case of religious groups, a gift given by God for the service of God's people, usually described as 'Church'. In the Greek New Testament, charism means gift, bounty, benefit, favour, grace, which is given freely. The charism of a religious congregation forms a set of core values which gives it identity. These core values are embraced by the members of any religious group, in every culture and every age. Charism is the way by which members of religious institutions follow Christ.

In the case of Benedictines, the core values which form charism are: the daily celebration of the Liturgy of the Hours, silence for continuous prayer, *lectio divina* (primarily prayer with the Sacred Scriptures), manual work, reverence, obedience, stability, humility, and renunciation of possessions. There is a reference to the Eucharist in RB80 63:4, but this celebration of *communio* is not mentioned in the liturgical code of the Rule of Benedict. The opinion of the editors of RB80 is that there was at the time 'a ritual of Communion (outside Mass) that included the exchange of the kiss of peace'.[1] The core values which form the charism of the Benedictine monastic life are not presented in the form of an inventory or directory. They are situated throughout the Rule of Benedict, and the formation of a Benedictine monk or nun introduces them to these values which will characterise their lives.

Since no monastic community or Church community stands alone apart from the wider Australian story, the research and assessment of primary and secondary sources behind this book was carried out against a background of sociological and historical awareness. This involved the reading of historical works exploring the Victorian era in Australia, the effects of Federation, two world wars, and the great depression of the 1930s. The book also briefly refers to post-World War II industrialisation because of its adverse effect on the community in question.

Catholic emancipation in England

After a prolonged absence since the dissolution of the monastries under Henry VIII (1535–1540), Benedictine monasticism returned to England in the Nineteenth Century, when the English Government began permitting monks and nuns to re-found monasteries in the British Isles, albeit very cautiously. Catholic Emancipation was a process which began with the Catholic Relief Acts of 1778 and 1791, and culminated in the Catholic Emancipation Act of 1829. When this final Act was passed in England, there were four houses of Benedictine nuns and two houses of Benedictine monks. At that time, some of these Benedictine houses had a school or boarding school attached. Daniel Rees notes that the two Benedictine houses of men, Downside and

---

[1] Fry, *RB 1980*, 411.

Ampleforth, 'lived in discreet obscurity, running their modest schools and serving remote mission chapels'.[2] Other houses were established in the 1850s and throughout the remainder of the Nineteenth Century. Just prior to the end of the Eighteenth Century, the houses of Benedictine nuns were: Brussels, Paris, Ghent, Cambrai, and Montargis. Never one of the 'historic English houses in exile', the Montargis community was rather a French refugee community.[3] Returning to England in 1795, the community of Cambrai became the Stanbrook community, settling at Callow End, Worcester, in 1838, before moving 170 years later to its present-day situation in North Yorkshire.[4] From the nuns of Stanbrook and those of Montargis came the two foundresses of an Australian Benedictine monastery: Dame Magdalen le Clerc, and Sr Scholastica Gregory.

Figure 1: Catholic Emancipation in England

1778	Catholic Relief Act	Permitted Catholics to join the army and purchase land, if they took an oath of allegiance. Still no freedom of worship.
1791	Catholic Relief Act	Granted freedom to worship. Removed a wide range of other restrictions. Allowed Catholics their own schools, to hold junior public offices, and to live in London.
1800	Act of Union	Subsequently political rights for Catholics driven largely by Irish politics.
1823		Irish barrister, Daniel O'Connell, forms the Catholic Association. Mass movements in Ireland demand full public and political rights.
1828	Sacramental Test Act	Repealed requirement that government officials take communion in the Church of England.
1829	Catholic Emancipation Act	Allowed Catholics to sit as MPs, vote in elections and hold most senior government offices.

Source: https://www.parliament.uk

2 Rees, 'Benedictine Revival', 327.
3 Rees, 'Benedictine Revival', 327.
4 https://www.stanbrookabbey.org.uk/page-ourroots.html.

Transition from England to eastern Australia

The passing of the Act of 1829 removed and reduced many of the restrictions on Roman Catholics. The Sacramental Test Act of 1828 (England) had removed the barrier that required certain public officials to be members of the Established Church. The effects of this Act were seen immediately within the penal colony of New South Wales, Australia.

On 21 November, 1829, the first Catholic Irishman to be appointed to high office in the colony of New South Wales, Roger Therry, was appointed as Commissioner of the Court of Requests in New South Wales and Victoria. O'Farrell notes that Roger Therry soon became 'a champion of Catholic causes'.[5] The second Catholic Irishman to be appointed to high office in the colony of New South Wales was John Hubert Plunkett. Plunkett, a barrister and politician, had worked with Daniel O'Connell in the emancipation movement of Ireland, and yet ironically he received the position of Solicitor General of New South Wales, arriving in 1832.[6]

The first two Catholic chaplains had been in the colony since 1820. These chaplains, the Rev. John Joseph Therry and the Rev. Philip Connolly, worked under Governor Macquarie and in accordance with the restrictions imposed upon them. John Hubert Plunkett brought a third Catholic priest with him: Father John McEncroe. In the beginning, his ministry was to convicts. In his private life, he battled alcoholism. 1840 saw him conquer the demon, and he then became a 'vigorous campaigner for Total Abstinence'.[7] Eventually he was someone the Irish community could look up to. McEncroe led the Irish 'towards temperance and social equality against Protestantism—and against Polding's [Benedictine] dream',[8] which was to found the Archdiocese of Sydney on the pillars of Benedictine monasticism. The Irish McEncroe was a diocesan priest who favoured his own version of ministry.

Within five years of Therry's ministry, he manifested a turbulent

---

5   O'Farrell, *The Catholic Church*, 30. Roger Therry's daughter, Jane, entered the Subiaco community with the women brought to Sydney by Polding. Therry's 'Last Will and Testament' is held in trust by the community of Jamberoo Abbey.
6   O'Farrell, *The Catholic Church*, 81.
7   O'Farrell, *The Catholic Church*, 81.
8   O'Farrell, *The Catholic Church*, 81.

personality, willing to work neither within the system of the established religion, nor with the Government of the colony of New South Wales. Governor Darling had Therry dismissed and his salary discontinued. The Government made money available for his fare back to England, but he refused to leave the colony. It would be twelve years before Therry would be reinstated as a Catholic priest authorised to work in the colony.[9]

The Rev. Daniel Power replaced him, at the request of Governor Darling. The position rendered the priest powerless to minister to the Catholic community because of Therry's constant undermining of Power's official position, using both religious politics and financial power. After Power died in the colony in 1830, another request was made for a Catholic chaplain. This time the lot fell to Christopher Dowling, an Irishman and a member of the Dominican order. For the same circumstances as endured by Power, Dowling was no more able to carry out his duties as chaplain.

It was the arrival in the colony of Governor Richard Bourke in 1831 that 'seemed to mark a revolution in the attitudes of authority [...] towards Catholics'.[10] Brownrigg describes Governor Bourke as possessing a 'consideration of the Rights of Man and a clear-sighted vision of his mission to assist with the rehabilitation of human beings who had erred'.[11] As a mark of his magnanimity, he went so far as to give a grant of five hundred pounds towards the building of St Mary's Church. Even then, Therry managed to foster dissent, dispute, and opposition, threatening physical violence against workmen trying to mark out the boundary for the building. This was the final act which led Governor Bourke to request the appointment of a Catholic prelate with ecclesiastical power. The man appointed was William Ullathorne, an Englishman, and a Benedictine Monk of Downside Abbey—the more prominent of the two Benedictine houses of men which were

9   O'Farrell, *The Catholic Church*; Birt, *Benedictine Pioneers*, 117–265. O'Farrell, *Documents in Australian Catholic History*, 7–74. Butler, *Life and Times*, 26–54.
10 O'Farrell, *The Catholic Church*, 81.
11 Brownrigg, 'Notes on Sir Richard Bourke', 2, who refers to Cleary's description (*Australia's Debt*) of Richard Bourke, Roger Therry, and John Hubert Plunkett as 'the Great Irish Triumvirate', 50.

in existence in England in 1829. He had been exposed spiritually and intellectually to the teaching of John Bede Polding, his novice master at Downside. Polding himself cherished a desire to 'devote himself to missionary life in Australia [...] and enkindled this fire in some of his novices'.[12]

Downside Abbey, Bath, England

With the arrival of William Ullathorne, and his appointment as Vicar General,[13] the Benedictine tradition was planted in the colony of New South Wales, a tradition which in the Nineteenth Century responded to the contemporary needs of Church and society. The Benedictine missionary trend, as Marie Gregory Forster has noted,[14] was shaped by the missionary trend of the wider Catholic Church, by the reality of colonial expansion, and by the wave of new 'thought' following the French Revolution and industrial development. Suttor describes the English Benedictine Congregation as that which 'became the main actuation of England's Catholic remnant'.[15]

Ullathorne met opposition to his appointment from Irish Priests

---

12 *Stanbrook Abbey Chronicles*, Chapter XXXVI, 659, 'The Parramatta Foundation in Australia'. Stanbrook Abbey Archives.
13 Ullathorne was appointed Australian Vicar General by Bishop Morris of Mauritius, Australia being under the ecclesiastical jurisdiction of Mauritius.
14 Forster, 'Monks–Monasteries–Mission', 39–74.
15 Suttor, 'Polding's Intellectual Formation'.

and Irish Catholics. The need for more clergy led him to write to his superiors in the English Benedictine Congregation. At the same time, the Irish turned for support to the Archbishop of Dublin. What O'Farrell calls 'an Irish ecclesiastical imperialism'[16] blinded the Irish clergy and Catholics to the peace and unity which could have prevailed on the Australian mission had Irish/English differences not held sway.

In September 1835 the first Roman Catholic Bishop arrived in Sydney—John Bede Polding, English and Benedictine—Ullathorne's novice master. This appointment had been the result of Ullathorne's request for more priests for the colony. Polding had finally been able to fulfil his own desires for evangelisation within the penal colony of New South Wales. Henry Norbert Birt notes: 'on that momentous 29th June [1834], Dr. Polding received the unction of Episcopal consecration in Bishop Bramston's private chapel in London, and Australia received its first [Roman Catholic] Bishop'.[17]

Birt also informs readers that Polding was highly regarded at Downside, and that his appointment as Bishop to Australia was a great loss to the Downside community. Birt cites the letter written by the prior of Downside to Pope Gregory XVI, asking that Polding's appointment [to Sydney] be reconsidered. In the *Downside Review* of April 1881, Polding is described as the column and mainstay of the establishment [Downside], the one 'on whom the entire studies of the college depend'.[18] O'Donoghue places Polding at the centre of an education which attracted 'the sons of old Catholic squires like the Vaughans'.[19] Australia, it seemed, was in for its own version of formation, education, and ministry.

The Rule of Benedict

Benedictine men and women profess to live under a rule and an abbot/abbess. The Rule of Benedict is a sixth-century Rule which, in

---

16 O'Farrell, *The Catholic Church*, 39.
17 Birt, *Benedictine Pioneers*, 231. Polding received the appointment of Vicar Apostolic of New South Wales—Bishop *Hiero-Caesaria in partibus*.
18 Birt, *Benedictine Pioneers*, 232.
19 O'Donoghue, *The Bishop of Botany Bay*, 6.

INTRODUCTION 11

its precepts and values, is Christological. As stated in the Prologue to this book, it begins with the word *obsculta* (listen carefully).[20] The first sentence of this ancient rule, 'listen carefully my son [child] to the master's instructions and attend to them with the ear of your heart',[21] is anchored in the wisdom tradition of the Old Testament; therefore, it sets the 'wisdom' tone of the Rule and is related to the key notion of the monastery as a 'school of the Lord's service'.[22] The Christology of the Rule is most evident in its application to the incarnation of Christ in the form of humanity.

A contemporary writer takes up the *obsculta* of the Benedictine Rule and makes the strong connection with verses 9–13 of its Prologue: 'Let us [...] open our ears to the voice from heaven that every day calls out this charge: "If you hear God's voice today, do not harden your hearts" (Ps. 94:8)'.[23] Through the ages of Benedictine monasticism, the first duty of a Benedictine monk or nun has always been responsive listening to the Holy Spirit. John Bede Polding described it as the 'susceptive and responsive quality of soul' necessary for Benedictine monks and nuns.[24] In the Twentieth Century, the 1967 Congress of Benedictine Abbots saw *obsculta* as the 'primary duty of a Benedictine: achieving and maintaining a constant sensitivity to the working of the Holy Spirit within, and a readiness to respond'.[25]

In the spirit of the *obsculta* of the Benedictine Rule, the first Benedictine missionaries came to New South Wales to minister to the spiritual needs of the Catholic population by administering the sacraments of the Catholic Church, visiting those in prison, ministering to the sick in

---

20 *Auscluta* is the form of this word which is used in the oldest extant manuscript of the Rule of St Benedict, the Codex Hatton 48, held in trust in the Bodleian Library in Oxford. The form *obsculta* is used in the Codex *Sangallensis* of 914.
21 Fry, *RB 1980*, Prologue, v.1.
22 Fry, *RB 1980*, Prologue, vv.1,45.
23 This is clearly evident in William Ullathorne's pamphlets, printed while in England in 1836–38: *The Catholic Mission in Australasia*, and *The Horrors of Transportation Briefly Unfolded to the People*. He also gave first-hand evidence to the Select Committee on Transportation. His Ministry to convicts on Norfolk Island filled him with a passionate revulsion for the degradation of human beings caused by the penal system: Ullathorne, *The Catholic Mission in Australasia*.
24 Stanbrook Abbey Annals – Memorial to Polding.
25 Congress of Benedictine Abbots. A Statement on Benedictine Life, 1:15, 8.

Sydney and the outer regions, presiding over funerals, and giving catechetical instruction.[26] What emerged as one of the dominant needs of the time was education of the young. This led to Polding establishing St Mary's Seminary in Sydney in 1838. He foresaw that the school would bring forth 'a native race of priests and statesmen, of lawyers and physicians, of soldiers, sailors and artists',[27] who would be leaders in the colony and strengthen the influence of Roman Catholicism.[28]

Suttor, interweaving the words of Ullathorne with his own, states that 'the nineteenth-century English Benedictines knew their heritage'.[29] That heritage celebrated Benedictines having been at every major turning point in European history and contributing to the arts, to industrial work, and inventions which advanced civilisation in the Middle Ages. Polding, like monk-missionaries before him, was filled with the ideal of monasticism as a driving force of evangelisation in the New World—specifically Australia. The need for education also led to Polding's request for a foundation of Benedictine nuns in the colony. In the Eighth Century, Boniface of Devon had made a similar request for Anglo-Saxon nuns to join him and his apostles in their mission to the Teutonic people. If the heart of history is story, this and similar stories would have been firmly implanted in the missionary spirit of Polding.[30]

Method

To understand why specific methods have been chosen in the research behind this book, it is perhaps important to begin with Benedictine

---

26 O'Farrell, *The Catholic Church*, 41. More lengthy summaries of Polding's early missionary work can be found in Birt, *Benedictine Pioneers*.
27 Haines et al., *The Eye of Faith*, 225.
28 Polding's plan for Benedictinising the Catholic Church of Sydney would, in the end, fail. But the failure, as Suttor describes, was 'his failure to transplant his intellectual milieu, one he himself helped create, in Australian soil'. Suttor, 'Polding's Intellectual Formation, 15–28. This is what most disappointed and disillusioned Roger Bede Vaughan, who came as Polding's coadjutor in 1873.
29 Suttor, 'Polding's Intellectual Formation', 15.
30 This history is part of the formation classes given to all sisters in initial formation at Jamberoo Abbey.

methodology and its components, especially that of 'continuity'. As one of the foundations of Benedictine monasticism, the principle of 'continuity' is lived out in the Benedictine vows of obedience, stability and conversion of life. Christ is the foundation of the Benedictine vows, which are lived in community. The word used by the Benedictine Rule for 'community' is *coenobium*.[31] In the *coenobium*, Benedictines willingly take on the precepts of the gospel of Jesus Christ, as expressed in the charisms and tradition of the Benedictine Rule. This effectively enables monks and nuns of any historical period to continue what was begun by Benedict of Nursia, Italy, in the Sixth Century AD.

By understanding the Benedictine Rule and method, this book employs a variety of parallel methodological tools. It draws on historical research based on the analysis of primary and secondary sources, such as church histories; canonical documents; correspondence between church authorities and the leaders of the community under scrutiny; community chronicles and letters; archival documents and Vatican documents. It will also apply some elements of discourse analysis as it speaks to 'history from below'.[32] Using this variety of tools enables reading, assessing, comparing, and analysing the history of the continuation of Benedictine charism and tradition in the context of the first one hundred years of the women's Benedictine mission in New South Wales.

In part, this book also performs a genealogy of the Benedictine tradition from Nursia, Italy, the birth place of St Benedict and his twin sister St Scholastica (c. 480), to the new and changing Australian landscape of the mid-1800s in New South Wales, where the Benedictine mission flourished. By mapping the historical and epistemological fields in this way, this book bridges the gap of representation that has left many histories of oral and epistolary nature on the periphery of dominant discourse, and therefore not considered as legitimate history.

Hence, this multi-faceted method enables the consolidation of some of those previously under-written histories of Benedictine women within the broader framework of the Benedictines of New South Wales, and the general history of the times. In defence of the work being

---

31   The *coenobium* is literally the coming together as a community.
32   Jenkins, *Re-thinking History*; Rediker, *The Slave Ship*; Port, 'History from Below', 108–113.

undertaken and the method employed, Jenkins can be cited:

> [...] no historian can cover, and thus re-cover, the totality of past events because their 'content' is virtually limitless. One cannot recount more than a fraction of what has occurred and no historian's account ever corresponds precisely with the past: the sheer bulk of the past precludes total history.[33]

Genealogy

If genealogy is an analysis of descent[34] and a search for traces, then it seems appropriate to include whatever traces and lines of descent from Nursia, Italy, are available and which inform the legacy that the Australian Benedictine movement inherited. The first section of this book therefore undertakes a rudimentary genealogy of the Order of St Benedict prior to its mission to Australia. This serves to develop an understanding of how such an Order—with its own particular method—undergirded the establishment of the Benedictines in Australia.

The genesis of the Rule of St Benedict—beginning with the word *obsculta*—is analysed within this genealogical thread. To that end, the method of discovery in the genealogy gives access to, and close analysis of, two original texts written by or about St Benedict during (or shortly after) his life.

The most important of these is the 'Rule for Monasteries', written by Benedict of Nursia for his own monastery of Monte Cassino. The second is 'Book Two of the Dialogues of Pope Gregory the Great (540–604), the Life and Miracles of St. Benedict'.[35] While Benedictine historians once used only these two texts, they have become aware, through research in the latter half of the Twentieth Century, that the genuine facts stated in Gregory's work need to be separated from, and even sifted out of, imagination and symbolism. While historians would prefer more facts and fewer miracles,[36] it is not always possible

---

33 Jenkins, *Re-thinking History*, 11.
34 Foucault, *Archaeology*.
35 Vogüé, *Benoit*.
36 Fry, *RB 1980*, 76–77.

from available literature to distinguish between the two. At this point, however, it is important to note the place St Scholastica had in the emergence of the Benedictine tradition. 'That Pope Gregory the Great was moved to write their story (not just Benedict's story), [… and] records the visit of St Benedict to his twin sister Scholastica' three days prior to her death, provides some testimony for her value in the early development of monastic/Benedictine tradition and for Pope Gregory, beyond any speculation to the contrary.[37]

It is the first text, the actual Rule of Benedict, which guarantees continuity of genealogy because of the author's awareness that 'a new beginning had to be made to meet the needs of the times'.[38] It is this 'new beginning' with its freshness that would guarantee the longevity of the rule for monasteries, and would travel through the centuries, adapting to the religious, political, and social needs of every age, while grounded in its own charisms and tradition.

Primary sources and epistolary collections

In relation to primary sources, this book examines and analyses material held in the Jamberoo Abbey Archives (JAA). The nature of these texts varies as follows:

- Canonical documents, such as the report of a canonical visitation carried out by the Catholic Archbishop of Sydney.
- Epistolary collections written to and from church authorities, and letters written home to England by the two foundresses.
- Chronicles of the community from 1849 to 1957.
- Financial records from 1856 to 1949. (In 1856, a ledger was begun with incoming earnings and outgoing expenditure.)
- Relevant archival documents from the English Benedictine Congregation, and archives of the communities of the two

---

37 Hawke, 'Seeking Matrology', 242. See also Farrell, *Solesmes,* 1934, reproduced by Jane Morrissey, 'Scholastica and Benedict': 'The antiphon *Cum Sanctus Benedictus,* speaks of St Benedict seeing the soul of his sister entering heaven in the form of a dove', and appears in the *Monastic Antiphonal.*
38 Fry, *RB 1980,* 72.

foundresses: Stanbrook Abbey, and Princethorpe Priory (no longer in existence).[39]
- Vatican Documents addressed to enclosed nuns of contemplative and monastic communities. The most important of these in its effect on the community in question was the 1917 Code of Canon Law.

It is important to note at this stage that even some of this archival material is biased in the handling of the 'truth'. As in journalism or the media of the present age, often a monastic chronicler consciously or unconsciously stated her preference in any given situation, encouraging the reader to see things from a particular point of view.[40]

Since no monastic community or church community stands apart from the wider Australian story, the research and assessment of primary and secondary sources will necessarily be carried out against a background of socio-cultural and historical awareness. This draws upon selected historical and sociological works which explore the Victorian and Edwardian eras in Australia, the effects of Federation, World War I, World War II, and the Great Depression of the 1930s. It will also briefly consider the impact of industrialisation post-World War II, because of its adverse effect on the Australian psyche generally, and the Benedictine community in question—in particular the relocation of the community from 'the ideal spot whereupon [its] foundation'[41] rested for almost one hundred years.

Australian history

Broader Australian histories are also included in this project to provide historically documented stories. In addition, however, this part of the research includes more recent and at times contested versions of

---

39 All relevant documents from the Princethorpe Archives were gathered and filed in the Jamberoo Abbey Archives through the 1990s.
40 For example, most events are recorded in favour of the prioress. The reason for this is clearly seen in the Rule of Benedict, where a monk/nun is to see Christ in the abbot/abbess (2:2 and 63:13). Any writing to the contrary would be in opposition to the Rule of Benedict.
41 Birt, *Benedictine Pioneers,* 141.

Australian history and identity. A brief account of the empirical works of authors such as Henry Reynolds and Manning Clark has been embedded to provide the reader with a more inclusive history of Australia through its many transitions. This, however, acts as an adjunct to the primary historical focus of this book, which has previously received insufficient attention: the history of Benedictine women's monasticism in Australia.

Discourse analysis and 'History from below'

Discourse analysis critiques existing and accepted research methods and discourses, such as dominant historical and political accounts of events, to glean the lesser-known perspectives from the periphery. In brief, discourse analysis investigates the questions of who speaks for whom and why, who is remembered and why, and who or what is intentionally (and also unconsciously) left out of the telling—and furthermore, what motivates such erasures.

In the Australian historical context, this would include women, indigenous Australians, people with disabilities, and the under-class, contrary to the famous words of Henry Parkes, Father of Federation, who said: 'The crimson thread of kinship runs through us all'.[42] 'All' is a bold claim and as history has shown, 'all' doesn't include everyone. As David Hitchcock says of the past and the present: 'The recovery of voices missing from the historical narrative is a central purpose of history from below'.[43] The intention of using this discourse is to rigorously include marginalised voices and histories, thereby giving the under-written and under-valued a valid place on the contemporary page, and attending to the ethical imperative of full representation. As Port makes clear, 'people's history makes a radical departure from traditionally mainstream historiography which long tended to

---

42   Henry Parkes: 'The Crimson Thread of Kinship'.
43   David Hitchcock, 'Why History from below matters more than ever'. Hitchcock is an active and world-renowned practitioner on 'history from below'. He concentrates not on the traditional subjects of history, but on ordinary working-class people, not simply for what they experienced in the past but for their ability to shape the way history happens.

concentrate on high level politics and diplomacy, warfare, and the lives of great statesmen'.[44]

Literature review

This is the first time, since the Benedictine nuns began their Australian foundation on 2 February 1849, that a study like this has been undertaken. A few papers found in the Abbey Archives reveal attempts to consolidate the said history at crucial times of change in the life of the community, and to claim an Australian identity for women's monasticism. Prior to the 1970s, a lack of resources and the limitations of papal enclosure for nuns (from 1921) prevented communication between the nuns and historians of the Australian Catholic Church. The Second Vatican Council brought the freedom needed to begin publication of papers in the newly-founded Australasian Benedictine Review. This Journal, known as *Tjurunga*, began publication in 1971.[45] Bearing the restrictions of papal enclosure in mind, and because no single history of the Benedictine women in eastern Australia yet exists, the literature review for this project is divided into four sections.

The first will survey sources specific to Benedictine history, such as *Life and Miracles of St. Benedict: Book Two of the Dialogues*, by Pope Gregory the Great; the Rule of St Benedict in its own historical setting. The two volumes of Henry Norbert Birt will be considered as 'a later history'. The second section includes other religious histories in Australia that make some reference to the Benedictine story. For example, *A Dynamic of Hope: Institutes of Women Religious in Australia* by M. R. MacGinley will be a priority. Archives and Epistolatory Correspondence, thirdly, provide invaluable insights into some insiders to this story and, finally, sources dealing with the evolution of Australian society paint the backdrop against which these under-written women made their quiet contribution.

---

44   Port, 'History from Below', 108–113.
45   *Tjurunga* was the offspring of the Benedictine Union of Australia and New Zealand. The name is an indigenous word for sacred stones or sometimes pieces of wood. A full explanation of the choice of the title can be found in the first edition of the periodical (1971).

Benedictine-specific history

The *Life and Miracles of St. Benedict* is the second of four books written by Pope Gregory the Great, collected under the title, *The Dialogues of St. Gregory the Great*. It is presented by 'adopting the ancient form of the dialogue, which goes back at least as far as Plato'.[46] Gregory uses 'his deacon, Peter, as the eager listener who asks naïve and sometimes rather obtuse questions to elicit the pontiff's teaching'.[47] In the preface to *Book Two*, Gregory sets out the course of Benedict's call to a life of prayer and asceticism, and in so doing, sets the nature of the call of every 'monastic'[48] who will follow in his footsteps. Pope Gregory

> accompanies him [Benedict] from his home in Norcia, to Rome, the scene of his studies. Then comes the saint's flight from the city to Affile and shortly after to the wilderness at Subiaco, where he spent three years in solitude, preparing for his future work by a life of prayer and fasting.[49]

As with all desert mothers and fathers, Benedict also confronted the 'tempter', and continued to do so, constantly opposing the temptation to destroy the monastic environment.

Gregory presents a sequential genre: temptation, victory over temptation, an increasing light of holiness for the benefit of others. It is Gregory who witnesses to the fact that Benedict wrote a Rule for monasteries, a rule anchored in Christ and in the wisdom tradition of the Old Testament. The first word of that Rule provides the title for this book: *Obsculta* (listen carefully).[50] Another characteristic of the Rule marks it as acceptable, adaptable, and gospel oriented: moderation. The editors of RB80 cite the fact that Benedict

---

46 Fry, *RB 1980*, 74.
47 Fry, *RB 1980*, 74.
48 Since the 1990s, the term 'monastic' has been used to replace 'monk' or 'nun'. It is an inclusive language word and with poetic licence is used as a 'noun'.
49 Pope Gregory the Great, *Life and Miracles*.
50 Proverbs 1:8; 4:1; and 6:20. The same word 'listen' (hear ye Him) is used twice in Luke 8:8b and once in Luke 9:28. In both Greek and Latin the word implies both a listening and a response.

was aware of the forms of monastic life that had preceded him in both East and West, and drew copiously upon their literature, [but] [...] saw that a new beginning had to be made to meet the needs of the times [...] the collapse of Roman civilization [...] the end of western civilization [...] a seriously troubled ecclesiastical society, [and a] general moral decline that accompanied the decay of an ancient culture.[51]

Henry Norbert Birt's *Benedictine Pioneers in Australia* provides the most factual, insightful and courageous history of the Benedictine mission to colonial New South Wales, specifically to Sydney, from 1835 onwards.[52] It is compiled from statistical records, mission statements and other material sent from Australia to Downside Priory in England. Like most of the early monk-missionaries of Sydney, Birt was a Benedictine monk and member of the same community and therefore had access to letters, historical records, and progress reports concerning the Benedictine mission, so firmly grounded within the English Benedictine Congregation. Of particular interest to this book is his reference to the Benedictine women of Subiaco near Parramatta (New South Wales). Birt relates, with some emphasis, the unsatisfactory financial arrangements between Polding and the nuns, and the frugal regime the nuns endured in the early years of their foundation.[53]

Ann Prendergast researched and wrote 'The Benedictine Schools and Students of Colonial Sydney'.[54] Part of this paper, presented as the Gavin Cashman Memorial Lecture (June 1999), included a generous contribution on the Benedictine school of Subiaco, near Parramatta. In this research, Prendergast was assisted by the community historian and archivist of that time, Marie Forster. Through the 1990s, both women also produced the unpublished document, 'Alumnae Subiaco'. This valuable source consists of an alphabetical list of every pupil who attended the Subiaco school from the first two pupils in 1849 through

---

51 Fry, *RB 1980*, 65–94.
52 Birt, *Benedictine Pioneers*.
53 Birt, *Benedictine Pioneers*, 400–401.
54 This was published in the *Journal of the Australian Catholic Historical Society* 21 (2000), 67–79.

to the official opening of the school in 1851, and up until the close of the school in December 1921.⁵⁵

The Good Samaritan Sisters published the three-volume work, *The Letters of John Bede Polding* in 1998. The editorial board consisted of Forster (a member of the community at the centre of this study), and six Good Samaritan sisters. The letters from Polding to individual members of the Subiaco community are published in Volume 2 and Volume 3. They are an important source of information for assessing the relationship between the Archbishop and the community.⁵⁶

In the 1970s and 1980s, articles written for *Tjurunga* included a well-researched study by Marie Forster on one of the foundresses, Magdalen le Clerc.⁵⁷ Forster used a significant portion of archival material on hand at that time. Then came a series of obituaries for the Benedictine nuns of the community which hold rare biographical material relevant to this volume. These obituaries focused on those women who had died between 1850 and 1987. While presenting interesting sociological background of family life in nineteenth- and twentieth-century Australia, a significant number of biographical details now appear inaccurate. This has emerged from the capacity to access information through advanced technology and the high percentage of Australians researching and writing their family history that at times stands counter to remembered history, mostly in relation to dates. New information is coming into the Abbey Archives on a regular basis. Births, deaths, and marriages are now for the most part available online, through various research engines.⁵⁸

---

55 Forster and Prendergast, 'Alumnae Subiaco'.
56 Sisters of the Good Samaritan, *Letters of John Bede Polding*.
57 Forster, 'Magdalen le Clerc', 259–337.
58 In my role as Abbey Archivist, I have been updating the obituaries since 2003, assisted by the Kiama Family History Centre, and the research carried out by Terry and Wendy Nunan, professional researchers who have assisted me, and who carry out research for the local councils on the South Coast of New South Wales.

General religious history

In 1982, Frances O'Donoghue's *The Life of John Bede Polding, Australia's First Catholic Archbishop* was published, and included a few sentences about the Benedictine women who are the focus of this work. Ronald Fogarty's earlier two-volume work on the History of Catholic Education in Australia from 1806–1950 (1959) refers comprehensively to the contribution of the Benedictine nuns in the field of Catholic education, which is presented as a limited contribution compared with other teaching orders of nuns.

Patrick O'Farrell, in his two-volume work, *Documents in Australian Catholic History*, cites Dr Gregory's Report to Rome on the Australian [Catholic] Mission, c.1850. Focused upon their school, this report contains a reference to the Benedictine nuns as 'recently being established'.[59]

A Dynamic of Hope, the most comprehensive account of religious orders in Australia by M. R. MacGinley, was published in 1996 and re-published in 2002.[60] It includes background on Benedictine monasticism from the Fifth Century to a more recent historical summary on the specific Benedictine community in focus in this volume.[61]

In 2015, Sr Aquinata Böckmann's book, *A Listening Community*,[62] provides a 'Commentary on the Prologue and Chapters 1–3 of Benedict's Rule'. Aquinata Böckmann OSB is a member of the Benedictine Missionary Sisters of Tutzing, Germany. Since 1973, she has taught in Rome, both at the Pontifical Institute for Spirituality and Moral Theology (Regina Mundi), and as the first woman professor at Sant'Anselmo. She is also the author of *Perspectives on the Rule of Benedict* and *Around the Monastic Table*. These sources help flesh out the Australian religious setting, as well as providing useful data on particular religious groups. A close reading of these sources renders a more thorough general history accessible, in relation to specific Benedictine history.

---

59   O'Farrell, *Documents in Australian Catholic History, Vol. 1*, 303–310.
60   Dr MacGinley's book is used as a text book for teaching religious and community history to sisters in formation, so that the wider history of women religious in Australia can be incorporated to prevent an 'isolationist' approach.
61   MacGinley, *A Dynamic of Hope*.
62   Böckmann, *A Listening Community*.

Archives and epistolary correspondence

All letters written by Dame Magdalen le Clerc from Australia to Stanbrook Abbey, England, were transcribed by Marie Therese Malone in the 1980s. Similarly, Sr Scholastica Gregory's few letters have been transcribed and are held in Jamberoo Abbey Archives, but her early death in 1850 limits the historian's research. Ruth Woods Wallis, the first elected prioress of the community, wrote copiously when away from the monastery on two pilgrimages arranged by the archbishops of Sydney during 1876–77, and then 1888–89.

The letters from the community councillors to Cardinal Moran during the 1890s, and the brief replies they received, form the only material which has survived from that era, giving a description of those turbulent and desperate years in which the community fell prey to malicious gossip. Included in this file is the letter from the first Abbot Primate of the Benedictine Confederation, begging Moran to visit the nuns of Subiaco. In addition, the original letters written by Polding and Vaughan to the nuns of Subiaco provide evidence of the written history of Australian Catholic church leaders.

Evolving Australian Society

The backdrop of an evolving Australia is critical to this inquiry with each source contributing something unique. In 1992, Rheem Australia Limited produced a large booklet with a brief history of Subiaco Rydalmere. Most of the nuns' land was purchased by Rheem in the early 1950s, and the Rheem factory commenced work in 1953. Some of the sweeping statements about the nuns and their monastery reveal a lack of serious research. However, its purpose was to collate 'The History of Rheem at Rydalmere', not the history of Subiaco Rydalmere.[63]

2017 saw the published research of Judith Dunn OAM, FPDHS, and Rosemarie Morris FPDHS: *The Parramatta Cemeteries. Saint Paul's, Carlingford, including Private and Demolished Cemeteries of the Parramatta*

---

63   Rheem Australia, *History*.

Area.⁶⁴ This research included the cemetery at Subiaco, Rydalmere, which was exhumed by Rheem in the early 1950s and moved to North Rocks Catholic Cemetery.

C. M. H. Clark, *A History of Australia* IV, covers the initial period of general Australian history relevant to this book, 1851–1888. In 1851, the beginning of the gold rush or 'gold fever' was also the beginning of a boarding school for girls, opened and staffed by the Benedictine nuns of Subiaco, near Parramatta. In his preface to Volume IV, Clark outlines the more serious issues of this period, which also had an impact on the Subiaco community:

> This volume sums up the themes introduced in those earlier volumes—the influence of the spirit of the place on human behaviour, the struggle between classes for the ownership of wealth, the struggle for political power, and the confrontation between Catholic Christendom, Protestant Christianity and the Enlightenment.⁶⁵

Clark is at his best in Chapter 12, 'The Kingdom of Nothingness', in which he exposes those who opposed harmony and unity in the education of children, and those who perpetuated sectarian bitterness. Since the Benedictine women of Subiaco educated Catholic and non-Catholic children alike, their story needs to be inserted into the pages of Australian history as being formed by a charism and a tradition which educated them to take the gospel for their guide,⁶⁶ and to let peace be their quest and aim.⁶⁷

Working with the theories of Keith Jenkins, *Rethinking History*, more light is shed on this fact: 'Women have been "hidden from history", that is, systematically excluded from most historians' accounts'.⁶⁸ The Benedictine women of Subiaco have been overlooked by Australian church histories because when written, the manner of transmission of knowledge was not considered legitimate. Included

---

64   Dunn and Morris, *The Parramatta Cemeteries*.
65   Clark, *History of Australia IV*, vii.
66   Fry, *RB 1980*, Prologue v.21.
67   Fry, *RB 1980*, Prologue v.17.
68   Jenkins, *Re-Thinking History*, 7.

here would be letters, archives, and documents not found on the shelves of public or state libraries. Hence the reparative gesture to mention those women and sources here, and have that testimony legitimated through scholarly discourse.

This book is an attempt to write the women of Subiaco back into Australian history and into Australian Catholic Church history. It is a 'history from below', because it focuses on the 'lives and struggles of ordinary people, social relations at the grass roots, attitudes, beliefs, practices, and behaviour'.[69]

By combining traditional modern history with the more controversial histories, the dominant and the marginal, the second-nature history and the obscure, this book offers not just a re-thinking of history in the Australian Benedictine context, but a re-reading.

Outline and content of chapters

Chapter One will argue for the continuity of Benedictine charism and tradition in the lived vocation of the two foundresses for the Australian Benedictine women's community. Brief biographical details, and the origins of their monastic communities, will be presented. Their transition from England to Australia on H.M.S. *Saint Vincent* will form a large section of the chapter, because of its foundational importance for the future: continuity of teaching of the Rule of Benedict, teaching on the Scriptures, fidelity to the Liturgy of the Hours, to the Mass and Sacraments; theology classes (for the monks), and spiritual instruction for the women. The clash of cultures, French and English, will be assessed from the letters and documents of the first two years. The effect of this situation on continuity of charism and tradition will be noted. A brief but significant account of the individual response of each foundress to the *obsculta* of the Benedictine Rule will be given.

Details of the beginnings of the community's life will be presented in order to emphasise that, as far as possible, the women kept to the charism and tradition of Benedictine monasticism. Details of their first home, 'The Vineyard', will be noted, with a short history of the house

---

69 Port, 'History from Below', 108.

and references to its owner, Hannibal Hawkins Macarthur. The date of the official foundation and the renaming of the house 'Subiaco', after the cave where Benedict of Nursia took refuge from a corrupt Roman society follows, and then an account of the first women to join the community; brief biographical details for the purpose of establishing a community which began and grew from a colonial society, from immigrants with like-minded vision; a new beginning in a new land; the division of authority between the two foundresses and the tensions which adversely affected the fledgling community; the issue of suitable constitutions;[70] and the daily monastic *horarium* of prayer and work—the *ora et labora* of the Benedictine life.

The chapter will end with an examination of the regular observance of the monastic life, and with the response in faith to the challenges of the Catholic mission in the colony of New South Wales.

Chapter Two focuses on the initial work of the community; efforts to remain faithful to the monastic tradition of the Liturgy of the Hours, with paucity of numbers, without a monastic church, and with the heavy laundry work the nuns were asked to undertake for the monks of St Mary's. The continuity of charism and tradition will be woven into Chapter 36 of the RB80, care of the sick, with its Christological foundation. The chapter will end with the death of the first foundress, Scholastica (Jane) Gregory in October, 1850.

Chapter Three argues that the birth of the Benedictine community of Subiaco near Parramatta was hampered rather than helped by the addition of three nuns from Princethorpe Priory, Warwickshire, England. This was organised by Polding. The growth of the Australian foundation was stifled by the imposition of more French customs. An analysis of some of these customs will be undertaken. It was a situation whereby tradition became a tyrant. During this period (1856–1861), racial tensions prevailed and inhibited the freedom to listen to the movements of the Holy Spirit in the Australian Benedictine mission.

---

70   This issue would be a cause of difficulty until early in the Twentieth Century when a set of constitutions, written specifically for nuns, would come into use.

Such tensions ran contrary to the precepts of the Rule of St Benedict, and contrary to Polding's Lenten Pastoral of 1856: 'Australians we should all be. We owe it to each other, we owe it to duty, we owe it to Christianity'.

The chapter notes an example of Polding acting contrary to the rule of Benedict, in a decision which resulted in much of the conflict of this period. It also includes the community's request of Polding to elect their own prioress; the 1864 election of Ruth Woods Wallis; the tensions that emerged between Wallis and le Clerc; the initial difficulties faced by Wallis; and the integrity of Polding in opting for Benedictine tradition when a major difficulty was reported to him.

Chapter Four argues that the Benedictine nuns were 'disposed and responsive to the call of God and the working of the Holy Spirit' in meeting one of the immediate needs of colonial society—the need for education. A 'School for Young Ladies', the official title for the Subiaco School, was established in March 1851. It was, in its essence, a boarding school for Catholic girls, even though Protestant girls also attended the school. In their role as educators, the nuns were listening, in the spirit of the *obsculta* of the Benedictine Rule.

The chapter examines the school curriculum, and the kind of pupil who attended the school. A brief history of Charles Henry Bishop Davis, Polding's coadjutor bishop, in his role as pastor/father of the Subiaco community of nuns and the girls of the Subiaco School, is also considered. Davis' death in 1854 and its effects in the Catholic Church of Sydney,[71] and on the infant Subiaco community warrants significant mention in this chapter. The chapter ends with 1856, when Polding was told by Roman authorities to 'regularise' both the women's and men's communities he had founded.

Chapter Five. This chapter relates the story of the Subiaco School, opened on 25 March, 1851; the school met one of the needs of the colony – the need for education; the school was another continuity of

---

71 See Graeme Pender's ThD thesis on the life of Charles Henry Bishop Davis, for which I was able to share the resources of the Jamberoo Abbey Archives.

a Benedictine tradition which was familiar to both foundresses. Their communities in England were involved in education as a means of earning an income. Sr Scholastica Gregory was educated in the Stanbrook school, and had Dame Magdalen le Clerc as one of her teachers.

Polding had worked closely with the Subiaco community, and from time to time relaxed some rules to accommodate the different climate and culture of Eastern Australia.

Chapter Six argues in favour of Vaughan regarding Catholic education and the closing of Lyndhurst Academy, the Benedictine School founded by Polding. The chapter will conclude with Vaughan's death (1883) and lead into Chapter Seven, the second pilgrimage to England and Europe made by Ruth Woods Wallis to obtain suitable constitutions for the community of Subiaco.

Chapter Seven begins with Wallis' second journey to England and Europe, her exposure to the neo-monastic revival of the Nineteenth Century, and her acceptance of the Beuronese Constitutions, given to her by Maurus Wolter OSB. These constitutions were written for a community of Benedictine Nuns in Prague. Discussing both sides of the problem, the chapter argues that Moran was right in rejecting much of this document. The issue of the Beuronese Constitutions was discussed in *Tjurunga* in the 1980s by Br Terence Kavanagh and Sr Marie Therese Malone. This article will be a point of reference. The chapter traces the years 1888—1902, arguing that the Benedictine community of Subiaco, in spite of opposition from Patrick Francis Moran and other clerics, managed to remain faithful to living the charisms and tradition of the Rule of Benedict. These years are noted in the community's history as years of great suffering, which were confronted with the spirit of the Rule of Benedict: *We shall through patience share in the sufferings of Christ that we may deserve also to share in his kingdom.*[72] The chapter concludes with the death of Ruth Woods Wallis in 1902.

---

72   Fry, *RB 1980,* Prologue, vv. 50, 167.

Chapter Eight considers the Benedictine continuity of charism and tradition as lived by the community in question, from 1902–1915, under the leadership of the second elected prioress, Mother Ignatius (Elizabeth Louisa) Harnett. Brief biographical details, and the colonial background of her family; her Benedictine education (attended the Subiaco School); entrance into the community; formation as a novice; her role as a teacher in the Subiaco School; her service in the community as novice mistress; and her election as prioress of Subiaco, Rydalmere, on 8 December 1902. (The suburb of Rydalmere was founded in 1886). Prioress Harnett inherited a united and stable community, one which had been strengthened by the adverse situation through the 1890s when Cardinal Moran was the Catholic Prelate of Sydney. She had a two-fold focus: to implement the Beuronese Constitutions, and to build a church. The Beuronese Constitutions were implemented with modifications suggested by Cardinal Moran, on 15 January 1903.

The chapter offers an assessment of how these constitutions manifested the Benedictine continuity of charism and tradition. Other relevant material includes first vocations after Federation; biographical details for sociological reasons; completion of the monastic church; further vocations; their biographical details and sociological backgrounds illustrating the nature of Australian society at the beginning of the Edwardian Era; changes in Catholic education; diminishing numbers in the Subiaco School; the outbreak of World War I; the death of the third elected prioress on April 23 2015; financial difficulties, compounded by the war years; the declining numbers in the school; and the number of pupils who couldn't afford school fees. The overall effects of war and poverty on the living of Benedictine monasticism is evidenced in these events.

Chapter Nine documents the period of monastic leadership under Prioress Brady, the third elected prioress: 1915–1945. It will assess the impact of the 1917 Code of Canon Law on the Subiaco community and the ways in which the community had to adapt to meet its norms. These adaptations will be assessed against the charism and tradition of the Benedictine Rule, arguing in favour of continuity.

Chapter Ten turns to the early years of the next prioress, Mildred (Gladys) Potts and her leadership; listening to the precepts of the Rule of Benedict and acting under the influence of the Holy Spirit—the susceptive and responsive quality which shaped this monastic story within the story of Australia; the influence of Columba Marmion; the prioress' grasp of the Christology of the Rule of Benedict; the adverse effects of post-war industrialisation on the health of the nuns; and the need to relocate.

Finally, a brief **Conclusion** bridges the historical community with the community of today.

Figure 2: Timeline for the Order of Saint Benedict
From Europe to the Australian Mission, AD 480–1847

YEARS	EVENT	COUNTRY
480	Birth of St Benedict and St Scholastica—twins	Nursia, Italy
	Early Education at home, further education in Rome	Rome
c. 497	Religious Conversion—renounces material world. Encounters the monk Romanus, entrusts his calling to him and receives the monastic habit	Rome
500	Lived for a while with Romanus in Enfide (now Affide), 'detained by the insistent hospitality of the people' associated with the Church of St Peter (David Hugh Farmer)	Affide, Italy
500	Lived in solitude for three years in a cave	Subiaco, Italy
c. 505	Became abbot for monks who couldn't accept his ideals, and who later tried to poison him	The Subiaco region
c. 510	Returned to Subiaco and was joined by many disciples	Subiaco, Italy
Over a number of years	Established 12 monasteries with 12 monks each / divine administration via number 12	The Subiaco region
529	Founded Monte Cassino Monastery	Monte Cassino, Italy
529–543	Annual visits to his sister Scholastica. On one visit, he witnesses her power of prayer	Cassino Region
543	Death of Scholastica. (Benedict had a vision of the death of his sister, on her way to heaven)	Cassino Region
543	Death of Benedict (depending on source) entombed with his sister	Cassino Region
590–604	Reign of Pope Gregory the Great	Rome
596	Pope Gregory sends Augustine (later known as Augustine of Canterbury) and other monk-missionaries to England	Anglo-Saxon England
c. 598	Royal Family conversion to Christianity traced back to the missionary work of Augustine and friends broadly understood to be Benedictine	Anglo-Saxon England
c. 695	Benedictine Rule brought to Northumbria, by Wilfrid	Northumbria, England
600	Benedictine nuns	Medieval England
664	Benedictine Abbess, Hilda of Whitby, attends Synod of Whitby representing male and female monasteries	Whitby, Anglo-Saxon England
800	Spread of abbeys	Europe
768–814	Charlemagne and Carolingian reform adopt Rule of St Benedict	France
800	Intentional use of word Benedictine, via Benedict of Aniane and Cluny	Aniane, near Montpellier, the south of France
810–820	Benedict of Aniane wrote *Codex Regularum,* and *Concordia Regularum*	Probably his own monastery on his estate at Aniane

817	Benedict of Aniane was recognised by Louis the Pious, successor of Charlemagne, as the reformer who would unify monasteries in his kingdom, under the Benedictine Rule. At the imperial city of Aachen, in 817, the reform was launched	France Aachen (Germany)
909	11 September, foundation of Cluny by William of Aquitane	France
1000–1200	The Benedictine centuries	Europe and the British Isles
1215	Fourth Lateran Council (Pope Innocent III) to reform monasteries	Rome
1300	Benedictine monopoly reduced, new religious orders emerged	Europe and the British Isles
1300	Sylvestrine Congregation founded—still exists, with one monastery in Australia: Arcadia, Sydney, NSW	Italy
1400	Bernard Tolomei founded Olivetan Congregation (still active in Twenty-first Century)	England and Northern Ireland
1517–1564	The Reformation period on the Continent. Disappearance of monasteries	Europe
1540	Reformation in England. Suppression of monastreries by Henry VIII	England and UK
1540s	Monastic houses in exile on continent	Europe
1545–1563	Council of Trent starts the Counter-Reformation	Trent, Italy
1625	9 Catholic women led by granddaughter of Thomas More, Dame Gertrude More, formed a Benedictine community at Flanders	France
1789	The French Revolution	France
1793	France at war with Europe	Europe
1795	Return to England for monastic survivors of war	England
1795–1796	9 Benedictine women establish Abbots Salford	England
1798	14 October, Magdalen (Constantia) le Clerc born. Educated at Abbots Salford	Darrington, Yorkshire, England Abbots Salford
1814	21 October, Magdalen le Clerc entered English Benedictine Community	Abbots Salford
1815	21 April, Magdalen le Clerc clothed in monastic habit	Abbots Salford
1816	12 August, Magdalen le Clerc made profession of Benedictine vows of Obedience, Stability, and Conversion of Life	Abbots Salford
1823–1846	Magdalen le Clerc held office of novice mistress	Abbots Salford and Stanbrook
1838	Relocation of Salford Benedictines to become Stanbrook Benedictines	Stanbrook England
1847	As a Stanbrook Abbey nun, Magdalen le Clerc volunteered for the Benedictine mission to NSW, Australia	Stanbrook England

CHAPTER ONE

Foundresses for the Australian Benedictine Women's Community

Departure from England

This chapter will argue that Benedictine charism and tradition continued in the lived vocation of the two foundresses for the Australian Benedictine women's community: Dame Magdalen (Constantia) le Clerc, and Sr Scholastica (Jane) Gregory. Brief biographical details and the origin of their monastic communities will form part of the narrative. The individual response of each foundress to the *obsculta* of the Benedictine Rule will be discussed. Their transition from England to Australia on H.M.S. *Saint Vincent* will also be discussed at length. The pastoral care of the monks and nuns by Archbishop Polding, on this long voyage, calls on his ministry to the sick, and his teaching skills. He held classes on the Rule of St Benedict and the Sacred Scriptures, the importance of daily fidelity to the Liturgy of the Hours, the Mass and the Sacraments. Theology classes were added for the men and spiritual instruction for the women. Cultural clash and its effect will be noted as a force which militated against the harmony of the Benedictine women's community. The chapter ends with the nuns in residence at St Mary's monastery in Sydney, responding in faith to the challenges of the Catholic mission, and yet in a tenuous situation, awaiting their own house and property.

The principal characters in this history are Benedictine monks and nuns, who are simultaneously missionaries of the Catholic Church. They carry, in a spirit of continuity, the Benedictine tradition and its many charisms. The analysis of Benedictine charism and tradition given here, draws on the insights of Cistercian writer and lecturer, Michael Casey ocso in his paper 'Tradition, Interpretation, Reform. The Western Monastic Experience'. Interestingly, the Latin verb *tradere* means not only to hand on, but also to betray. Casey presents the etymological notion that 'something is changed in the very act of being passed on. Receiving what is handed on modifies the content of what is received'.[1]

Casey asserts that tradition is 'not a thing, nor an archive, nor a school of thought, nor a series of rituals. It is more like the human memory which continually reshapes its contents according to present interests and concerns'.[2] Casey also cites the Pre-Socratic Greek philosopher Heraclitus of Ephesus, and his insistence on the fact that ever-present change is the fundamental essence of the universe. For the purposes of this discussion, tradition and the way charism is expressed is an ever-changing, ever-flowing reality.

Heraclitus: 'No man ever steps in the same river twice'.

1   Casey, 'Tradition, Interpretation, Reform', 400.
2   Casey, 'Tradition, Interpretation, Reform', 400.

The ordained priests of Archbishop Bede Polding's early monastic community of Sydney were monk-missionaries[3] whose missionary work at times took the place of the Liturgy of the Hours in choir, silence, and the daily monastic *horarium*. Only the flexible survived such a challenge—one which found a priest riding long hours on horseback to reach a centre like Campbelltown or Liverpool. This necessitated overnight accommodation, away from the monastic community, to rest the priest and the horses. The laws of fasting for priests were severe,[4] hence socialising over a meal taken at a venue after Mass (or several Masses), or the sacraments, became the norm as time passed and the demands of the mission increased. What began as a monastic foundation, empowered by the Benedictine tradition and charism, grew into an apostolic, evangelistic stronghold for convicts first of all, for lapsed Catholics, for Protestants, and for the indigenous people of Australia. Since all denominations were evangelising according to their traditions, all were sharing a piece of the great event called 'Christianity'.

The process of involving Benedictine women in the passing on of Benedictine continuity of charism and tradition to New South Wales began when Polding first approached Princethorpe Priory in Warwickshire, England. This initial approach 'brought no immediate results'.[5] After further discernment, the prioress of Princethorpe agreed to another proposal: to 'train for the Australian mission two young women the archbishop had interested in his project'.[6] The two young women were Miss Gregory and Miss Edgar. They entered Princethorpe Priory for the purpose of first being formed in the Benedictine life and

---

3   A double role such as this usually means that one triumphs over the other. In the case of the monastic foundation made at St Mary's monastery in Sydney, it was the role of the missionary which triumphed, and eventually led to the closure of the St Mary's community. (This monastic history/theology was part of a conference given by Michael Casey OCSO to the nuns of Jamberoo Abbey in 2016. The conclusion drawn follows upon a discussion I had with Casey at that time).
4   Priests fasted from midnight, in order to celebrate Mass and take Communion before giving the consecrated bread to those in attendance at Mass the following morning. A priest could be fasting from midnight to midday, if he had been assigned a number of Masses the next day (Sunday).
5   Forster, *Subiaco Resource Book*, Vol. I, 8.
6   MacGinley, *A Dynamic of Hope*, 76–77

then going to Sydney with Polding, to found the first female Benedictine monastic community.

Archbishop John Bede Polding (1794–1877), c. 1840s

In a letter Polding wrote to the two women at Princethorpe on 30 July 1844, he refers to them as being in the monastic habit one year, and 'sufficiently fledged and feathered to take your flight across the vast ocean—on the wings of Divine Love and, buoyed up by all the motives holy religion provides—space and distance lose their terror'.[7] This, despite their being in the monastic habit for less than one year.[8] In the same letter, he refers to Benedictine monasticism as having Christianised the northern hemisphere for more than one thousand years, and as now 'taking its flight into the Southern Hemisphere for

---

7   Forster, *Subiaco Resource Book,* Vol. I, 8.
8   The women referred to here were clothed in the monastic habit on 14 September 1843 and made monastic profession (vows) on 21 November 1844.

purposes equally noble and good'.[9] As summarised by Birt, a letter to his former superior after his episcopal consecration on 29 June 1834, Polding 'foreshadowed his resolve to work out the conversion of Australia on the lines laid down by the Apostle of England, St. Augustine [of Canterbury]. That is, he hoped to put the beauty of religion before the gaze of the colonists in the exemplary Christian lives of a religious community, thus setting an example of what an ideal Christian-like life should be'.[10] 'Just as Anglo-Saxon Benedictine nuns were part of the eighth-century evangelisation of Germany by Boniface of Wessex and his fellow monks, Benedictine women were a vital part of his mission.[11]

Polding would have known that the Carolingian reform movement undertaken by Charlemagne (768–814) saw a return to 'the culture of the Roman empire, thoroughly Christianised, [where] the monasteries were centers of genuine spirituality and culture'.[12] This was achieved by securing uniformity of observance, and the basis for such uniformity was to be the 'Roman Rule' of St Benedict. This plan was extended by Louis the Pious, son of Charlemagne. In the centuries which followed, the Rule of Benedict continued to be the preferred Rule for monasteries.[13]

The encouragement Polding gave to the two young women who entered Princethorpe Priory did not fully strengthen Miss Edgar, who was professed as Sr Mary Benedict. She withdrew her commitment

9   Jamberoo Abbey Archives (JAA), *Collection of Letters from Bishop Polding to the Nuns at Princethorpe*. (Box marked 'Polding—original letters'). There are also the three volumes of Polding's letters published by the Good Samaritan sisters. While there is no proof for the following, it is probable that Polding was well-versed in English and European Catholic history. Polding was aware of the Anglo-Saxon mission by English monks and nuns to convert the people of Germany.
10 Birt, *Benedictine Pioneers*, 237–38, reproducing Polding to Dr Birdsall, 29 June 1834.
11 At the end of the 7th Century 'the Anglo-Saxon monks from both the north and south of England were undertaking missionary enterprises on the continent' (Fry, *RB 1980*, 20). Boniface of Wessex 'was commissioned by the Holy See to evangelize Germany' (120). This work was carried out from 718–754. In this work, he was assisted by his cousin, the Anglo-Saxon nun, Lioba, of the Abbey of Wimbourne. She and her companions helped with the missionary venture. One of the stained-glass windows in the Abbey Church at Jamberoo depicts the Anglo-Saxon women going to join Boniface and his companions.
12 Fry, *RB 1980*. Part One, Historical Orientation, 121.
13 Fry, *RB 1980*, 113–151.

to the Australian mission and asked instead to be admitted into the Princethorpe community. Miss Gregory, now professed as Sr Mary Scholastica, was left as the only foundress, and member of a new establishment in New South Wales, which led Polding to approach Stanbrook Abbey in Worcestershire. MacGinley notes that 'Polding's desire for a women's foundation in his mission-field had not been encouraged by the English Benedictine Congregation, thus precluding an approach to Stanbrook'.[14]

At Stanbrook Abbey, Dame Magdalen (Constantia) le Clerc, who had recently been relieved of her duties as novice mistress, volunteered to be the second Benedictine woman for Polding's Australian missionary venture. Le Clerc was born on 14 October 1798 at Darrington, Yorkshire. Her father was French and had sought refuge in England after the Revolution. Constantia's mother was Ann Day, who would, in her will, leave £2,300 to her daughter Constantia. This would go to the building of a new school building. Constantia's uncle and a brother were priests. Her sister Apollonia and two cousins were all nuns of Stanbrook. Polding had known her since 1834, when, on his appointment as bishop, she had supplied ecclesiastical garments for him, some ornately embroidered.[15]

Dame Magdalen le Clerc (1798–1878), c. 1848

14   MacGinley, *A Dynamic of Hope*, 76.
15   Forster, 'Magdalen le Clerc', 264.

Two foundresses, two monastic influences, an emerging tension

Dame[16] Magdalen (Constantia) le Clerc had been one of Jane Gregory's school teachers when the Stanbrook Community was in residence at Old Salford in Warwickshire.[17] Dame Magdalen le Clerc was approaching the age of fifty. Scholastica Gregory was just thirty years of age.

The Princethorpe Benedictines were founded from Montargis in France,[18] and came to England in 1792, during the upheaval of the French Revolution. Headed for the Lowlands, their ship was diverted by elemental forces, and they landed off-course in Brighton. Here, at the height of the holiday season, the Prince of Wales (later King George IV), and his wife, Mrs Fitzherbert, took the responsibility of seeing to the welfare of this group of nuns, encouraging them to remain in the safety of England, instead of returning to the Lowlands of Europe.[19]

The Stanbrook nuns had been part of the English Benedictine Congregation since they were founded in 1625 under the leadership of the great-great-granddaughter of Thomas More, Lord High Chancellor of England. Thomas More, as a person in public office, had to swear allegiance to Henry VIII as the supreme head of the Church of England.[20] When he failed to do so, he was imprisoned and later executed for treason. Gertrude More, with nine young English women, exiled from their native land at the time of the English Reformation, were professed at Cambrai, Flanders. Thomas More's 'love of learning and spirit of hospitality' led them to follow 'Fr. Augustine Baker into the way of an interior search for God based on the training of will, mind

---

16 The title 'Dame' (Lady) was used in England at this time in history for a choir nun. The title 'Sister' was used for a lay sister (those who entered the monastery as domestic workers). The title 'Dom' (Lord) was used for choir monks. The title 'Brother' was used for lay brothers (who entered as domestic workers). The title 'Dame' is still used in Stanbrook Abbey of the present day. A choir nun was well-educated, and therefore able to cope with the Latin Office.
17 This community purchased Stanbrook Hall Estate in 1838, and today resides in Wass, York, while keeping the identification 'Stanbrook Abbey'.
18 As noted in the Introduction.
19 Summarised from Author, *A Short History*.
20 This was known in Reformation history as the Oath of Supremacy, and was the result of the Act of Supremacy of 1534.

and heart'.²¹ The blending of the two traditions, English and French, for the purposes of the Benedictine mission to Australia, created its cultural tensions. This was all the more so because Polding favoured the Princethorpe Priory.²²

**Dame Gertrude More
(1606–1633)**

Magdalen le Clerc's *obsculta* is poignantly expressed in her farewell letter to her abbess and community:

> Since I have listened to the voice which has long been calling for the sacrifice of all that is dear to me on earth, and being assured by those who hold the place of God in my regard, that the call is from God, I tear myself from you […] to fulfil the gracious designs of God and impart to others a share of those spiritual treasures I have gathered among you.²³

---

21 Entry for Stanbrook Abbey, in the Annual Benedictine Yearbook. The Yearbook is a guide to the abbeys, priories, parishes, and schools of the monks and nuns following the Rule of Saint Benedict in Great Britain, Ireland, and their Overseas Foundations. (*The English Benedictine Congregation Trust*, 111–112).
22 Princethorpe Priory no longer exists as such. The Princethorpe Archives are housed at Douai Abbey, Upper Woolhampton, Reading, Berkshire. Canonically, the community will continue to exist under the care of the Abbot Visitor until the last member dies. The remaining nuns live in different religious houses.
23 *Stanbrook Abbey Annals*, September, 1847.

Scholastica Gregory's *obsculta* and her conviction that the Benedictine mission to Australia was God's will for her, did not lessen the pain of her departure from Princethorpe Priory.

The Princethorpe Chronicles record that on September 16 1847 Dame Magdalen le Clerc of Stanbrook Abbey, who has been 'destined by God to be the foundress of the new house', came to Princethorpe 'accompanied by Fr. Barber [of Downside Priory][24] [...] to be joined by her companion [Sr Scholastica Gregory], that they might set out together'.[25] She stayed three days at Princethorpe, during which time

> she edified [the nuns] greatly and inspired [the nuns] with a lively interest in [the Australian Mission]. We could not sufficiently admire her entire abandonment to God's designs upon her, her unshakeable confidence in Divine Providence and her peace of soul.[26]

The next entry in the Princethorpe Chronicles is of great significance in the light of later decisions made by Polding. The prioress of Princethorpe gave Dame Magdalen le Clerc 'a copy of our Constitutions so that she might compare them with her own to see which would be the more suitable for the new foundation'.[27] This comparison never took place. Once the foundation was made, Polding insisted on the use of the Princethorpe Constitutions and Customs, even though they were grounded in the French Benedictine tradition and not his English Benedictine tradition. The Princethorpe nuns were never members of the latter tradition, having been founded from Montargis. Montargis was a daughter house of Montmartre.[28]

The reason for Polding's choice was a simple one: the Princethorpe Constitutions and Customs were written for women (for French Benedictine nuns). Being himself a member of the English Benedictine Congregation he was aware that the Constitutions of the English houses

---

24   St Gregory's Priory Downside was raised to the status of an abbey by Pope Leo XIII on 29 June 1899. Cf. Birt, *History*, 248.
25   The Princethorpe Chronicles, September 1847.
26   The Princethorpe Chronicles, September 1847.
27   The Princethorpe Chronicles, September 1847.
28   Author, *A Short History*, 13.

were written for men.[29] Certainly, the Princethorpe Code was a living one, and was, at this time, observed by the nuns of Princethorpe. On the other hand, the Cambrai/Stanbrook [Code] was obsolete, inasmuch as Magdalen le Clerc had never observed it, nor seen it enforced.[30]

Marie Forster, former archivist and historian of the community which is the subject of this book, notes that neither set of Constitutions was suitable for colonial Australia, and that during his lifetime it was Polding himself who actually determined the lifestyle of the nuns who formed the Australian foundation.[31] Birt describes it thus: 'the Archbishop reserved supreme authority to himself as founder'.[32] This being the case, there is no evidence that he challenged the Princethorpe Code which was used from 1849 until 1856, as a document that was flexible under his direction. This same document was used more rigidly from 1856–1861, with no interference from Polding. These were the years when three additional nuns would come from Princethorpe to help the Subiaco community. This will be discussed later in this book.

There are further considerations regarding this question of suitable constitutions. Polding's observation about the Constitutions of the English Benedictine Congregation being written for men, does not tell the whole story. The Cambrai Code was also a code for women, as the Princethorpe Code was. It is documented by Dom Basil Whelan, OSB, that 'the upheaval at Cambrai, in the years 1793–1795 during the French revolution, followed by the years in England up to the coming of the community to Stanbrook in 1838, had made the observance of the Cambrai Constitutions impossible'.[33]

Whelan states that even the living of religious life was carried out with great difficulty. Catholic emancipation reached its finality in 1829. The wearing of religious habits and veils was done with great

---

29 The assumption that the Cambrai/Stanbrook Code was the same as that written for the men of the English Benedictine Congregation is not correct, as will be shown in the next paragraph.
30 These Constitutions and Codes form the guide for the practical daily living of the Rule of Benedict. Dame Magdalen (Constantia) le Clerc entered the Stanbrook community on 21 October 1814, after the Cambrai nuns had settled back in England.
31 Forster, 'Fragment', 70.
32 Birt, *Benedictine Pioneers*, Vol. II, 400.
33 Whelan, *Annals*, 10.

caution. The women had a school, and worked to earn a living. This too was done with caution. It wasn't until 1868, thirty years after the nuns had settled at Stanbrook, and twenty years after Dame Magdalen le Clerc had been in Sydney, that the Stanbrook community moved towards obtaining new Constitutions—those of the women's abbey of Ste Cécile. In July, 1872, they finally signed a petition for adopting the code. The business concluded in 1878 when the 'Abbot President of the E.B.C.[34] received final approbation at the General Chapter'.[35] Thus, Polding's observation about the Constitutions of the English Benedictine Congregation being written for men, is misleading. The nuns of Stanbrook, until 1868, observed 'no fixed mode of life, and the form of observance changed from [Canonical] Visitation to the next [Canonical] Visitation and even sometimes in accordance with the whim of the abbess at the time'.[36]

It could be argued that it was Polding's intention to remain overall in charge of the new Benedictine women's community. However, his intention to remain in charge may have been to safeguard against the already strained relationship between Dame Magdalen le Clerc and Sr Scholastica Gregory. For most of the voyage from England to New South Wales, Scholastica Gregory had been ill. Not very far into the voyage, she developed toothache. She was so ill 'that Dame Magdalene was obliged to call His Grace to come to me about midnight'.[37] This became the pattern. The former infirmarian of Downside was gifted with the sick.

Once in Sydney, Dame Magdalene le Clerc writes that 'her [Jane's] health is wonderfully improved'.[38] In a letter written in February 1849,

---

34 English Benedictine Congregation.
35 Whelan, *Annals*, 15.
36 Whelan, *Annals*, 10. This sexist comment is a window into nineteenth century Victorian society. Women in general were thought to be weak, frivolous, mostly useless, and needing a chaperone when out of their home. The 'whim' of the abbess could be a situation where an entire community is ill, and therefore, some of the *horarium* (timetable) is adjusted. 'The Sabbath was made for human beings. Human beings were not made for the Sabbath' (Mark 2:27).
37 Forster, 'Fragment', entry for December 15, 1848.
38 Magdalen le Clerc, 'Letter to the Lady Abbess of Stanbrook'—no date given, but from the content, it was written soon after their arrival in Sydney, on 6 February 1848. (JAA, Complete collection of the Letters of Magdalen le Clerc, both original and transcribed. File marked 'Magdalen le Clerc', Letters).

Magdalen le Clerc comments that 'Sr Scholastica is enjoying pretty good health. She is a famous, busy procuratrix on her legs all day long, putting all things in order'.[39] As a monk of the English Benedictine Congregation, Polding would have been aware of the Stanbrook Constitutional history. The Princethorpe nuns were not members of the English Benedictine Congregation. In the affirmative, their Constitutions and Customs were written for women. Remaining in close proximity to the two nuns during 1848, he would have been aware of a strained relationship between the two foundresses. Whatever the reason, Polding remained overall in charge, with the Princethorpe Code in place, until the community elected their own prioress in 1864.

The comment that neither set of Constitutions was suitable for colonial Australia gradually became a reality, at least in the case of the Princethorpe Code. In a letter she wrote to the Lady Abbess of Stanbrook in January 1861, Dame Magdalen le Clerc says:

> I have a copy which I wrote out myself, of the Cambrai Constitutions – the essentials are precisely the same as those of Princethorpe […] but the latter are more modern and require fewer modifications to suit present circumstances, which was the very motive that induced His Grace to adopt them. What other modifications may be required by the wants of this community or the peculiarities of climate His Grace will make at the time of Visitation. When I mentioned this to the Archbishop, that I knew it was the intention of some nuns[40] to petition for Cambrai Constitutions, he replied: 'You will have neither Princethorpe or Cambrai, but Subiaco Constitutions.' I daresay the visit will be made during Lent, and I feel sure his Grace will settle everything to the satisfaction of all, and that we shall henceforward progress, happily, peaceably.[41]

Before departing England, the two foundresses spent up to five days at Pugin's Convent of Mercy in Handsworth, learning the method of

---

39   Le Clerc, 'Letter to the Lady Abbess of Stanbrook' (JAA).
40   The names of the nuns have not been entered into the community chronicles.
41   Le Clerc, 'Letter to the Lady Abbess of Stanbrook', 23 January, 1861.

Ecclesiastical Embroidery which was part of the Gothic Revival of the Nineteenth Century, brought to birth by Augustus Northmore Welby Pugin.[42] On 24 March 1850 the St Mary's Monastic Journal records the first wearing of a Gothic chasuble in Sydney, with the likelihood that it was made by Dame Magdalen le Clerc and Sr Scholastica Gregory. Magdalen le Clerc was already skilled in the art of ecclesiastical embroidery.[43] Scholastica Gregory's first introduction to it may have been at the Convent of Mercy in Handsworth.

Monastic life at sea after leaving England

One of the hermeneutics of tradition is verbal communication, and exposure to such communication on a three-month voyage resulted in both a 'handing on' and a 'betrayal'. The Australian mission was the focus for Polding, as he gathered monks, nuns, priests, and deacons into his passion for the Benedictine dream: to make the Catholic Archdiocese of Sydney a Benedictine stronghold. He had had little success with the Irish orders in Sydney, because of Henry Gregory's authoritarian manner. To sum up a very long saga, Henry Gregory (when Polding was in Europe in 1842), acting as Vicar General, was the 'authority' in the Sydney Archdiocese, and insisted that all authority resided with him. When Polding was in Europe again in 1846, Gregory continued his autocratic rule, even deposing Mother de Sales O'Brien as Head Superior of the Sisters of Charity in Sydney, and stating that all offices [of the Sisters of Charity] had ceased. He appointed new offices 'and acted [...] as Head Superior'.[44]

---

42 As noted earlier in this chapter, Polding had known Dame Magdalen le Clerc since 1834, when, on his appointment as Bishop, she had supplied ecclesiastical garments for him, some ornately embroidered. Her obituary notes that she was 'intelligent, musically accomplished, and highly skilled with the needle. She was 25 years of age when she was appointed novice mistress, and she held that office until 1846': 'Obituary: Dame Magdalen le Clerc', in *Tjurunga* 8, 39–40.

43 All the Pugin treasures of Australia, including those held in trust at Jamberoo Abbey Heritage Centre, are documented in Andrews, *Creating a Gothic Paradise*. Brian Andrews notes that 'before the [Benedictine] nuns' departure from England, they had spent just over a fortnight at Pugin's Convent of Mercy, Handsworth, conveniently close to Lucy Powell's Birmingham vestment establishment' (161).

44 Shanahan, *Out of Time*, 91–92.

Dom Henry Gregory OSB, (1813–1877),
c. 1840s

With Polding, the handing on of tradition was first of all subject to the Benedictine dream, in that the underlying force was to make it successful, no matter what obstacles were encountered. Therefore, a 'betrayal' was also present and active. A modification of tradition was in process. From the time the ship left England until its arrival in Sydney, Polding instructed the founding sisters, the Benedictine priests, monks, and deacons who made up his small community at sea. The missionary group set sail from Liverpool on 7 October 1847 and arrived in Sydney on 6 February 1848. The group travelled on the H.M.S. *St. Vincent* under Captain Young and included: the two nuns, three priests (Frs Peter Magganotto, CP., John Gourbeillon, OSB, Emmanuelle Ruggiero, OSB), two deacons (Messrs Ryan and Luckie), candidates for the diocesan clergy; three professed monks (Brs Edmund and Bernard Caldwell, and Br Edmund Moore), three postulants (Messrs Connery, Sheridan, and Nevil), and Victor, a French servant for Polding.[45]

---

45 This summary has been adapted from Br Edmund Moore's diary. The original diary is kept in the Downside Abbey Archives, which also keeps the fragment of a diary written by Sr Scholastica Gregory during the voyage to Sydney.

Of the first day at sea, Brother Edmund Moore, in his journal, describes the *horarium*[46] thus:

> Got up at 8, said Matins and Lauds before breakfast – after breakfast copied a little piece of English music, the words of which Dr. Polding thinks are calculated to please the sailors because it is something about the deeps. The music and words are from a book His Grace has, entitled: 'Manual of Catholic Melodies', printed in Baltimore, bought in Liverpool.[47]

Already then, the monastic day at sea is shaped by prayer, study, and work of a modified nature. Edmund Moore's reportage of the work assigned to him by Polding, is a vital piece of information in regard to Polding's missionary spirit, and his anticipating the evangelical nature of worship once back in colonial Sydney. Catholic education too would require such a hymnal. This would be the case with both the monks and nuns—that there would be hymns in the vernacular language of a primarily English/Irish colony. The *obsculta* of Polding led to modification of tradition. Hymns in English, as opposed to hymns in Latin, made the spirit of Catholic worship more relevant. Hymns in the vernacular would become a means for evangelisation. In July 1856 Polding would write a Pastoral Letter, encouraging Catholics to sing Hymns:

> [G]et, read carefully and study the hymns, they are well worth it. You will find them the most exquisite voice of all you hold dear, and then, being fully possessed with their meaning. Come here and sing them with your fellow worshippers, as humbly, or as well as you can.[48]

It is clear in the Princethorpe Annals for 1847 that Dame Magdalen le Clerc was to be the Superior of the Australian Foundation. However, the voyage from Liverpool to Sydney proved to be the catalyst for

---

46 The Latin term *horarium* is the word used for timetable in a monastic community.
47 The 'Manual of Catholic Melodies' was first published by John Murphy and Co. in Baltimore in 1845. It was a Manual of Catholic Melodies, Hymns, Psalms. The book was compiled, along with other text books for Catholic schools, by Martin Kerney, a Catholic teacher of the 1840s. It appears at the top of a list of school books advertised in 1846 by Murphy and Co.
48 Haines et al., *The Eye of Faith*, 234.

changing this arrangement. Scholastica Gregory's voyage was dominated by illness. Polding, gifted in nursing the sick,[49] ministered to her. Her walks on the deck of the ship were mostly taken with Polding. He shared with her the treasured aspects of his Australian mission, gave her lessons in Latin, talked 'over several precepts of the Rule [and] Constitutions and asked her to write to St. Mary's Princethorpe, in order to obtain the Règlements des Emplois'.[50]

On 7 January 1848, Polding spoke with her on domestic economy —in regard to the Australian foundation. A further meeting followed on January 12, on the manner of speaking of religious institutions in general. Polding spoke from the nineteenth century-understanding of religious life: virtues such as subduing the imagination, practising interior mortification, and the perfection to which the religious soul is called. Such perfection, for example, taught one to receive a rebuke in silence and without interior murmuring.[51] This, of course, was not solely Benedictine spirituality, but rather more the spirit of religious life in general.

Polding gave other meditations to the group as a whole: one on the tepid and fervent soul based on Revelation 3:16. Scholastica Gregory wrote that the comfort Polding gives her 'falls like dew from heaven'.[52] Overall, the relationship forged between Polding and Scholastica Gregory on that long voyage would determine the shape of early governance in the new foundation.

All Polding's meditations, provided to his 'sea' community during the voyage, were grounded in the spirituality of the Rule of Benedict which in turn is grounded in the Gospel. Various topics concerned the

---

49   Polding had been the infirmarian at Downside School. O'Donoghue, *The Bishop of Botany Bay*, 5, describes him as 'an excellent infirmarian, kind and attentive when pupils were ill'. Van Zellar, *Downside*, 39, says of Polding: 'he had filled every important office in the house except that of Prior'.
50   Forster, 'Fragment of a Diary', entry for 3 January 1848. This book translates best as Regular Observances—how the day was structured around the Liturgy of the Hours, Mass, Work, Meals, Rest, and Recreation.
51   The same kind of Catholic spirituality prevailed in boarding schools for girls, right up to and immediately after the Second Vatican Council (1960s). This type of discipline was expected in the élite English schools for boys or girls, and in the British armed forces. There was an understanding that one accepted a rebuke without complaining.
52   Forster, 'Fragment', entry for 15 January 1848.

enemies of one's spiritual household, taking up one's cross daily in order to follow Christ, refraining from sins of the eyes and from gluttony, holding firm to faith in Jesus Christ as one's food, medicine, and light for the soul.[53] These meditations were led by Polding as a practical exercise in *Lectio Divina*. The meditations were given in addition to the celebration of the Mass, the Liturgy of the Hours, the Sacrament of Reconciliation, theology classes (for the men)[54], and often a musical gathering of a more informal nature in the evenings.[55]

It is recorded in Br Edmund Moore's diary that Dame Magdalen was the organist, being already a skilled musician. Moore notes that she often accompanied Br Caldwell on the flute during the long voyage.[56] This combining of monastic women and men on the three-month voyage modified the customary tradition where the only male who dwelt in close proximity to Benedictine women, in any Benedictine monastery, was the chaplain. Both Sr Scholastica Gregory and Dame Magdalen le Clerc were enjoying a freedom they had not experienced since entering their respective monastic communities.

Christmas 1847 is recorded as being celebrated liturgically in Polding's cabin with the *Adeste*, and the *Hodie*. It was Dame Magdalen le

---

53 This theological and doctrinal concept would find its way into a hymn composed by Charles Henry (Bishop) Davis, for the community and school at Subiaco, Rydalmere, c. 1850. It has been recorded by the Jamberoo monastic community. It is still used on the annual anniversary of foundation.

54 Polding and his companions, in initial formation at Downside, had been the recipients of teaching by a Sorbonne Professor, who so advanced his students in philosophy and theology that by 1813 they were ready for minor orders; see O'Donoghue, *The Bishop of Botany Bay*, 3. Birt, *Benedictine Pioneers*, Vol. I., 247, notes that 'Polding, from the time of entry to the community of St. Gregory (later Downside Abbey) had imbibed the history of Benedictinism'. This, coupled with his strong theological formation, equipped him to take up the challenge of missionary-ministry in colonial Australia.

55 This activity was part of the daily *horarium* in Benedictine and other religious communities of the time, and still is the case in the present day. Its familiar term is 'recreation' which enables the community to come together and share the events of the day, or as Edmund Moore has recorded, listen to music together. In the 21st Century, the mode differs from one community to another. It may combine a short meal together, and a commitment to news broadcast on ABC or SBS. This responsibility is taken seriously by the Jamberoo community, with its focus on social justice on a national and international scale.

56 Moore, 'Diary', *Tjurunga* 6, 109–124; *Tjurunga* 7, 77–93; *Tjurunga* 9, 77–92. The instrument she played was the seraphine, sometimes spelt incorrectly (serafin, or seraphim).

Clerc who had the copy of the *Hodie*.⁵⁷ Again on St Stephen's Day the group met in the same venue for more singing and celebration.

Arrival in Sydney. A year at St Mary's

The H.M.S. *St. Vincent* arrived in Sydney on 6 February 1848. The nuns were placed in temporary accommodation at St Mary's in Sydney. Dame Magdalen le Clerc comments on the fact that she and Sr Scholastica Gregory had two comfortable rooms which Scholastica's brother, Henry Gregory, had given up for their use.⁵⁸ Henry Gregory had been appointed Vicar General in 1844. He was Polding's assistant and confidante.⁵⁹ In this same letter which Dame Magdalen wrote from St Mary's, she shares that she is already engaged in meeting the needs of the Australian Catholic Benedictine mission:

> I have many under instruction, particularly old women who cannot read […] among the rest a family […] who will in a few weeks be received into the Catholic Church. ⁶⁰

Her attitude and spirit emerge as adaptable, willing,⁶¹ attuned to missionary activities and the Sacraments. Le Clerc mentions the ordinations to the priesthood, the fact that 130 children received First Communion,⁶² and that 540 received the Sacrament of Confirmation. She notes that so many of these candidates for the Sacraments

---

57 *Hodie Christus Natus Est* was and still is the Magnificat Antiphon for Vespers of the Nativity of the Lord and for Vespers throughout the Octave of Christmas: (Today Christ is born, today the Saviour has appeared. Today the angels sing on earth, and the archangels are rejoicing. Today the just exult, saying: 'Glory to God in the highest, alleluia'.) The *Adeste* is the *Adeste Fideles* by John F. Wade (1711–1786).

58 *Collection of 32 Letters written by Dame Magdalen le Clerc, from Australia to England, during her lifetime on the Australian Mission.* Letter No. 2, 1848, written from St Mary's, Sydney, to her Abbess at Stanbrook. Archive box marked 'Letters, Dame Magdalen le Clerc, from Australia to England', JAA. These were transcribed by Marie Therese Malone during the 1980s.

59 O'Farrell, *The Catholic Church*, 78.

60 Le Clerc, Letter No. 2 to the Lady Abbess of Stanbrook, written early in 1848.

61 The Stanbrook Abbey Archives record that the Stanbrook community felt her loss but submitted 'to the designs of an all-wise Providence, who called our Sister to a distant land, there to labour for the good of souls and extend the holy Benedictine Rule'.

62 During the long sea voyage, Polding had shared with Scholastica Gregory his procedure for preparing child communicants.

are converts to the Roman Catholic faith. She responds profoundly to the offering of young boys to God. Witnessing the reception of a child oblate, she comments that about twelve boys are brought up in the monastery, aspiring to the religious life.[63] Overall, then, she immersed herself in the flourishing religion of Sydney in 1848. There is no mention in letters or archival sources that Sr Scholastica Gregory was involved in missionary activities. There is mention of the fact that she contracted scarlet fever in 1848, and that this left her with a hearing impairment. In spite of her illnesses, Polding continued to favour her and the Princethorpe contribution to the Australian mission.

St Mary's, Sydney, c. 1840s

In the school attached to St Mary's monastic community, O'Farrell notes that there were 'eighty-five boys, well taught by Messrs Sconce and Makinson, former Anglican clergymen who, in February 1848, had embraced Catholicism'.[64] Such a choice, as that made by Sconce and Makinson, must have stirred up public opinion. This is referred to by Sr Scholastica in a letter of 12 August 1848, written first of all to the

---

63   Le Clerc, 'Letter to the Lady Abbess of Stanbrook'. In the 20th Century this policy prevailed in some Religious Orders. It was called a 'Junior-ate', or Pre-Novitiate.

64   O'Farrell, *The Catholic Church,* 88

Benedictine nuns of St Mary's Princethorpe, who then shared sections of the correspondence with the nuns of Stanbrook Abbey. She comments on the living faith of Sydney Catholics. The situation far surpassed her expectations. She is right in her observations and experiences: according to Patrick O'Farrell, in mid-nineteenth-century Australia, despite all the early obstacles, Catholicism was in vibrant health.[65]

Her letter, though, does not reveal anything of the anti-Benedictine rumblings already beginning because of Henry Gregory and his lack of ability to handle the monks in his care, his 'stern demands for subjection to authority and his seeming arrogance'.[66] In fact, she wrote that it is 'most gratifying to me to see how much my dear brother [Henry Gregory] is beloved and respected, not alone by clergy and community, but by the majority of the inhabitants both Protestant[67] and Catholic'.[68] This is obviously what she observed.

Communication between Sr Scholastica and her brother, or between her and the other monks would have been limited by both nineteenth-century social convention, and nineteenth-century monastic etiquette. It is not likely that a monk would have confided in her about his difficulties living under her brother's rigid régime. The Rule of Benedict Chapter 7:35–37 states: 'The fourth step of humility is that in this obedience [for the love of God] under difficult, unfavourable, or even unjust conditions, [the monk's heart] quietly embraces suffering and endures it without weakening or seeking escape'.[69] Since obedience was one of the vows they had taken or were preparing to take, the application of RB80 7:35–37 was expected of them.

---

65 O'Farrell, *The Catholic Church*, 88.
66 O'Farrell, *The Catholic Church*, 78.
67 'Protestant' was the term used by Roman Catholics when referring to other Christians whose allegiance was to churches of the Reformation. The term continued to be used through the 20th century. Ecumenical relationships were among the outcomes of the Second Vatican Council, even though the World Council of Churches had been founded in 1948. The Roman Catholic Church was hampered by its policy of superiority: claiming to be the one true church above all others. The Australian Catholic Bishops Conference of the 21st Century appoints one bishop to facilitate ecumenical gatherings, workshops, and prayer meetings.
68 Sr Scholastica Gregory, 'An excerpt from a letter written to the nuns of St. Mary's Priory, Princethorpe'. No date is given, but it is written early after arriving in Sydney (JAA).
69 Fry, *RB 1980*, 197.

What wasn't expected is Edmund Moore's description of Henry Gregory's authority. Moore wrote to the Abbot President of the English Benedictine Congregation (EBC), on 18 October 1849, describing obedience under Gregory's rule: 'The monks had to be abject, grovelling and slavish' in order to live under Henry Gregory's authority.[70]

Education

Scholastica Gregory's first mention of education is in the same letter of 12th August 1848:

> Parents are sighing for a conventual[71] education for their daughters. Numbers of young ladies are settling in life before even they are fully grown. It is really quite distressing and to me quite revolting to see mere children [as] mothers of families […] and such numbers of children without any means of education so that a convent for that purpose is quite necessary for the colony.[72]

Added to these impressions are the more caustic comments of Dame Magdalen, in a letter dated February 14 1849, written to 'Venerated Father', most probably Fr Barber:

> I am told the children here are very indolent indeed; to tell the truth, independence being the spirit of the land, there are no children: a child of ten is like one of fourteen at home, and to see their consequence—it is quite laughable as they strut about the streets. We must try to bring down their spirits a little when we get them under our tuition. [73]

---

70 Shanahan, *Out of Time,* 57. (Edmund Moore's letter of 18 October 1849 to the Father President of the English Benedictine Congregation).

71 The word 'conventual' is the adjective she uses to describe the type of education desired by parents for their daughters: that conducted in a convent of nuns, in quietness, simplicity, and discipline, and which included the finer graces and skills which a woman would need in Victorian society and family life.

72 Gregory, 'Letter to the nuns of Princethorpe Priory 12 August, 1848'. (In file Sr Scholastica Gregory, JAA.)

73 Le Clerc, 'Letter to [most probably] Dr. Barber, President of the English Benedictine Congregation. Letter transcribed by Marie Therese Malone, OSB. (JAA.)

Dame Magdalen and Sr Scholastica were not alone in their initial impressions. The English of the colony of New South Wales, and the English in Australia generally, had difficulty with the independent spirit of the young. An English male visitor to Australia, Mark Kershaw, was 'annoyed to see "nice-looking, stylishly-dressed creatures, who looked as if they would hardly condescend to a Duke, talking and walking with ill-dressed young larrikins"'.[74] Twopeny, in his 'Southern Lights and Shadows' commented that 'at thirteen years of age, they [Australian girls] have more ribbons, jewels, and lovers, than perhaps any other young ladies of the same age in the universe'.[75] The 'strutting' described by Dame Magdalen is expressed similarly by H. R. Rae, in 'Pencillings by Land and Sea'. He sees the 'walking' of an Australian girl as 'peculiar to herself—she swings and sways her right arm to and fro'.[76] These first impressions do not appear to have negatively affected the teaching of girls who would attend the educational establishment run by Benedictine nuns in the colony. The spirit of Benedictine *obsculta* prevailed in the case of Dame Magdalen and Sr Scholastica who refrained from allowing first impressions to blind them to the work of the Holy Spirit in the Australian mission.

> This particular reference to *obsculta* cannot conclude without a reference to a woman, who, attending Mass on Easter Sunday 1841 at St Mary's in Sydney, heard God calling her. This recipient of grace was Caroline Chisholm. She listened, and received what Campion calls 'a singular grace […] which underpinned her dedication'.[77] Her first response can be contrasted with the response of Dame Magdalen le Clerc. While le Clerc wanted to bring down a little the spirits of independent and indolent children, Caroline Chisholm responded with more compassion:

---

74   Cannon, *Australia*, Vol. 3, 224. Cannon is referring to a document called 'Colonial Facts and Fictions' by Mark Kershaw.
75   Cannon, *Australia*, Vol. 3, 224. Cannon is referring here to a document entitled 'Town Life in Australia' by R. E. N. Twopeny, London, 1883.
76   Cannon, *Australia*, Vol. 3, 224.
77   Campion, *Australian Catholics*, 24.

I was enabled at the altar of our Lord, to make an offering of my talents to the God who gave them. I promised to know neither country nor creed, but to serve all justly and impartially.[78]

Caroline Chisholm was English born, with a strong humanitarian spirit. She was progressive for her time in history. Campion notes that her school at the immigrants' home had Anglican and Catholic chaplains and a Presbyterian teacher; that clerical jealousies handicapped her work; that Polding didn't like her and thought her to be unfeminine.[79] One may wonder whether she was too strong a character for Polding, a woman who wasn't under obedience to the Catholic hierarchy of New South Wales. She was not a nun, and not in alliance with the Benedictines of Sydney, nor Polding's Benedictine vision.[80]

For the year of 1848, the two nuns continued to live at St Mary's monastery in Sydney, and observed the monastic *horarium* accordingly.[81] The handing on of Benedictine tradition had been modified to meet the initial missionary project into the colony of New South Wales.[82] This being the case, there comes into play a second hermeneutic of tradition, that of 'monuments', to use a term proposed by Alfred Shutz. Shutz considers monuments as 'social institutions which embody and express the conscious choices of those who have gone before us and who have established or developed the form of life which we follow'.[83]

---

78 Campion, *Australian Catholics*, 24.
79 Campion, *Australian Catholics*, 25.
80 One of the three women who would become the first lay sisters (entering on 2 February 1849) was Susannah Diamond, who was a free immigrant, a passenger on the *Lallah Rookh*, arriving in Sydney on 26 December 1841. On the shipping record, her occupation is noted as 'Domestic Servant' and her place of work Caroline Chisholm's Immigrant Home at Parramatta.
81 Not as a comparative study, but by way of interest, it was usual for women to be part of the evangelical thrust into the British Empire. In regard to Australia, women evangelists worked with the Primitive Methodist Religion, and 'women shared the task of soul-winning and crusading for the right': Breward, *History*, 63.
82 This consisted of a catechetical approach, combined with the simple rudiments of education, such as teaching the illiterate how to read. Magdalen le Clerc was a teacher, as is noted earlier in this chapter.
83 Shutz, 'Dimensions', 58–59, cited in Casey, 'Tradition, Interpretation, Reform', 402.

Cover for the Rule of St Benedict
Hand tooled by the Benedictine Nuns, Jamberoo. c. 1990s

Benedictine monastic communities of both men and women are by nature cenobitic, that is, communal. The Benedictine Rule is written for cenobites as opposed to hermits. The cenobitic Benedictine community is a social unit. The monument which remained in place for the Benedictine missionaries who came to New South Wales was the Benedictine Rule and the Benedictine history of England and Europe. This has been documented at the beginning of this chapter: Polding's intention was to convert Australia as Augustine of Canterbury had converted the English, beginning with the Royal family, and as the Anglo-Saxon monks and nuns had converted Germany. For Sr Scholastica Gregory, the monument would have been the French origins of her community, and its interpretation of the Benedictine Rule.

Chapter Two will examine the details of the beginnings of the Benedictine women's life in Australia, and argue that as far as possible the women kept to the charisms and tradition of Benedictine monasticism. This will be shown by the *horarium*, with a strong focus on prayer and work: the attention to the Liturgy of the Hours, and the enthusiasm of both foundresses in passing on to newcomers the rubrics of the Liturgy, and Benedictine life in general. A strong focus will be on prayer and work, the *ora et labora* of the Benedictine life.

CHAPTER TWO

Beginnings

*A*s far as possible, the Benedictine nuns kept to the charisms and tradition of Benedictine monasticism. Their *obsculta* is demonstrated by their attention to the *horarium*, with a strong focus on prayer and work,[1] by their adaptability to country and climate, and by their frugal lifestyle.

Purchase of a house for the Benedictine nuns

In October 1848 Polding purchased a house for the two nuns which cost £5,600 with 'three years to pay it. […] The property was valued at £30,000' some years before 1848.[2] The owner, Hannibal Hawkins Macarthur (nephew of John Macarthur, famous, amongst other things, for his contribution to the development of Australia's merino wool), fell victim to the financial depression of the 1840s. He was one of the founders of the Bank of Australia. When it collapsed in 1843, he and

---

1. In Latin *ora et labora,* (prayer and work), has been parallel with *pax inter spinas,* (peace through a crown of thorns), as a motto of Benedictine life.
2. Sisters of the Good Samaritan, *Letters of John Bede Polding*, Vol. II, 123. Letter of Polding to the Prioress of Princethorpe, Warwickshire, dated 16 November 1848. Birt, *Benedictine Pioneers*, Vol. II, quotes another letter of Polding to Hepton, in which the purchase price and assessment value of the house are £5000 and £32,000 respectively. Rev. T. Heptonstall (Hepton) was Polding's friend and the one who looked after Polding's English interests. He was thus a supporter of the Australian mission.

his co-founders were liable for its losses. The house had only been completed in 1836. Macarthur was married to Anna Maria King, the daughter of the third Governor of the colony, Philip Gidley King, and the couple had a family of eleven children, born in the cottage on the property, where the family had lived since 1813. The property was called 'The Vineyard'. The original grant of '54 hectares was made to Philip Schäffer by Governor Phillip on 30th March, 1791 […] it was the fourth land grant to be made in New South Wales'.[3] In 1797, Captain Henry Waterhouse acquired the property to run Australia's first flock of Merino sheep, which he had brought from the Cape of Good Hope, supplementing Schäffer's holding by the grant of a further four and a half acres. Most of the thirteen sheep were soon sold to others, including John Macarthur, who was later credited for their development in the colony. After Waterhouse returned to England in 1800, the farm was left in the care of others—without much success. In 1812, Waterhouse died, and the property was sold by Liverpool magistrate, Thomas Moore, who held his power of attorney. With 'the Fences and Buildings having gone to utter Ruin' and the valuers concluding that 'the said Premises are worth no more than One Hundred and Sixty Pounds Sterling',[4] on the 17th March 1813, the property was sold. The purchaser was Hannibal Hawkins Macarthur, freshly back in the colony to assist with the Macarthur flocks just as the value of Australian wool began to be recognised in England.[5]

---

3   Latta, *Memorial*. Sections of this document are in Jamberoo Abbey Archives, a gift from an historian friend. The pages are not numbered. Although Schäffer occupied the land in 1791, all four original land grants were registered in the Colonial Sectretary's office on the same day, 22 February 1792, when his grant was recorded as 140 acres. See Waterhouse Papers: 13 - List of Grants and Leases. The indenture made with Waterhouse refers to Schäffer's grant being made on 25 April 1787, the date of Arthur Phillip's instructions from the Crown.

4   The property was valued by Rev Samuel Marsden and Rowland Hassall, who also brokered the deal with Hannibal Macarthur. Samuel Marsden and Rowland Hassall to Thomas Moore Esqu 17/3/1813; Waterhouse Papers: 7c_7d - Valuation of Waterhouse Farm at Parramatta 1813. See page 62.

5   The documents relating to 'The Vineyard' from its first lease to its sale to Macarthur were amongst the papers of Thomas Moore, and are now housed in Moore College library as the 'Waterhouse Papers'. For Hannibal Macarthur, see Nairn, 'Macarthur, Hannibal Hawkins (1788–1861)'. For Waterhouse's introduction of the Merino, see Bolt, 'Moore and the Merino'.

Figure 3: The Early History of 'The Vineyard'

June, 1790	Philip Schäffer arrives in Sydney on the *Lady Juliana* as a supervisor of convicts, amongst whom was Rachel Turner, future wife of Thomas Moore
Ap 17, 1791	Schäffer settles on 'the north side of the creek leading to Parramatta'
Feb 22, 1792	Arthur Phillip issues lease for Schäffer's property, known as 'The Vineyard'
Aug 17, 1797	Henry Waterhouse buys 'The Vineyard' from Schäffer to provide for his flock of merino sheep which he purchased at the Cape of Good Hope
Mar, 1800	Henry Waterhouse returns to England, leaving his farm in the care of others
Ap 24, 1812	Hearing that the farm is not going well, Waterhouse sends his Power of Attorney to Thomas Moore, with a view to its disposal
July 27, 1812	Henry Waterhouse dies
Sep 21, 1812	William Waterhouse, Henry's father, asks Thomas Moore to sell the property and remaining stock, to provide for Henry's daughter Maria
Mar 17, 1813	'The Vineyard' valued and subsequently sold to Hannibal McArthur
May 6, 1813	Waterhouse's remaining stock sold by auction

Philip Schäffer's land grant (Top right corner)

Dear Sir,

We the undersigned being appointed to value the Farm of Captain Waterhouse on the North Side of Parramatta River, have this day taken the same into Consideration, and from the Fences and Buildings having gone to utter Ruin, we are of the opinion that the said Premises are worth no more than One Hundred and Sixty Pounds Sterling to be paid on demand; as nothing can be taken into consideration but the Land and Situation except what Sawed Timber may be found in the Ruins which may help the Purchaser in his Improvements.

The above we have mentioned to Mr Hannibal McArthur who has agreed to become purchaser upon your giving him possession and a regular Transfer.

We are &c
Saml. Marsden
Rowland Hassall

P.S. Inclosed is Mr H. McArthur's Note relative to the Purchase of the same to which he requests an immediate answer.

Letter of Valuation (1813) and View of The Vineyard, c. 1830s

The house that the new owner caused to rise from the ruins of Waterhouse's derelict estate, became one of the venues for Sydney's élite. Among those who stayed at Macarthur house were Charles Darwin (when visiting Australia), the explorer Ludwig Leichhardt, and Governor and Lady Fitzroy, awaiting the completion of Government House at Parramatta. The house was designed after the Petit Trianon, Marie Antoinette's Garden Palace in the grounds of the Palace at Versailles.[6] These details—the spaciousness of the house, the number of guest rooms, the ballroom, would all be to the advantage of the monastic community and those who assisted them to adapt the house for monastic living.[7]

Remaining firmly attached to his Benedictine plan, Polding re-named the house Subiaco, after the cave where Benedict of Nursia lived and first took refuge from the amoral Roman society of his time. Also on this property was a dwelling which Polding re-named Monte Cassino, after St Benedict's first monastery in Italy, founded AD 529. It was this dwelling which he used for his own monks, those from St Mary's monastery in Sydney, who would later benefit from a sojourn at 'The Vineyard', and those who would initially be placed there for the protection of the women. In October 1848, preparations began in order to bring about adaptations within the colonial mansion—making it a suitable dwelling for a monastic community. Sr Scholastica Gregory and two lay-sister postulants[8] occupied the house soon after October 17. It wasn't until November 19 1848 that Dame Magdalen

---

6   Latta, *A Memorial*.
7   At this time in Australian architectural history, there was not a characteristic Australian-style residential dwelling. Just as the architect John Verge did with this mansion, so those who emigrated to Australia from England and Europe brought their own understanding of residential dwellings: Georgian, Victorian, Gothic, Italian, Swiss, Danish, and Norwegian. The land on which Jamberoo Abbey stands today was first settled by a Norwegian family, who built their home in the style they knew. Even when architects were employed to design Jamberoo Abbey, the nuns had to stand against their pre-conceived and mostly European ideas of what an abbey should look like.
8   Lay sisters date from the Middle Ages. Their genesis lay in the incorporation of servants in the monastic domain into a form of religious life under the auspices of the monastic community, cf. MacGinley, *A Dynamic of Hope*, 318–319. A postulant in this case was a woman waiting for the official foundation of the community, so she could begin her formation as a lay sister.

le Clerc, with two Sisters of Charity,[9] went to Subiaco with the community of St Mary's for the first Mass celebrated by Polding. Dame Magdalen did not go into permanent residence until 29 January 1849. By this time, relations between Dame Magdalen and Sr Scholastica had already become strained. Marie Gregory Forster says of the two foundresses:

> They were separated by age, by the difference of the traditions in which they had been formed, by temperament and by the ambiguity of their position where jurisdiction was divided between Polding as 'sole superior' and the two nuns, one of whom had charge of the monastery's temporalities, the other of the more spiritual tasks. [10]

Canonical foundation

The monastery was canonically established on 2 February 1849. That was the day a novitiate was established and the day on which the Divine Office (Liturgy of the Hours) began.[11] Polding placed the house under the protection of the Mother of God, and called it the Convent of the Presentation of Our Lord.[12] Printed in private and public documents, this could appear as an inaccuracy to some. However, the answer lies in Luke 2:22–39, which combined the Presentation of Our Lord in the Temple and the Purification of the Mother of the Lord.[13] It took place forty days after his birth.[14] From at least 1700, the title for 2 February in the liturgical calendar was 'The Purification

---

9   The Sisters of Charity had been in the Colony since 1838.
10 Forster, 'Monks–Monasteries–Mission', 39–74.
11 The official document from the Roman Catholic authorities for permission to establish the foundation and novitiate was given ahead of the actual need of it—February 1848. The Divine Office is the Liturgy of the Hours, the *Opus Dei* (Work of God)—the main Prayer of Benedictine monks and nuns.
12 A stained glass window, depicting this biblical event, has been built into the church of the Benedictine Abbey, Jamberoo. The original is in the church of the Benedictine Monastery, Arcadia.
13 Cross, 'Candlemas', 226.
14 Leviticus 12:1–4.

of Our Lady' and was a Double Second Class Feast.[15] In the Church's Liturgical Calendar it is also known as 'Candlemas'.[16]

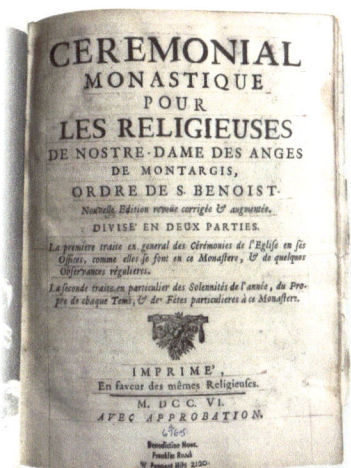

This book translates best as Regular Observances
How the day was structured around the Liturgy of the Hours,
Mass, Work, Meals, Rest and Recreation. Printed 1706.

Five women were present as entrants to the Subiaco community, bringing into focus different aspects of colonial society. Alicia Lett,[17] and Elizabeth (Eliza) Burrows entered as candidates for the choir.

---

15 Noted in the *Ceremonial Monastique pour Les Religieuses de Notre-Dame des Anges de Montargis, Ordre de S. Benoit. Nouvelle Edition reveüe, corrigé & augmentée, MDCCVI*. In the *Breviarium Monasticum pro Omnibus sub Regula SS. P.N. Benedicti Militantibus*, 1860, 2 February is noted as the 'Purification of the Blessed Virgin Mary', and was celebrated as a Double Second Class Feast. Current Liturgical Dictionaries note that the feast has been the celebration of a double event, originating in Jerusalem, as early at the 4th Century. There it was celebrated under the title of the 40th day after the Epiphany. In the 6th Century it spread to Byzantium and became the feast of the 'Meeting' of Jesus and Mary with Simeon. In the 7th Century it came to the Church from Rome and took on the title the 'Purification of Mary'. See Davies, *Dictionary of Liturgy*. No source states that Pius IX changed the title to 'The Purification of Our Blessed Lady', as has been noted in the Community Chronicles.

16 Throughout Church history, this day has been known as Candlemas Day, the Feast of the Purification of the Mother of God, and the Feast of the Presentation in the Temple. Since the liturgical reforms of the Second Vatican Council, the last title applies, and the Mass begins with the Candlemas Procession.

17 In her book *Ancient Tradition*, MacGinley traces a niece of Alicia Lett's: Josephine de Lauret, who entered the Dominican Order, and provides some information on both families.

Legal Document signed by those entering the community (post-1900)

I, the undersigned Sister and Member of the Benedictine Order, Subiaco, Rydalmere, New South Wales, HEREBY TESTIFY that in consideration of the spiritual benefits, and also in consideration of the boarding, clothing and education, which I am to receive gratuitously in said Order, I RENOUNCE all right to demand or claim any other compensation whatever for any work or service which I shall do for, or render to, the said Community. AND FURTHER, that if I ever leave voluntarily, or be compelled to leave the said Community, I shall not be entitled and will have no right to demand or claim in any way for whatsoever reason or pretext, any salary, wages or compensation for whatsoever work or service of any kind performed or rendered by me during my connection with the said Order.

Signed..................................

Susannah Diamond, her cousin Margaret Diamond, and Angela Guilfoyle entered to become lay sisters. Susannah and Margaret Diamond were born in Ireland. It is possible they came to Australia and worked as domestic servants in Sydney before entering Subiaco. Their ages at the time of entering were thirty-six and forty-five respectively, which would indicate a previous working life. Angela Guilfoyle, who didn't find the monastic life within her capabilities, left the community.[18]

Alicia Lett became Sr Benedict. She was one of seven children of Helen Maria Magdaline Lett (née Murphy) and her husband John. The Letts, an Irish family, sailed from London as Free Emigrants on the *Ann*—May 15 1839. When settled in Sydney, Mrs Lett, a talented educated woman, established a school for young women in the Rocks [Sydney]. This school was at 15 Upper Fort Street. Some of her daughters may have taught in this school. Sr Ursula Trower, in a personal interview undertaken in 1997, said that Agnes Hart, one of the first women to enter the Sisters of the

---

18   Community Chronicles.

Good Samaritan, had been educated at this school.[19] The school was in operation at the time Alicia entered the Benedictine community.[20] Elizabeth Burrows became Sr Placida (feminine of Placid, one of St Benedict's disciples). Elizabeth is listed as Eliza on the Immigration Record. She was born in Ireland, being the second youngest child of Stephen Burrows and Mary Kennedy of Co. Longford, Ireland.[21] She was four years old when her family emigrated on H.M.S. *Cleopatra* in 1828. From 1851–1903, it is recorded in Irish County Records that over four million men women and children emigrated.[22] The five women, two to be choir nuns, and three to be lay sisters, joined with Sr Scholastica Gregory and Dame Magdalen le Clerc to begin Benedictine women's monasticism in Australia.

Monastic *horarium*

The daily *horarium* consisting of prayer, work, rest, and recreation, is the traditional structure of the monastic day. As described by Dame Magdalen le Clerc in her letter of 1850 to the Abbess of Stanbrook, it is noted as being the same as the *horarium* for the monks of St Mary's, but, in fact, the monks had the freedom to choose a time.[23] For the women, the Liturgy of the Hours, work, rest, and recreation was as in Figure 4.

---

19   This interview was carried out by Sr Peter Damian McKinlay, sgs, on behalf of Sr Marie Gregory Forster towards the end of the 1990s. This is also attested by Margaret Walsh, in her book *The Good Sams*. Agnes Hart and her widowed father emigrated to Australia when she was sixteen years old. Her father, because of his protection of his only child, placed her in 'Miss Lett's Private Boarding School, Fort Street, Sydney, for 1 month and there she completed her education' (50). Walsh, TITLE, p., notes that it was Miss Lett's Private Boarding School, rather than Mrs Lett's Private Boarding School. This could indicate that one of Alicia Lett's sisters was then in charge of the school [emphases in the text].
20   Walker, 'Old Sydney', 313. The 'Sydney Commercial Directory for 1851' notes Mrs Lett's school still being in operation.
21   Her surname is spelt with one 'r' in the Irish Record, obtained from www.rootsireland.ie, and with a double 'r' on the shipping records.
22   Curtin et al., *Irish Heraldry*, Part II, 41.
23   Graeme Walker notes that the monks of St Mary's had a choice: 'All monks should free themselves for a full half hour's meditation and prayer daily, before or after Prime' (Walker's translation): 'The 1855 Monastic Constitutions', 44–80. The Benedictine women did not have this freedom.

Figure 4: The daily Horarium at Subiaco

4.30 a.m.	Rise
5.00	Meditation, followed by Prime
7.30	Mass
7.00	Breakfast
9.00	Tierce and Sext
	Work followed Tierce and Sext
12.45 p.m.	There was no 'break' between work and dinner at 1.00 p.m. A bell was rung at 12.45 p.m. This was the signal for morning *examen* and a visit to the Blessed Sacrament. The community then walked in procession to the refectory, praying the *De Profundis* (Psalm 129), a Psalm of repentance and trust.
	The Hour of *None* was prayed after Dinner
	One hour of 'recreation' then followed which was shortened according to the length of the meal or the length of the Hour of *None*.
	Then one hour of 'strict silence'. The first quarter of this was given to spiritual reading, then to prayer, work or rest. This time would have been shortened according to the Liturgical Hours of the day. Sometimes it may have been forty minutes or less.
2.30	Work followed at 2.30 p.m. This varied according to the Liturgical Hours of the day.
4.00	Vespers and Compline were combined and prayed a little before 4.00 p.m.
6.30	Supper was taken at 6.30 p.m.
8.00	The Hour of Matins was prayed at 8.00 p.m.
9.30	The Community retired for the night at 9.30 p.m.

Forster comments that on a first reading of this *horarium*, it is noted that one important element of prayer has been omitted—the practice of *Lectio Divina* (Holy Reading—primarily of the Sacred Scriptures), as taught in Chapter 48:1 of the Benedictine Rule:[24] *Otiositas inimical est animae, et ideo certis temporibus occupari debent fratres in labore manuum,*

---

24   Forster, 'Magdalen le Clerc', 259–336.

certis iterum horis in lectione divina.[25] Chapter 48 of the Benedictine Rule, as it is opened out and explained in the first Constitutions and Declarations of the Subiaco community, adopted from Princethorpe, places the direct focus on the Benedictine charisms of 'prayer and work'.[26]

Chapter 48, Declaration 1 of the *Princethorpe* Constitutions begins:

> DECLARATION 1: The Church, instructed by doctrine and by the example of the Apostles, has always shown a great aversion to idleness and high esteem for work. It is for this reason that the sisters will be conscientious about occupying themselves usefully outside the Hours of Office as laid down by our father Saint Benedict in this chapter. They will zealously do whatever needs to be done in the monastery; and the Mother Prioress will see to it that their work is done carefully, charitably and to the best of their ability. Outside the times of Offices, the sisters will work in their cells, remaining secluded therein in a saintly manner, being very scrupulous about coming and going within the monastery unless their Offices, obedience or necessity requires it. They will apply themselves faithfully to carrying out what they have been called upon to do by the Mother Prioress or by those replacing her, and when there is extra work to be done, they will be informed so they will be in the assigned place.
>
> DECLARATION 2: The sisters will not excuse themselves from joint [community] or individual work without permission and after their work they will not stop anywhere in the monastery where they have no reason to be. On Feast days and Sundays, because of the length of the Office, and [the next two lines are illegible – the meaning seems to be that there is extra time between Sext and Vespers, and therefore this time] can be spent visiting the sick [in the Infirmary], or in prayer in the Church, Chapels

---

25 'Idleness is the enemy of the soul. Therefore, the monks should have specified periods for manual labour as well as for prayerful reading'.

26 This *Ora et Labora* has always been in focus in Benedictine history, sometimes thought to be the real motto of the Benedictine life. It is acceptable only as an adjunct to the Benedictine Motto: *Pax inter Spinas,* 'peace through a crown of thorns'. This too has been shortened to *Pax*—which leads to an erroneous understanding of Benedictine life.

or at the monastery altars. And if there are any shrines in the garden [there were seven at Princethorpe], they may also go there, provided there be at least two chosen by the Mother Prioress, and strict silence be observed. However, one sister may be separated from the other during these holy visits for reasons of meditation, provided the sisters are not too far apart and they come back together in the same silence.[27]

Princethorpe Monastic Ceremonial, c. 1600s

This excerpt from the Princethorpe Constitutions, opening out Chapter 48 of the Benedictine Rule as it was meant to be lived in the monastery, immediately presents difficulties for the small community at Subiaco. There were no cells as such in the Macarthur house; there was no church, nor private chapels, nor outdoor shrines. There were a

---

27 At first this may appear as a serious lack of trust on the part of the prioress. However, this was the 19th Century and monastic customs for women were not so far removed from social customs. Jennifer Phegley in *Courtship and Marriage* is clear on this issue: 'Social encounters were heavily monitored by chaperones until late in the [19th] century, when standards were loosened to allow more natural interactions'. (Chapter 2, Courtship Conduct.) Monastic life was not so far removed from social life, where a woman, especially one of the upper class, would not wander very far on her own, would take her place in the garden where she could be easily seen by family or friends, and when away from the house would be chaperoned. In 'The Essential Handbook of Victorian Etiquette' it is clearly stated that, 'A single woman never walked out alone. Her chaperone had to be older and preferably married'. *Etiquette in the Victorian Era*. www.avictorian.com/etiquette.html.

few office bearers. The traditional office bearers in a Benedictine house were and still are: Abbess (or Prioress), Subprioress, Cellarer, Refectorian, Novice Mistress, Infirmarian, and Sacristan. In a numerically large community, there was an assistant novice mistress, the Zelatrix. There were also assistant Infirmarians and Sacristans. At Subiaco, there were two founding mothers, two women who entered for the choir, two out of three remaining who entered to be lay sisters, and two girls aged twelve, who lived in the monastery with the nuns, because the school was not yet open. While the monument remained stable, the continuity of custom had to continually reshape 'its contents according to present interests and concerns'.[28]

What Polding had given to Scholastica Gregory in the way of spiritual education also required a 'handing on' and a 'betrayal'.[29] The concept of 'perfection' for religious and monastic men and women of the Nineteenth Century provides an example. While it was a common denominator across religious and monastic orders, and lingered well into the Twentieth Century, it would presuppose, in the case of Subiaco, a functioning monastic community, which would foster the fruits of the Holy Spirit expressed through the Benedictine Rule, the choral Liturgy of the Hours, public reading, private reading, and monastic work. It is noted in Sr Scholastica Gregory's fragment of a diary, as already noted in this book (page 50), that Polding had spoken to her of the ways of religious perfection, and of religious institutions in general and their spiritual doctrine, during the sea voyage from England to Australia. She listened ardently to the teaching of the bishop. When the reality of 1849 set in, a more earnest listening was called for.

The Princethorpe Constitutions state that an 'obedience until death' is required of the nuns, as Christ was 'obedient until death, death on the Cross' (Philippians 2:8). A significant excerpt of the Constitutions dwells on the Passion of Jesus Christ, and the gift of salvation. The nuns are exhorted to imitate the suffering of Christ, for their own immolation of 'self'. This understanding of immolating the 'self' was the spirituality of the time. The term 'precious blood' (of Jesus) was

---

28 Casey, 'Tradition, Interpretation, Reform', 400.
29 Casey, 'Tradition, Interpretation, Reform', 400.

incorporated into prayers and hymns of the Catholic Church until the time of the Second Vatican Council.[30]

Lectio divina / Spiritual reading

Chapter 48 of the Benedictine Rule, with its *lectio divina* (holy reading), was catered for not with the Sacred Scriptures but with 'spiritual reading' (what Augustine Baker called 'private reading'), meaning the reading of spiritual books in print and available at this time in the Nineteenth Century.[31] Part of this reading would have included books on religious perfection. One of the preferences of Polding and Dame Magdalen le Clerc was for the conferences of Fr Frederick Faber (of the Oratory).[32] The Princethorpe Constitutions and Declarations make a gesture towards *lectio divina* in the following words:

> It was the intention of the holy Patriarch, [Benedict of Nursia] that the time given to work should be partly employed in reading, and partly in manual labour. (RB 48:1) The Sisters therefore shall devote themselves to these exercises in such manner as the Superior shall arrange for each one individually. (Princethorpe Constitutions: declaration on RB 48)

Forster makes reference to the *devotio moderna* which appears to replace the authentic monastic manner of prayer.[33] And yet this type of devotional spirituality was Catholic prayer at its best, the prayer of the saints of the Catholic Church at this time. There are several mentions

---

30 I have written extensively on this after examining a collection of hymnals, hand-written or professionally printed, and held in trust in the Abbey Archives. The intention of my writing was to contradict the error of 'presentism' by those who hurriedly write an historical paper or journal article, freely mocking the sacred music of the past. [insert reference to HR writing?]

31 Baker, *Commentary*. Two copies of this commentary have been transcribed: one for His Grace Dr Polding (1846) and one for the Benedictine Nuns of Subiaco (1869). Both were gifts from the Benedictine nuns of St Mary's Abbey, Colwich.

32 Fr Frederick Faber was received into the Catholic Church in 1845, two weeks after Blessed John Henry Cardinal Newman. Both men were associated with the Oratory of St Philip Neri which Newman introduced into England in 1847. For the founding of the Oratory, see Cross, 'Oratorians', 985–986.

33 Forster, 'Magdalene le Clerc', 304.

of the saints and their holiness in the Princethorpe Constitutions. In the final paragraph, the sisters are exhorted to love, esteem, and practise the example of the great number of persons who are already sanctified by the Church. There is a specific mention of the saints of the Benedictine Order, though no names are given. The women saints of the Benedictine Order will be mentioned specifically in the Beuronese Constitutions obtained by Prioress Walburge Wallis from the Abbey of Beuron in 1888–89.[34] The case for and against *devotio moderna* will be discussed more fully in Chapter 8 below.

What Forster calls 'Subiaco's devotional excesses'[35] were characteristic of nineteenth-century religious and monastic life. Devotions as a form of prayer were particularly characteristic of French spirituality. Virtues such as self-sacrifice, obedience, and humility were foundations of all religious institutes. Books which grounded religious and monastic women in the pursuit of perfection were 'États d'oraison', and 'Meditations on the Gospel', by the French Jesuit Bossuet, 'The Way of Perfection' by St Teresa of Avila, 'The Herald of Divine Love' by St Gertrud the Great of Helfta, the works of the Ven. Blosius, Benedictine abbot and spiritual writer of the Sixteenth Century, the 'Institutes and Conferences of John Cassian',[36] and the lives of the Saints.

Rule of St Benedict and other spiritual reading

The oldest exposition of the Rule of St Benedict in possession of the Benedictine Abbey of Jamberoo is one transcribed by the nuns of St Benedict's Priory, Colwich in 1846, as a gift to Polding. Another transcription of the same document was written in 1869, and given to the community then resident at Subiaco. These transcriptions were

---

34 Casey, 'The Rule of Benedict and Inculturation', 24. *Devotio moderna* has come into popularity again in the present era of the Catholic Church to the extent that those entering monastic life may experience, in the words of Michael Casey, a 'piety void', similar to what many experienced after the liturgical changes initiated by Vatican Council II. Newcomers may feel deprived of what have hitherto been their most potent sources of spiritual energy.
35 Forster, 'Magdalen le Clerc', 304.
36 Because the edition used by the Subiaco Nuns was written in French, it is probable that it came from Princethorpe Priory.

Fr Augustine Baker's Exposition on the Rule first written in English in 1631.[37] Chapter 48 is interpreted as work and prayer, with the addition of a distinct comparison between private reading and public reading. Baker notes that private reading is done by a monk in his cell or in the Oratory; public reading is that which is done in the Liturgy.[38] He explains Chapter 48 of the Rule as praying, reading (in private), and corporal labours—work assigned by the Abbot to the individual monks.

Other books still extant from these times at Subiaco are *The Following of Christ*—in four volumes, dated 1851, printed with the approval of the Cardinal Archbishop of Westminster. Thomas à Kempis, *The Imitation of Christ*, in one volume was also used by the nuns for spiritual reading, as was a small volume in Latin containing the Rule of Benedict, the Life and Praise of St Benedict, followed by the Exercises of St Gertrud the Great[39] and significant excerpts from the writings of Blosius. *The Imitation of Christ* 'is regarded as the finest example of the spirituality of the *devotio moderna* [...] It focussed on the interior life and the Eucharist [...] and placed insistent emphasis on repentance and conversion'.[40] The Exercises of St Gertrud are what they say: exercises in prayer, carefully orchestrated by the writer, a mystic of the Thirteenth Century and a Benedictine nun. Gertrud of Helfta, known as Gertrud the Great, was a woman educated within the cloistered life, and thus fluent in Latin. The Monastery of Helfta was a 'center of mysticism and culture in 13th century Germany'.[41] The 'Exercises' are specifically con-

---

37   Fr Augustine Baker was the spiritual director of Dame Gertrude More—a direct descendant of Thomas More, martyr of the English Reformation—who, in 1625, led nine young English exiles to form a Benedictine community at Cambrai in Flanders. The community returned to England in 1795, after a period of imprisonment in France at the height of the Revolution. This is the community to which Magdalen le Clerc belonged in England.
38   Baker, *Commentary*.
39   See the stained glass window at the Benedictine Abbey, Jamberoo, Australia, in 'our Lord's side' of the Chapel (p. 264), depicting St Scholastica (front) and from left to right, St Gertrud (with The Exercises), St Lioba, St Hildegard and St Mechtild.
40   According to Upton, 'Thomas à Kempis', 832, Thomas à Kempis, supposed author of the *Imitation of Christ*, joined the monastery of the Canons Regular of St Augustine at Zwolle in 1399. Writing in the same collection, Walter Principe, 'Western Medieval Spirituality', 1036, associates him with the school of Windesheim, 'the Brethren of the common Life [...] Theirs was a practical devout life, without legal formal status or vows'.
41   Lewis and Lewis, *Gertrud the Great*, 2. Every Benedictine nun of the Subiaco community had a copy of the Spiritual Exercises in Latin.

structed for Benedictine nuns, focusing on all stages of the monastic journey: rebirth, spiritual conversion, the dedication of the self to God, the following of Christ, mystical union, and death. They are anchored in the Sacred Scriptures and the Rule of St Benedict.[42]

The familiar image of the Twentieth Century, which depicts a nun or monk sitting alone with a Bible, engaged in *lectio divina*, was unknown in monastic life at this time,[43] being inhibited by the need for literacy in Latin and the availability of copies of the Bible. Not only was this the language of the Breviary used for the Liturgy of the Hours, but the texts of the Sacred Scriptures, integrated into the Hours, were also in Latin. Dame Magdalen le Clerc therefore had the task of teaching newcomers to the Subiaco community the rudiments of the Breviary.

The first Bible in English

The first Bible in English at Subiaco, the official community Bible, was one translated from the Latin Vulgate, and dated 1850.[44] There was another Bible in English, owned by Fr Bonaventure Curr, who was Chaplain at Subiaco from 1874–1888, and a second Bible in English dated 1875. This edition is also translated from the Latin Vulgate and published in Dublin in 1847. Bibles in English for the use of each nun (see note 206) were introduced around the time of the Second Vatican Council. Until then, *lectio divina* was carried out according to the canonical and spiritual books available at the time. These would have

---

42 See also Rev. Dr Jane Foulcher, writing on humility in relation to the Benedictine Rule through a twenty-first century lens: Foulcher, *Reclaiming Humility*.

43 Sr Elizabeth Funder who entered the Monastery in 1947 confirms that the term *lectio divina* came into use around the time of the Second Vatican Council, when a full edition of the Bible (Old and New Testaments) was provided for members of the community. When she entered, only a 'New Testament' was on the list of 'what to bring'.

44 This Bible was first published at the English College at Rheims in 1582. It weighs in at 6.2 kgs. It would have been used for Ceremonies or Chapter gatherings and was not available to individuals. 'Chapter' is the term referred to for the nuns in Solemn Vows who would gather to vote for a candidate or to be informed of serious matters such as the departure of a nun from the monastery. It may have been the Bible used in the School, to teach the children the Gospel for the coming Sunday.

been a source of *ruminatio*[45] for the choir nuns.

In a letter written by Dame Magdalen le Clerc to the Lady Abbess of Stanbrook in 1873, she refers to Dom Guéranger's *L'année liturgique*, volume three. It is the one dedicated to Paschaltide. It is her favourite, because it is 'like a continuous feast of the penitent saint whom I must try to imitate'.[46] She says that the first two volumes, given to them by Polding, are in the 'general Library' (community Library), but that this particular volume 'can be for our private use'—the 'our private' is underlined. What she means in monastic language is 'my'. Nuns and monks of this time and well into the Twentieth Century never used the possessive pronoun 'my' since all the goods of the monastery were held in common, and St Benedict was adamant that the 'vice of private ownership be rooted out of the Monastery'.[47] While it was for Dame Magdalen le Clerc's spiritual reading in a private way, it was always open to be shared in the spirit of the Rule of St Benedict. She mentions two other books sent to her by the Abbess of Stanbrook: *Meditations on the Passion* and *L'action de grâce*. Authors are not known.

This Chapter, grounded in Chapter 48 of the Rule of Benedict, has opened out one foundation of the life of a Benedictine monk, nun, or oblate: Prayer. The second foundation is 'work': 'Idleness is the enemy of the soul, and so [monastic men and women] should be occupied at some times with manual labour, and at certain times with holy reading [*lectio divina*]'.[48] Chapter Three will open out the second foundation of the Benedictine life: Work.

---

[45] One of the 'terms' used in *lectio divina*—pondering on the Word of God.
[46] Magdalen le Clerc was called after Mary Magdalene, the first person to witness the Resurrection of Jesus Christ, and the one therefore, who brought the news to the other disciples.
[47] Fry, *RB 1980*, Chapter 33: Monks and Private ownership.
[48] Fry, *RB 1980*, Chapter 48:1.

CHAPTER THREE

Obsculta: the *Labora* (work) of the Benedictine Rule

An old man [desert father] said: 'Never have I desired a work that was useful to me but that caused harm to my brother, for I have this firm hope: that my brother's advantage is for me a work full of fruit'.[1] In the Benedictine tradition, monastic men and women must 'serve one another in works of love'.[2]

Earning a living

This was the first major trial for the new foundation. Polding's vision was that the monks and nuns be as 'one' in accordance with the ideal community of the Acts of the Apostles, 4:32: 'And the multitude of them that believed were of one heart and of one soul; neither said any of them that ought of the things which he possessed was his own; but they had all things in common'. However, the relationship between the monks and nuns was strained by the financial arrangements. Polding

---

1 Feiss, *Monastic Wisdom*, 38.
2 Fry, *RB 1980*, 35–6.

had assured the nuns of a small income: thirty pounds per annum for the whole convent, which he considered to be sufficient for a comfortable subsistence.[3] It was expected that the nuns would be able to supplement this meagre income by the making and embroidering of vestments and other liturgical garments, and eventually by opening a school. The arrangement was tried, in a spirit of obedience to Polding as their superior, but it soon proved to be impractical. The five postulants and two girl boarders had to be fed and cared for with basic necessities. Added to this was the fact that the making and embroidering of vestments was minimised by the assistance which the monks of St Mary's required: heavy laundry work for the monastery and Cathedral, the making and mending of habits for the monks, and the endless darning of stockings for the fourteen boy postulants.[4]

The work described here speaks loudly of the Benedictine *obsculta*—Benedictine women, listening to the direction of the Holy Spirit as it came to them through their founder, Polding. Their acceptance of a meagre income for the rendering of such heavy work was not by any means an isolated case in religious life within the history of the Catholic Church, or society at large. For Benedictine nuns, obedience was one of their vows taken in faith: obedience to the Church, to their immediate superior, Polding, and within the monastery, to their prioress or novice-mistress.

Beginning of the School

Under arrangements made by Polding, two twelve-year-old girls arrived in September 1849 forcing the premature beginning of a school. One girl was Edith Makinson, daughter of Thomas Makinson, one of the two Church of England ministers who had resigned in February 1848 to join the Catholic church. In 1849, he was already

---

[3] John Bede Polding, 'Letter to Barber, 10 August, 1847'. Rev. L. Barber, OSB was the President of the English Benedictine Congregation at this time. The letter in its entirety can be read in Sisters of the Good Samaritan, *The Letters of John Bede Polding*, 89. The Melbourne *Argus* of 23 June 1851 notes that £30 per annum was the annual salary of one gardener. Downloaded from: https://guides.slvvic.gov.au/what the cost/earnings on 19 October 2019.

[4] Forster, 'Magdalen le Clerc', 276.

employed by Polding as a teacher at the college attached to St Mary's Seminary, and would later teach at St Mary's College, Lyndhurst, in Sydney after it opened in February 1852.[5] The second girl was Julia Marum, the niece of one of Polding's pioneer priests.[6] Both were accepted by the nuns at Polding's request, to be educated without a pension. Both were given into the care of Dame Magdalen le Clerc, already an experienced teacher.[7]

Lyndhurst College near Sydney, 1853

The educational venture embarked upon by the nuns was part of what one author calls 'Benedictinism'. Others write of Polding's 'Benedictine

---

5   In February 1848 two Church of England ministers, Thomas Makinson and Robert Sconce, resigned their parishes, and were soon received into the Catholic Church. It was considered by the Anglican Church to be a betrayal. Sconce had been a disciple of [Bishop] Broughton. 'He and Makinson were thought to be influenced by John Henry Newman's position on the authority of the Catholic Church'; . Judd and Cable, *Sydney Anglicans*, 51. See also Daly, 'Makinson, Thomas Cooper (1809–1893)'. The backlash against Broughton from Sydney's Church of England laity led to the collapse of his St James College, which he had opened in 1844 and three years later transferred to Lyndhurst, Glebe. Subsequently Polding bought the property to house St Mary's College.
6   Forster, 'Magdalen le Clerc'. Born in Ireland, Julia Marum was also the niece of two Sisters of Charity, Srs Augustine and Vincent Marum. Sr Augustine Marum was the first religious woman to be professed in Australia.
7   Forster and Prendergast, 'Alumnae Subiaco'.

Dream'[8] that Roman Catholic New South Wales would gather as 'one' under the leadership and influence of Benedictine monasticism. Because the nuns constituted a significant part of Polding's Benedictine dream, they were free to settle into the Australian mission and go on 'listening' to the Holy Spirit at work in the mission, and to the Benedictine Rule and its precepts which would guide their journey.

Sisters of Charity and the Christian Brothers

The Sisters of Charity and the Irish Christian Brothers did not enjoy the same freedom. At the end of the 1840s, while Polding was preparing to return to Sydney with the two foundresses for the women's community, his assistant, Vicar General Henry Gregory, blinded by the Benedictine dream, dealt a death blow to both the Sisters of Charity and the Irish Christian Brothers. He had 'endeavoured to force both the Sisters of Charity and the Christian Brothers to forsake their own congregations and either come under a modification of the Benedictine Rule, or become purely diocesan congregations'.[9] Their refusal was met by Gregory's insistence and so the Christian Brothers returned to Ireland and some of the Sisters of Charity went to Tasmania.

A more detailed description of events has been addressed in Chapter One (pp. 47, 54–55). Henry Gregory's actions would prove to be a major setback for Catholic Education in Sydney and surrounds. While the nuns and girls at Subiaco awaited the opening of a school, the girls lived with the nuns. Such was the adaptability and flexibility of the first three years. The school did not officially open until March 1851, six months after the premature death of Sr Scholastica Gregory, from tuberculosis.

---

8   O'Farrell, *The Catholic Church*; Birt, *Benedictine Pioneers*; Campion, *Australian Catholics*; Shanahan, *Out of Time*.

9   Fogarty, *Catholic Education*, 245.

Non-remunerative work: care of the sick

Chapter 36 of the Rule of Benedict addresses care of the sick. Its theology rests on one foundation: Christ Incarnate. Benedict uses Matthew 25:36 and 40 to support his teaching:

> Care of the sick must rank above and before all else, so that they may truly be served as Christ [...] sick brethren must be patiently borne with [and] the abbot should be extremely careful that they suffer no neglect.[10]

Allowances are made for the sick in diet, separation and hygiene. Mohler suggests that 'the lack of meat, except for the sick, probably reflected the Italian peasant diet'.[11] Daly refers to Chapter 36 of the Rule of Benedict, explaining first that each monastery had an Infirmary and a 'botanical garden where [medicinal] plants could be raised'.[12]

Daly also addresses the subject of monastic buildings, placing the Infirmary 'outside the main group of monastic buildings' and describing who would be eligible for a place there:

> the sick ... the old monks who could no longer follow the full monastic routine, as well as those who had been through the medieval periodic blood-letting and were given a few days for recuperation.[13]

As the centuries evolved, the monasteries became places of therapeutic healing, not only for monks and nuns but for the poor and pilgrims. Guenter B. Risse traces the history of hospitals as originating from the 'hospitality' of monasteries which extended to care of the sick, and the dispensing of welfare. They were, says Risse, 'providers of organized medical care after the fall of the Roman Empire'.[14] Herbal medicine and bathing became trusted sources of healing, alongside spiritual comfort or pastoral care. In the history of monastic women, perhaps the most outstanding example of this therapeutic healing is the work carried out by Hildegard of Bingen (1098–1179).

---

10 Fry, *RB 1980*.
11 Mohler, *Heresy*, 210.
12 Daly, *Benedictine Monasticism*, 306.
13 Daly, *Benedictine Monasticism*, 197.
14 Risse, *Mending Bodies*, 95.

Premature death in the life of the Subiaco community

The first death in the infant community occurred on 8 October 1850. To the great sorrow of this small band of women, it was Sr Scholastica (Jane) Gregory who died. In 1848 she had contracted scarlet fever while living at St Mary's in Sydney. She had been nursed by a Sister of Charity for a period of three months in isolation. In June 1849 she was ill with influenza,[15] and yet endeavoured to carry on the heavy laundry work for St Mary's, and introducing the novices to monastic ways. Letter 7 written on 9 June 1850, describes Scholastica Gregory as 'worn to a mere shadow' with 'a terrible cough, no appetite, little sleep [...] no strength'.[16]

On 20 October 1850, Magdalen le Clerc wrote to Princethorpe Priory, Warwickshire, to inform the prioress and community of Scholastica Gregory's death which had occurred on 8 October. It was tuberculosis (described as consumption in Magdalen le Clerc's letter) which finally claimed her life and the lives of a number of young women under Magdalen le Clerc's care. Following the death of Scholastica Gregory, Magdalen le Clerc was left with two women in vows, and three lay sisters, one of whom, Angela Guilfoyle, left the monastery.[17]

In addition to opening the school in 1851, and keeping up the monastic observance, the nuns nursed Eliza Regan, who entered in 1853 and died in 1859 of tuberculosis. Also requiring nursing was Victorine Hawthornthwaite who entered the monastery in 1851. Following her Profession of Vows in 1853, she became chronically ill, and spent thirty years as an invalid before her death in 1882. Elizabeth Burrows entered the monastery in 1849 and died from tuberculosis in 1859; Bridget Shortall entered in 1851 and died from tuberculosis in 1861. The same illness would claim the lives of six more women before 1870.

---

15 Le Clerc, 'Letter to the Lady Abbess of Stanbrook, June, 1849'. Letter 6 in a collection of 31 letters written by Magdalen le Clerc during her life in Australia. (JAA).
16 Le Clerc, 'Letter to the Lady Abbess of Stanbrook, June 9, 1850'. Letter 7 in a collection of 31 letters. (JAA).
17 During this time, when Sr Benedict Lett contracted a 'rheumatic infection in her hand, which caused inflammation of the left eye, obliging her to be shut up in a dark room for upwards of three months, under a severe course of medicine' (le Clerc, Letter 9), le Clerc was without her right-hand person and co-worker in the school.

Forster notes that during Dame Magdalen le Clerc's years at Subiaco the average age of death in this one monastic community was thirty-six.[18]

The following table shows statistics for deaths from tuberculosis, length of illness, numbers in community (choir nuns, lay sisters), and numbers in the school.

Figure 5: Deaths at Subiaco from Tuberculosis 1850 to 1900

YEAR	DEATH	NUMBER OF CHOIR NUNS	NUMBER OF LAY SISTERS	DATE OF DEATH	LENGTH OF ILLNESS	AGE AT TIME OF DEATH	NUMBERS IN THE SCHOOL
1850	1 choir nun	3	2	01.10.1850	1 year	33	2
1855	1 choir nun	4	4	18.12.1853	5 years[19]	23	No record
1859	1 choir nun	10	6	28.04.1859	Not recorded	34	29
1861	1 lay sister	8	5	18.06.1861	Not recorded	33	39
1867	1 lay sister	10	6	25.11.1867	Not recorded	54	20
1876	1 lay sister	11	4	29.05.1876	4 months	47	24
1877	1 choir nun	11	3	09.11.1877	1 year	34	30
1882	1 choir nun	10	4	07.01.1882	30 years	82	23
1891	1 lay sister	13	7	10.07.1891	Approx. 4 months	40	9
1894	1 choir nun	17	7	24.09.1894	Not recorded	56	14 – two unpaying
1900	1 choir nun	13	7	24.04.1900	15 months	39	12 – four unpaying

18   Community Chronicles, death certificates, and obituaries compiled by Marie Therese Malone in *Tjurunga* 28 (1985), 37–80.
19   This nun, Eliza Nagle, had sought refuge at Subiaco. She was already ill. Her father persecuted his daughter, the Subiaco community, and the Archbishop. He exchanged letters with Henry Gregory in *The Sydney Morning Herald*, expressing his opinions on why his daughter should not have become a Catholic, and why she should not be in the monastery. He threatened the Archbishop (through *The Sydney Morning Herald*), that he would remove his daughter from the monastery. She made her vows on her death bed. See further below, pp. 101–102.

There are no documented letters or notes describing the extent of Scholastica Gregory's physical suffering or how it impacted on her disposition, her response to the call of God, and the working of the Holy Spirit in her missionary commitment. Magdalen le Clerc's admiration of Scholastica Gregory, who, despite her illness and frailty, continued to work, portrayed both her fragility and her generosity.

Spread of tuberculosis in community

The seemingly rapid spread of tuberculosis in the community of Subiaco was caused by a lack of knowledge about the disease. Dr Livingstone Trudeau was the first American to promote isolation as a means not only to spare the healthy, but to heal the sick'.[20] The infirmary at Subiaco was not a separate building, nor were the sick able to be isolated from others who were sick with different illnesses. Jean Antoine Villemin was the first medical scientist who proved that the disease was contagious (1868). Before his time, it was thought by the medical profession to be hereditary, or from 'tubercular' parents. This theory is mentioned several times in the obituaries of the nuns who died in the Nineteenth and Twentieth Centuries from tuberculosis. It was the German microbiologist Robert Koch who discovered the 'tubercle bacillus', whereby a 'single cough or sneeze' on the part of someone with the disease 'might contain hundreds of bacilli' (1882). In the Nineteenth Century, such discoveries were slow in reaching the rest of the world, especially Australia.

Health facilities non-existent

Lesley Potter notes the fact that 'health facilities were practically non-existent in Sydney in the early 1860s, [...] as were the educational opportunities for both the medical and nursing/midwifery professions'.[21] The Benedictine community of Subiaco, while remaining faithful to Chapter 36 of the Rule in their care of the sick, were also doing what the majority of the population in Sydney and surrounding

---

20   For the information in this paragraph: University of Virginia, 'Early Research'.
21   Potter, 'Independent Women', 79–92.

areas did—cared for the sick at home, with herbal and other traditional medicines. Hospitals or Infirmaries were mistrusted because of a lack of hygiene, the infestation of vermin, and the ignorance of medical and nursing staff.[22]

Continuation of the planting of Benedictine women's monasticism

It appears that Magdalen le Clerc, despite the demands of her work in school and community, did not lose sight of her *obsculta* and carried on the planting of Benedictine women's monasticism in the colony of New South Wales. With the opening of the school in March 1851, the heavy laundry work and sewing for St Mary's came to an end.

Covering 1856–1864, Chapter Four will continue to emphasise that the Benedictine nuns were 'disposed and responsive to the call of God and the workings of the Holy Spirit'.[23] The addition of three more nuns from Princethorpe to help the fledgling community of Subiaco will also tell part of the story and objectively assess whether their contribution was positive. They too were called by the *obsculta* of the Benedictine Rule, although the conditions placed upon their commitment—conditions which gave them a way out—may have lightened their load.

---

22 Cf. Godden, 'Hospitals': 'If you were sick you called in a doctor to visit you at home, or you relied on family and friends for care, or you used herbal and traditional remedies'.
23 Polding to the nuns of Stanbrook, 1847.

CHAPTER FOUR

A Window into the Subiaco Community (1856–1864): Tradition as tyranny

This chapter is confined to eight years of Benedictine life at Subiaco into which came three nuns from Princethorpe, who did not have the mission as a priority, or the spirit of the *obsculta* manifest in their response to monastic life. This attitude did not prevail over that of Magdalen le Clerc and the women who had joined the community since its foundation in 1849.

Voyage to Australia

'The Journal of a voyage to Australia 1855–56' by Myles Athy, a recruit for St Mary's Monastery, Sydney, was transcribed by Anne Wark in 2017.[1] Along with other historical sources, the diary notes that on 23 October 1855 Polding left Liverpool for Australia, sailing on the *Phoenix*. The twelve-week journey which Edmund Athy[2] made with Polding, Gregory (Polding's Vicar General, and prior of the Benedictine

---

1   Wark, *Journal*.
2   Edmund was his name as a Benedictine monk.

monastery at St Mary's), and three nuns from Princethorpe Priory gives a reasonably transparent view of the different characters. Polding gave Edmund Athy, on this voyage, what he gave to Scholastica Gregory on the 1847–48 voyage: spiritual instruction, and lessons in Latin. Added to this was the praying of the Rosary[3] and reading aloud to the Archbishop from a spiritual book. For men and women who lived Benedictine monasticism, the Rosary would be considered as private prayer on the part of an individual monk or nun.[4] There is also mention of the Oratorian Hymns of the Rev. Frederick Faber. The prayers and hymns of Frederick Faber belonged in the liturgical tradition of the wider Catholic Church and were not part of Benedictine tradition. However, liturgical boundaries were often blurred, and the hymns of the Oratory reached into monastic, religious, and parish communities of the nineteenth-century Catholic Church. They sought to revive what was lost in the English Reformation of the Sixteenth Century.

In Athy's Journal, Henry Gregory takes on a different *persona* from the 'arbitrary, persecuting'[5] description of Gregory by the monks of his community in Sydney. If anything, Henry Gregory emerges as amiable, and fun-loving. One would have to ask if holding the office of prior brought out the ruthlessness in him.[6]

Polding returns to Australia with three more nuns from Princethorpe Priory

In January 1856 Polding returned from Rome on board the *Phoenix*, with three more nuns from Princethorpe Priory. Polding's orders

---

3 The Rosary had been prayed by Catholics since the 16th Century, but this appears to be the only reference to it in the community's history.
4 For Polding, the praying of the Rosary was an expression of his love of the Mother of God. While at Downside School, soon after his ordination to the priesthood, he 'was instrumental in bringing back into operation amongst the students, the ancient Sodality of the Blessed Virgin'; Fitzwalter, 'Archbishop Polding and Mary', 32–42. In the same article, Fitzwalter relates the story told by H. N. Birt of an elderly Irish woman, devoted to the praying of the Rosary, and the sacramental encounter between her and Polding.
5 O'Farrell, *The Catholic Church*, 91.
6 This wouldn't be a new phenomenon. In Benedictine houses up to the present time, monks and nuns are sometimes given trial periods in the various offices of the house so that the abbot or abbess can see how authority is handled.

from Rome were to 'regularise' the two Benedictine houses he had established.

The arrival of Polding and his party in Melbourne, on the way to Sydney, was recorded by Bishop James Alipius Goold, whose diary is accurate in numbers and names.[7] He records that 'the Archbishop's party consisted of the Vicar General (Dr Gregory), three priests, two students, three nuns, and a postulant'. The three nuns were Sr Scholastica McCarthy, Sr des Anges Chivot, and Sr Editha Amshurst. Unlike Sr Scholastica Gregory and her companion Miss Edgar, who had entered Princethorpe Priory specifically to be formed in the Benedictine life and then sail with Polding for the Australian mission, the three women who came in 1856 were committed members of their own community. They were formed strictly in the ways of Princethorpe Priory and they came with conditions imposed on them by their Prioress Madame du Chastelet, and agreed to by Polding on 3 September 1855, which seemed to relieve Princethorpe of any financial responsibility for their nuns while yet wielding authority over the new house at Subiaco. Polding replied to Madame du Chastelet, addressing her concerns:

> 1. I do not consider that they [the three nuns] will have any claim on the Mother House (Princethorpe) for support and maintenance except in the case of their return to it.
>
> 2. My object in taking out the Sisters [to the Australian mission] is that they may devote themselves to aid in the establishing of the Community of Subiaco according to the Constitutions of St. Mary's Priory, Princethorpe, with such accidental modifications as the circumstances of New South Wales require, and that may be introduced in strict harmony with the spirit of the Rule and Constitutions ascertained and regulated in [a]

---

7   James Alipius Goold was a member of the Augustinian Order, and the 'first of the Irish bishops of the [colonial] period. [He came to] Australia at Ullathorne's request'; cf. Molony, *Roman Mould*, 31–32. Goold was the historian for the Council of the Australian Catholic Church. The postulant referred to doesn't appear again in the history of the Subiaco community.

Canonical Visitation.⁸ No objection will be made on the part of the ecclesiastical authority in New South Wales to the return of the sisters to the parent house, if after a fair trial, it is found that their union with the sisters already of the community of Subiaco is not a happy and a useful one, or, that being the case they do not succeed in establishing a separate House governed by their own Constitutions.⁹

Since '[t]radition is not a thing [nor] an archive [nor] a school of thought or a series of rituals',¹⁰ Madame du Chastelet's inflexible and non-adaptable policy could have stifled, but fortunately did not, the growth of the Subiaco community. The Princethorpe tradition was one community's interpretation of Benedictine life for women, but, as Casey presents it: 'None of the many expressions of the Benedictine tradition has any inherent right to claim to be permanently normative. Each embodiment speaks to its own time and to its own culture'.¹¹

The community of Subiaco 1856–1861

During the period when the three Princethorpe nuns were in Australia, the Benedictine community of Subiaco was evolving into a mirror of colonial society, albeit a monastic one, and it is fair to say that in the beginning, all made the effort at harmonious living. A letter written by Magdalen le Clerc to the Lady Abbess of Stanbrook on 15 February 1856 provides a positive indication of this early harmony:

> Our union [between Princethorpe and Stanbrook] is almost miraculous—the Subprioress [Scholastica McCarthy] is but one heart and soul with me, and does not take one step in the establishment of discipline without consulting me and having my full consent—this you may be sure is readily granted as I have but one wish with her—viz. that my dear children should be

---

8   Shanahan, *Out of Time,* 109, sums up the conditions in a masterful way, saying: 'the nuns were going to [Australia] to change nothing except convent and climate'.
9   Forster, *Subiaco Resource Book, Vol. 2.*.
10 Casey, 'Tradition, Interpretation, Reform', 400.
11 Casey, 'Tradition, Interpretation, Reform', 401.

brought up in the true Benedictine spirit, so admirably carried out in the Constitutions of Princethorpe.[12]

Le Clerc goes on to speak about the 'humility and deference of this saintly Mother who is not three years younger than myself'[13] as filling her with astonishment. She describes Scholastica McCarthy kneeling before her in Chapter,[14] 'to make her accusation of faults', and how this action overwhelmed le Clerc. Although le Clerc entreated her not to do it, McCarthy insisted upon fulfilling the Rule that requires all, even the subprioress, to submit to this humiliation.

M. Magdalen le Clerc (top centre) with Dom Bede Sumner and Angelo Ambrosoli. c. 1860s

---

12   Le Clerc, 'Letter to the Lady Abbess of Stanbrook Abbey, February 15, 1856', Letter 19 of the transcribed Letters of Magdalen le Clerc. (JAA)
13   Le Clerc, 'Letter to the Lady Abbess and the community of Stanbrook Abbey, March 14, 1853', Letter 9 of the transcribed Letters of Magdalen le Clerc. (JAA)
14   In monastic communities, the Chapter of Faults was held weekly. It was the time when each member of the community would kneel before the prioress and confess faults against the customs and agreements of life in community. It did not consist of divulging serious sin, such as temptations against the monastic vows. Classic examples of faults which needed to be declared in Chapter would be: breaking the agreed times of silence, absenting oneself from a community exercise, handling the tools and goods of the monastery carelessly. In the Benedictine Rule Chapter 31:10, it is clearly stated that a monk/nun 'will regard all utensils and goods of the monastery as sacred vessels of the altar, aware that nothing is to be neglected' (Rule of Benedict, 80).

Polding appointed Sr Scholastica McCarthy to act in the capacity of subprioress and novice mistress.[15] Unfortunately the initial positive relationship between prioress and subprioress was not lasting. Within a couple of years of the three nuns' arrival from Princethorpe, Magdalen le Clerc developed an anti-French attitude. This was so marked that the nuns were forbidden by Polding to speak of nationality but not before factions had developed within the community. This development militated against the exhortation of St Benedict to 'let peace be your quest and aim' (Prologue v.17), to 'serve one another in works of love' (RB80 35:6) and to 'show to one another […] pure love' (RB80 72:8).[16] The continuity of Benedictine charism and tradition was beginning to be challenged by cultural tension.

Restructuring of the financial situation

In spite of cultural conflict, a positive contribution was made during the six-year period by Sr Scholastica McCarthy who set out to re-structure the financial situation, separating it from the finances of St Mary's in Sydney. This arose because of an equally dysfunctional situation at St Mary's,[17] and because of what McCarthy saw as injustice towards Subiaco.

The financial injustice was a situation which could only have been changed by an outsider, and not by Magdalen le Clerc, who was too closely associated with Polding and strongly supportive of the Australian Benedictine mission. Sr Scholastica McCarthy approached Polding on this matter, and it was decided that the nuns of Subiaco should manage their own financial affairs, separately from St Mary's. This meant that the school fees would substantially support the nuns of

---

15   Polding had thus appointed both the prioress (Dame Magdalen le Clerc), and the subprioress. This is 'deplored in Chapter 65 of the Rule of Benedict', as noted by Forster, 'Magdalen le Clerc', 304.
16   These quotations have been taken from Fry, *RB 1980*.
17   Butler, 'Jean Gourbeillon', 40, notes Edmund Moore's letter to Downside ('Moore to Alphonsus Morrall, 8 February, 1848'), lamenting that he found 'not so much as one rule of any kind by which the House was governed'.

Subiaco. The Ledger[18] she began was kept until 1945, and gives an annual account of choir nuns and lay sisters, pupils (numbers who paid, and numbers who didn't), workmen, housemaids, and domestic servants. It is probable that from a position of prejudice Magdalen le Clerc wrote in 1861 to the Lady Abbess of Stanbrook, asking for 'a model of the plans you use in drawing up the general accounts—as they were shown in the [community] Council every six months [...] your plan is so much clearer and better than the one adopted here after the Princethorpe style'.[19]

School numbers increase

During the period 1856–1861, while the three nuns from Princethorpe were at Subiaco, the numbers in the school rose to thirty-nine pupils. However, it is highly unlikely that the numbers rose because of the presence of the three nuns from Princethorpe. It is more likely to be because of the changing economy.

The 1850s also saw the discovery of gold in Australia. Edward Hargraves is the name associated with this period of prosperity, after his exaggerated and falsified claims about gold discovered near Bathurst triggered the 1851 Gold Rush.[20] The population grew. From the end of the 1850s the numbers in the school dropped to thirty and below, except for the year 1861 when there were thirty-nine pupils.[21]

---

18   This Ledger is a primary historical source and reference document for any scholar carrying out research on the history of the Subiaco community. It also bears the signatures of the various Prelates who carried out Canonical Visitations through the 19th and 20th Centuries. (JAA).
19   Le Clerc, 'Letter to a nun of Stanbrook Abbey, November 1861', Letter no. 22 of the transcribed letters of Magdalen le Clerc (JAA). Despite the request, the Ledger set up by Sr Scholastica McCarthy based on the Princethorpe model remained.
20   Molony, *A History*, 101–119; Mitchell, 'Hargraves, Edward Hammond'.
21   These statistics can be viewed in the Ledger which was set up by Sr Scholastica McCarthy.

Subiaco, Rydalmere c. 1850s

The effects of the Princethorpe nuns on monastic living at Subiaco

Forster notes that during the period 1856–1861, Princethorpe customs were perfected, devotions multiplied, strict discipline enforced, observance upheld, and an exalted spirituality aspired to.[22] On the issue of devotions, the English Benedictine Congregation published in 1861, a 'Manual of Devotions to Our Holy Father Saint Benedict, Abbot and Patriarch of Western Monks; to his Sister, Saint Scholastica, Virgin and Abbess; and to All Saints of His Holy Order'. This book contained the Little Office of St Benedict, prayers, and hymns in honour of St Benedict, the office of St Scholastica, and various hymns, prayers, and devotions relevant to this time in Benedictine history. The book was printed in London with the approval of Abbot Placid Burchall, Abbot President of the English Congregation of the Order of St Benedict. The book was in use at Subiaco. The copies which survive reveal a very personal use of these devotions. The annotations reveal a depth of individual responses to the sentiments therein. Such books catered for the affective dimension in the spiritual lives of monks and nuns, providing the opportunity to pray in English, rather than Latin. The Liturgy of the Hours, on the other hand, was prayed only in Latin, as was the daily Mass.

22 Forster, 'Magdalen le Clerc', 301.

The three Nuns returned to Princethorpe in 1861. Most of the reasons profferred for their return are speculative, one being that Polding did not honour his promise that the Princethorpe Constitutions would be adhered to according to the letter of the law. He made too many adaptations, and modifications to colonial living. Magdalen le Clerc disagreed with this:

> His Grace is accused of breaking his contract—that the Princethorpe Constitutions should be observed—which they are and have been to the very letter—as far as was in any way compatible with circumstances and—we are as strict here as they are there.[23]

From the evidence of his Pastoral Letters to the Catholics of Sydney, Polding was listening and seeking to respond to the movement and inspiration of the Holy Spirit in the Australian mission.[24]

The three nuns from Princethorpe, on the other hand, were in Australia for a limited time, living according to their own Constitutions and customs, according to the letter of the law. They were, because of their vow of obedience, under obedience to the then Prioress of Princethorpe, Madame du Chastelet. They were in Australia, but not of Australia; obedient to their own constitutions and customs, and forbidden to indulge in any exceptions to the rule. The Heraclitan principle that everything changes, nothing remains still, is one of the underlying forces in the process of handing on tradition. Stepping on to a new land was, for the Princethorpe nuns, just a continuation of all that was Princethorpe, not a new chapter in the history of Benedictine monasticism.[25]

In keeping with their new situation in Australia, Polding was, in many instances, compassionate and understanding towards the women of Subiaco, who were affected by climate-related illnesses. He made exceptions to a demanding daily *horarium*, and allowed rest during the Australian summer. He was also moving more and more

---

23 le Clerc, 'Letter to the Lady Abbess of Stanbrook Abbey, July 10, 1860'. Letter 24 of the transcribed letters of Magdalen le Clerc.
24 Haines et al., *The Eye of Faith*.
25 Shanahan, *Out of Time*, 109.

into a spirit of nationhood. In his Pastoral Letter of 1856, Polding wrote:

> Before everything else we are Catholics, and next, by a name swallowing up all distinctions, we are Australians [...] and the man who seeks by word or writing to perpetuate invidious distinctions is an enemy to our peace and prosperity.[26]

Such a position may have been distasteful to those whose ties remained with an English community, founded from France.

Other reasons given for the departure of the three nuns were the strained relationships in Sydney between those who supported the Benedictine plan and those who didn't. Scholastica McCarthy (from Princethorpe) was the sister of Helena McCarthy, the second Mother General of the Sisters of Charity in Ireland, and the contact person for the Sisters of Charity in Sydney, who had been treated so discourteously by Henry Gregory. Magdalen le Clerc refrained from verbal involvement. Scholastica McCarthy was outspoken on the matter. This issue is not the subject of this book, and so is left for other historical analysis. Still, it is supposed to have been one of the reasons for the recall of the nuns of Princethorpe—that, and the dying wish of their prioress at the time. After the departure of the three nuns, Magdalen le Clerc, previously restrained, took up her pen and wrote to the Abbess of Stanbrook:

> Mother Scholastica McCarthy's ideas of perfection are far too exalted for infant establishments, nor is she a person altogether calculated for government—notwithstanding her great virtue and eminent qualities [...] She feels most bitterly the disappointment of not being able to carry out the views which she had formed by herself in coming out here—and has not the slightest suspicion that any mismanagement of her own may have contributed thereto. It would have been well if Stanbrook alone had sent out missioners.[27]

---

26 Pastoral Letter for Lent, 1856, O'Farrell, *Documents, Vol. I*, 155.
27 'Missioners' is the word she used. 'Missionaries' is the term more familiar to people of the 20th and 21st Centuries.

A letter written by Sr des Anges Chivot, from Princethorpe to Stanbrook, in 1890, presents a different portrayal of the relationship between Magdalen le Clerc and Scholastica McCarthy. It is described as being one of 'perfect concord and charity in spite of the false position each one occupied'. It is probable that the term 'false' means 'in the wrong order'—that Magdalen le Clerc should have appointed her own subprioress and novice mistress, in accordance with the Rule of Benedict. She finishes the letter on a more realistic note, saying:

> Of course, we had our own crosses during these five years. The cross is everywhere, but for truth's sake add that these crosses were never caused by Dame Magdalen. What a religious model! What a soul of faith! What a heart burning with the love of God. She was devoured with zeal for the house of God and the salvation of souls.[28]

This nun may have been trying to build bridges between Stanbrook and Princethorpe. Communication between Magdalen le Clerc and Stanbrook Abbey continued until 1874, three years before Polding's death and four years before her own. Polding was eighty and Magdalen le Clerc seventy-six when she penned a witness statement of the way she and Polding had come to the final years of their commitment to the Australian mission:

> His dear old Grace is become such a Home Bird. He seldom can muster courage to come as far as Parramatta, but, thank God, he is wonderfully well; you know, on the 18th next Month he completes his 80th year! And somebody else (not worthy of mention) her 76th.[29]

---

28 Sr des Anges Chivot to Stanbrook, 1890 (JAA, copy of letter obtained from Stanbrook Abbey during the 1990s).
29 Extract from a letter dated 2 October 1874. Addressee is not given, but the letter appears to be a response to news she has had from England. Polding died on 16th March, 1877. Magdalen le Clerc died on 30th March, 1878.

The colonial character of the Subiaco community

The following nuns were in the community of the 1850s and 1860s: Benedict (Alicia) Lett, Placida (Elizabeth) Burrows, and Walburge (Ruth Woods) Wallis, an English woman who had first tried her monastic vocation at Stanbrook and was advised to leave. Also in the community was Angela (Eliza) Regan, born in Tasmania of Irish parents and a former pupil in the Subiaco School, who entered in 1853.[30] Sr M. Bernard (Victorine) Hawthornthwaite, an English woman, entered the community in 1851. She was well-educated and already an accomplished teacher. While the community had great hopes for her in regard to the Subiaco school, oral tradition has passed on that she was only able to make a limited contribution to the community's life and work after very early on she became chronically ill, and spent the next thirty years being cared for.[31]

The other nuns were: Sr Elizabeth (Mary Ann) Dwyer, the granddaughter of Michael Dwyer, the Wicklow Chieftain, and one of the leaders of the 1798 rebellion against the tyranny of the English. Michael Dwyer and his accomplices were sent to the penal colony of New South Wales in 1803, and became, in the words of Patrick O'Farrell, 'a colonial cynosure, hero-worshipped by their fellow Irish. They were, in fact, more exiles than prisoners'.[32] O'Farrell describes Dwyer as a 'gentleman leader', one who certainly gained from 'transportation'. Along with his fellow exiles, he became a land-holder in the Campbelltown area. Both his granddaughter and his great-granddaughter (Rose Dwyer) entered the Subiaco community.[33] His grandson, John, entered the Benedictine Community of St Mary's in Sydney.

Sr Evangelista (Joanna) Donovan was professed with Sr Walburge (Ruth Woods) Wallis. She was restless, and difficult in community. In

---

30 Her profession of monastic vows was delayed because of ill-health. She died, aged 26, of tuberculosis.
31 Malone, 'Obit List', 41, 39. Copied from an unpublished manuscript 'Torrens in Austra: "*Subiaco*", 1849–1864'. Based on twenty-five years of research, Higgins, *The Woman of Many Names*, presents Jane Hawthornthwaite in a much more positive light.
32 O'Farrell, *The Irish In Australia*, 30.
33 John O'Sullivan, a free Catholic immigrant, sent his three daughters to the Subiaco School. He was the husband of Bridget Dwyer, daughter of Michael Dwyer, the Wicklow Chieftan. See Forster and Prendergast, 'Alumnae Subiaco'.

1864 (22 April), Polding wrote in a letter to Henry Gregory (now in England) that Joanna Donovan was one of the two thorns afflicting the young prioress (Walburge Wallis).[34] In another letter of 1870, he wrote: 'They have had trouble at Subiaco from S. M. Evangelista Donovan. I have arranged for her to go to the Sisters of Mercy, Albury, as a visitor. If she has a vocation I shall apply to Rome for transfer'.[35] He did apply for this transfer in March 1871.[36]

As the real Superior of the Subiaco community, Polding's course of action in the case of S. M. Evangelista Donovan manifests an understanding and fidelity to the Rule of Benedict, in an *obsculta* which 'let mercy triumph over judgement'[37] and did not 'crush the bruised reed'.[38] Discernment in the Rule of Benedict is one of the duties of the abbot. It is found in Chapter 2, verses 16 and 21, the first chapter on the abbot. It is reiterated, though differently, in Chapter 63, verses 1 and 5, where it is stated that 'monks keep their rank in the monastery according to the date of their entry, the virtue of their lives, and the decision of the abbot'.[39] Finally, in Chapter 64, verse 17, the abbot is to:

> show forethought and consideration in his orders, and whether the task he assigns concerns God or the world, he should be discerning and moderate, bearing in mind the discretion of holy Jacob, who said: If I drive my flocks too hard, they will all die in a single day.[40]

---

34 Walburge (Ruth Woods) Wallis was elected as the first Prioress three years after the departure of the Princethope nuns.
35 This arrangement on the part of Polding is an early example of discernment which later, after the Second Vatican Council, and into the 1970s, became essential for the acceptance of candidates for monastic and religious life.
36 The Sisters of Mercy in Albury did not accept her for profession and no further information is held in the Archives of Jamberoo Abbey. Joanna's sister, Catherine, entered the Goulburn Sisters of Mercy, and was the first Australian-born woman to do so. (JAA – a small note in the Chronicles for 1865).
37 James 2:13; Rule of Benedict 64:10.
38 Isaiah 42:3; Rule of Benedict 64:14.
39 Fry, *RB 1980*, 63:1–5.
40 Cf. Genesis 33:13.

The novitiate of the 1850s and 1860s

In the novitiate during the 1850s was Sr Xaveria (Catherine) Heydon, who had been a pupil in the Subiaco School, as was her sister Emily. According to Magdalen le Clerc, Catherine Heydon had imbibed her father's spirit. Le Clerc called the *Freeman's Journal* (under the management of Catherine and Emily's father), the 'agent of Satan', and is relieved when Polding, on the twelfth anniversary of the nuns' arrival in the colony, could join them on an excursion, and escape the 'nest of calumny, the wretched Babylon of Sydney, and the mean abuse of the *Freeman's Journal*'.[41] Le Clerc also remarks in the same letter that she 'has come in for a bit of its abuse now and then'. Having said that, she then says that she never troubles her head about 'such nonsense, and would not read a line of a paper envenomed by the breath of "Old Scrat" [the devil]'.[42]

Freeman's Journal masthead

Catherine Heydon and the other two novices under the direction of Scholastica McCarthy formed a 'trio' of 'deserters'. According to Magdalen le Clerc, Sr Xaveria (Catherine) Heydon was the ringleader. She describes these three women as 'subjects of pity'.[43] Thus, three of six

---

41 le Clerc, 'Letter to the Lady Abbess of Stanbrook Abbey, March 14, 1853', No. 9 in the collection of transcribed letters.
42 Le Clerc, 'Letter to the Lady Abbess of Stanbrook Abbey, March 14, 1853'.
43 Le Clerc, 'Letter to the Lady Abbess of Stanbrook Abbey, February, 1860', No. 23 in the collection of transcribed letters. (No date is given for this letter, just the month).

novices left when Scholastica McCarthy was the novice mistress. One would have to ask if the tyranny of tradition, and the declarations and customs of Princethorpe Priory were unsuited to the younger women of the New World, called to a more magnanimous *obsculta*.

Le Clerc's letter to Catherine Heydon's father is more tempered by charity. At the end, she states her firm conviction that Catherine has a decided vocation to the religious state, but is troubled by a 'peculiar turn of her character' which seems to 'require more active employment [...] than existing circumstances' [at Subiaco] provide. Finally, le Clerc writes: 'She leaves Subiaco with my affectionate and fervent prayers that God may direct her to do whatever may [...] most effectually promote his glory'.[44]

The story of Catherine Heydon has been documented, in two parts, by her great-grandson, Fr George Connolly. The first part of this history researches Catherine's life from the time she left Subiaco until the time she went to the country as a governess (1858–1868).[45] Catherine married Nathaniel Connolly, a widower with a family. Born to Catherine and Nathaniel was Richard Hugh Connolly, whom they sent to Downside School for his education. Richard entered the Downside community to become a Benedictine monk. He was ordained a priest in 1899. He was the Head of Benet House, Cambridge, in the early years of the Twentieth Century. He was a prominent scholar in both early Church History and in Syrian Christianity.[46]

Sr M. Gertrude (Eliza) Nagle had become a Catholic in 1850, and endured the rejection of her family for doing so. She entered the Subiaco community, more for refuge than to live out a monastic vocation. She had no money, and was already ill from her circumstances with family. In the meantime, her father issued threats to Polding—that he would remove his daughter from the convent. Her father and Henry

---

44   Emily Heydon, 'Letter to her father, Jabez King Heydon', JAA. See pp. 120–121. Letter supplied by Fr George Connolly, direct descendant of Catherine Connolly (née Heydon). The letter was a part of the family archives. Fr George Connolly is now deceased.
45   Connolly, 'Catherine Heydon', 19–47.
46   These facts are summarised from Fr George Connolly's article, 'Catherine Heydon', 18–27; they can also be found in Cross, 'Connolly, Richard Hugh (1873–1948)'. It is also noted in Linane, *Biographies*, that Richard Connolly was the first Catholic Priest to take a Cambridge Degree since the Reformation.

Gregory exchanged letters on the matter in *The Sydney Morning Herald*. In one letter to *The Sydney Morning Herald*,[47] Charles Nagel concludes:

> To the laws of that Government under which I live, I am resolved to appeal for the redress for the intolerable grievance I complain of – the illegal act of trepanning a child from her father and near relatives. In those [laws of Government] I have the fullest confidence, and trust that so flagrant a breach of the ordinances of God and man will not be suffered to pass with impunity. From those laws, I claim the restoration of a child to her father and near relatives, her rescue from the fangs of the Roman Catholic priesthood.[48]

There is some doubt as to whether she was ever professed. The St Mary's Monastic Journal records that she took vows on her death bed. The Subiaco records note that she died on December 18 1855 of tuberculosis, and was buried the following day, 'holding the Form of Profession in her hands, but clad in the monastic habit of a Novice'.[49]

Sr Placid Loughnan (entered in 1860) was from a wealthy Melbourne Catholic family of Spanish/Irish origins. Before her entrance into monastic life, she was known in high society as the 'Belle of Melbourne'. Her sister also entered, but left during the novitiate. Sr Placid, Isabella Loughnan, was the daughter of an Officer in the British Army in Bengal.[50]

From a colonial pioneer family came Jane Therry (entered in 1858), one of the daughters of Sir Roger Therry.[51] Therry was Attorney-General in the colony in the early 1840s, and had a seat in the Legislative Council. By 1846 he was a judge of the Supreme Court of New South Wales. Jane Therry was well-known to Polding.

---

47 'Persecution by the Roman Catholic priests', *The Sydney Morning Herald*, 31 May 1850, 2.
48 The father's name is spelt 'Nagel' in *The Sydney Morning Herald*. His daughter's name is spelt 'Nagle' in Community records and those of St Mary's Cathedral.
49 Community Chronicles, 1850s. (JAA)
50 Death Notice: Sr Placid Loughnan, *Freeman's Journal* Saturday 4 August 1894, 15.
51 Sir Roger Therry (1800–1874), Lawyer, Judge, and Acting Attorney-General.

Mother Austin (Julia) Marum, formerly one of the first pupils in the School, entered the community in 1856.[52]

In 1860, Eliza Merewether entered the community. Daughter of Francis Lewis Shaw Merewether[53] and Kate Amelia Plunkett (John Hubert Plunket's sister), Eliza was born in Sydney and brought up with a healthy perspective on a maturing colonial society. Her father, through the 1840s and 1850s, held various positions in Government: Colonial Treasurer, Clerk of the Councils, Clerk of the Executive Councils. As Auditor-General from 1852–1856, he was successful in proposing that the University of Sydney should be granted the 128 acres of waste pasturage known as Grose Farm. He was an original Fellow of the Senate of the University of Sydney, and held the positions of both Vice-Chancellor and Chancellor. He also managed to secure the Main Building in stone rather than brick, and the Great Hall as well.[54]

It is probable that he educated Eliza and her sister Lavinia at home, as the family moved house a number of times for proximity to Merewether's work commitments. Alternatively, he may have employed a governess. Merewether was a graduate of Eton and Trinity College, Cambridge. The motto for the University of Sydney was successfully proposed by Merewether: *Sidere mens eadem mutato*.[55] After Eliza's Profession of Vows, the Merewether family returned to England. Eliza (Mother Justina) Merewether taught English and Music in the Subiaco School for many years, which indicates a solid educational background.

All the choir nuns mentioned here were formed under the Benedictine Rule as interpreted by the Princethorpe Constitutions. The question of fidelity to the *obsculta* of the Benedictine Rule arises. Michael Casey, writing in 2002 on the Benedictine Rule and culture, comments:

---

52 The title 'Mother' was later attached to her name as a mark of reverence for her early connections with the community. It was also given to other pioneer nuns, for example Benedict (Alicia) Lett.

53 Smith, 'Merewether'..

54 Mowle, *A Genealogical History*, 257. Some dates in this history differing from dates noted in other biographical accounts, have been omitted here.

55 Loosely translated as 'the same mind under a different Star' (or, a different constellation), expressing the same standard of learning as in the English Halls of learning: Oxford or Cambridge, or Eton. Cf. Smith, ' F. L. S. Merewether', 10.

> The interaction between a written text and ongoing experience may be represented as a circle or spiral in which tradition and life interact to guarantee a fidelity that is not only in continuity with its sources, but also responsive to what the Spirit is saying to the churches. (Prologue v.11).[56]

Casey also notes that the Benedictine Rule

> does not attempt to legislate by defining boundaries and having them enforced. It operates rather at the level of beliefs and values ... the abbot and monastic officials are expected to teach, to communicate values, to establish a climate of meaning.[57]

That 'climate of meaning' is built upon the Rule's *obsculta*.

The lay sisters of the 1850s and 1860s

The lay sisters at this time were Bridget Shortall (entered in 1851), the two Diamond sisters from Ireland (who entered on Foundation Day), Bridget Schahill, born in Ireland in 1833, and Margaret Fitzpatrick, daughter of two Irish convicts. Margaret's mother, Mary Walsh, had been transported on the worst of convict ships of 1828, *The Elizabeth*.[58] She was a farm servant, convicted for possessing forged notes. Margaret's father, Thomas Fitzpatrick, was convicted of horse stealing and transported for seven years.[59] Two of their daughters entered religious life, one joining the Benedictines of Subiaco, and one the Good Samaritan Sisters, the Religious Order founded by Polding in 1857. Mary Hogan was born in Ireland, and entered Subiaco in 1852. Catherine

---

56 Casey, 'The Rule of Benedict and Inculturation'.
57 Casey, 'The Rule of Benedict and Inculturation'. Casey is referring to his earlier journal article, 'Leadership'.
58 Of seventeen women who were given life sentences, fifteen were under the age of forty. Apart from two women there was no previous offence. Seventeen children accompanied their mothers to Australia. One was a teenager and the rest were under nine years of age; 'One of the saddest aspects of transportation is the number of children who were left behind in Ireland'; Voytas, *Elizabeth*, 25.
59 Thomas Fitzpatrick was transported on the convict ship *Henry Porcher*. His wife, Mary Walsh, came on the *Elizabeth*. Thomas and Mary were married on 20 July 1829.

Comyn was born in Co. Clare, and entered the Subiaco community in 1850, to be a lay sister.

While the Prologue of the Rule of Benedict states that Benedictine monks and nuns journey 'with the Gospel for their guide' (Prologue 21), it cannot be ignored that every lay sister, except one, was an Irish woman, and in some way inferior to the educated English women of the community. The Diamond sisters had come on the *Lallah Rookh*, arriving in Sydney on December 26 1841. Both had their 'calling' listed on the shipping record as 'domestic servant'.[60] Upon arrival in Sydney, Margaret Diamond was assigned to Mr John Terry Hughes at Albion House (corner of Mary and Albion Streets, Sydney). Susannah was assigned to the Caroline Chisholm House at Parramatta. This equipped them for their domestic service in the Benedictine community and by extension, the continuity of charism.

Election of the first prioress

In 1864, three years after the departure of the Princethorpe Nuns, the ten solemnly professed nuns of Subiaco applied to Polding for permission to elect their own prioress. Permission being granted, Polding presided at this election which saw Walburge (Ruth Woods) Wallis become the first elected prioress.[61] She was just thirty-two years of age, and eight years in vows. She suffered ill-health, and Magdalen le Clerc did not have much confidence in her. In the background was the fact that Sr Walburge Wallis had entered Stanbrook, le Clerc's community.[62]

---

60   *Lallah Rookh*, 26 December 1841. Shipping record: Susannah Diamond, unmarried female Immigrant. Calling: Domestic Servant. In good health and likely to be useful. Margaret Diamond, 22 year old unmarried female. This information was obtained from the Kiama Family History Centre. Susannah's death certificate lists her occupation as 'nurse'.

61   Even in the 21st Century, a Diocesan Bishop or an Abbot President (should the community belong to a Congregation as such) must preside over the election of an abbess. The first abbess of the community was elected in 1982, after the monastery was raised to the status of an abbey that same year.

62   Community Chronicles, 1864. (JAA)

Prioress Walburge (Ruth Woods) Wallis. c. 1870s

The Stanbrook Annals record that she was an orphan of twenty-one years of age at her time of entering, having been through painful family trials following the death of both parents, and in a state of vulnerability which won for her the motherly affection of the Abbess of Stanbrook, Lady Scholastica Gregson. Even at the age of twenty-one, Ruth Woods Wallis was highly educated and gifted intellectually. It was the Abbess of Stanbrook who discontinued her novitiate and who 'with tender solicitude, continued to watch over this unprotected child'.[63] Through her recommendation, Ruth Woods Wallis was introduced to Henry Gregory when he was nearing his return journey to Australia in 1854.

In the spirit of the Benedictine Rule, she was a listener, both to her abbess, to the chaplain of Stanbrook at that time, and, one could infer, to Henry Gregory on the long voyage to Australia. Her ability to listen to the promptings of the Holy Spirit in her life enabled her to find her 'climate of meaning'.[64] It was arranged for her to be conducted to the Subiaco convent, where her talents as a teacher in the school would be a real boon. It was also stated in the Stanbrook Chronicles that she

---

63   Excerpt from the Stanbrook Chronicles sent to the Jamberoo Abbey Archives, c. 1997.
64   Casey, 'The Rule of Benedict and Inculturation', 53.

might prove a future candidate for the Subiaco monastic community. In fact, after six weeks in the school, she asked to enter the community.

When she was elected in 1864, part of le Clerc's lack of confidence was because of Wallis's indecisiveness during the novitiate. Important to the discernment at the time was the fact that she did not relate to another novice, who was not well-educated, and who did not appear to have an authentic vocation to the monastic life. This sister was eventually dismissed by le Clerc. In the same novitiate was Evangelista Donovan, who, according to Forster, was struggling against the inactivity of monastic life.[65] Polding, in his capacity as canonical superior, assisted Evangelista Donovan to seek her vocation with the Sisters of Mercy. Despite le Clerc's misgivings about Wallis, and the fact that in 1864 Wallis took on a 'somewhat divided' community, her leadership proved to be strong, and she succeeded in 'stabilising and uniting the community'.[66]

Turning to the Subiaco School, Chapter Five will show how the work of the Benedictine nuns was set on a firm foundation, as they met one of the most pressing needs of the colony during 1856 to 1864—part of which was the road from financial insecurity to financial stability. Despite the tyrannical approach of the three nuns from Princethorpe, one of them effectively brought the money earned by nuns out of St Mary's control, and into Subiaco management.

---

65   Forster, 'Magdalen le Clerc', 291.
66   Malone, 'Obit List', 47.

CHAPTER FIVE

The Subiaco School (1851–1854)

The Benedictine nuns continued their fidelity to the Benedictine rule in a spirit of *obsculta* and their response to the call of God and the working of the Holy Spirit, in meeting one of the immediate needs of colonial society—the need for education. Set against the most significant events in Catholic society of the time, this chapter focuses on the Subiaco School, prior to the year 1856, when Polding was told by Roman authorities to regularise both the women's and men's communities he had founded.

The School

The school, advertised as being under the care of the Benedictine nuns, and near Parramatta, opened officially in March 1851 and began with four pupils.[1] Polding had insisted that the nuns were to provide schooling for young ladies at Subiaco, with an emphasis that the richer classes of society were the preference. The opening of the Subiaco School occurred three years after the colonial Government set up the dual system of education, operated by a Denominational Schools Board and a Board of National Education (January 1848). Both Boards received Government grants. The dual system was in operation until

---

1   This was also the year of the great rush for gold, which began in May 1851.

1867. The Subiaco School was not governed by either Board, and so was considered to be a private boarding school.[2]

1856 was also the year that the Anglican Church opened an independent school for the daughters of Clergymen, St Catherine's, Waverley. Fr Therry founded the first Roman Catholic school on Hunter Street in Parramatta in 1820.[3] In 1835, a year after Polding arrived in the colony of New South Wales, he took control of schools and by the end of 1836, there were thirteen Catholic primary schools: seven for boys, and six for girls. All these schools had Government support. Seven years after the Benedictine nuns officially opened a school, the Sisters of Charity opened a second boarding school for girls in East Sydney (1858), and two years after that, the Sisters of Mercy opened a third boarding and day school for girls in Geelong (1860).[4]

In 1851, when the Benedictine nuns opened their school, there was in operation across the colony a system of twenty-two National Schools, engineered by George Rusden, who was 'a great promoter of non-denominational government schools, publishing a significant polemic on the subject in 1853'.[5] By the beginning of 1856, there were ninety-two elementary schools in Sydney and across the Cumberland plain. There was no lack of education. From the chaplain on the First Fleet, Rev. Richard Johnson, onwards, the Anglican Chaplains had engaged teachers, built schools, and overseen education in New South Wales on behalf of Government. Through this means, even in what is defined as the early colonial period until 1830, the Government established schools 'for the children of convicts based in Sydney and even for Aboriginal children'.[6] There may have been a lack of convent schools, but no lack of schools.

Allan Grocott names the year 1822 as one which saw the growth of 'chapels-cum-school houses [...] located at Castlereagh, Richmond, Pitt Town, Wilberforce, Campbelltown, Kissing Point and Pennant

---

2   Molony, *The Penguin Bicentennial History*, 132–133, 216–217; Fogarty, *Catholic Education*, 26–113; Campbell and Proctor, *A History of Australian Schooling*.
3   Southerwood, *Time-Line*, 4.
4   Barcan, 'Education for a liberal democracy', 75.
5   Campbell and Proctor, *A History of Australian Schooling*, 43.
6   Sherington and Campbell, 'Education', 1.

Hills'.⁷ Sherington and Campbell speak of 'private venture' schools 'for the sons and daughters of free settlers'.⁸ The King's School at Parramatta was a Church of England School, opened in 1832.⁹ The Roman Catholic Church had St Mary's College on the site of the Cathedral in Sydney, since 1837, before being relocated to Lyndhurst Academy, Glebe, in 1852.¹⁰

The Denominational Board Office promulgated ten general regulations for the functioning of denominational schools. Regulation No. 3 listed the subjects which were to be taught: Reading, writing, arithmetic, grammar, geography, and history. Regulations 1 and 2 defined school hours as 9.00 a.m. until 4.00 p.m., and decreed that the beginning and end of the school day would include prayer. In the year 1851, when the official opening of the Subiaco School took place, the denominational schools were listed under the headings: Church of England, Presbyterian, Wesleyan, and Roman Catholic. Financial support was given in the following amounts: Church of England, £4,020; Presbyterian, £1,900; Wesleyan, £570; Roman Catholic, £1,860.¹¹ The grant for Roman Catholic Schools did not encompass the Subiaco School. It was a Catholic boarding school, with limited space for student occupation.

1851–1854

It was Magdalen le Clerc and Benedict Lett who made the Subiaco School a quality establishment. During this time, Bishop Charles Henry Davis was appointed Bishop of Maitland,¹² and Coadjutor to Archbishop Polding. Polding then appointed him Director and Vicar

---

7   Grocott, *Convicts*, 78.
8   Sherington and Campbell, 'Education', 1.
9   George Fairfowl Macarthur, third son of Hannibal Macarthur and born at The Vineyard in 1825, became an Anglican clergyman and was the Headmaster of The King's School from 1869–1886.
10 Lyndhurst Academy was at 61 Darghan Street, Glebe, and formerly occupied by Bishop Broughton's St James College.
11 'Minutes of the Legislative Council: The Estimates—Education', *Maitland Mercury*, 29 November 1851.
12 The See of Maitland was created by Vatican authority in 1847.

of Subiaco.[13] Unlike Polding, Davis was a skilled administrator, and provided encouragement and friendship for Magdalen le Clerc, who remained as the only foundress.[14] After the death of Scholastica Gregory in October 1850, Polding had appointed le Clerc as Superior.[15]

Bishop Charles Henry Davis OSB (1815–1854), c. 1850

Like Polding, Bishop Charles Davis was anchored in the *obsculta* of the Benedictine Rule and was thus 'disposed and responsive to the call of God and the working of the Holy Spirit' within the Australian Benedictine mission.[16] When he died in 1854, the situation at Subiaco became

---

13   Le Clerc, 'Letter to the Lady Abbess of Stanbrook Abbey, 1 February, 1860'. Le Clerc notes in this letter to Stanbrook that Bishop Davis' cousin is a Governess at Subiaco. She is 'deaf', but highly educated and manages the children well. Le Clerc was a devotee of Davis, and found in his pastoral care of the community the strength she needed to execute her missionary work of education.
14   Writing on the 1859 crisis in the Catholic Church of Sydney, John Hosie, '1859, Year of Crisis', 342–361, notes that it was William Bernard Ullathorne, the first Vicar General, who clearly delineated Polding's incapacity as an administrator. Ullathorne's letter on this matter is noted in Birt, *Benedictine Pioneers*, Vol. I, 438.
15   'Superior', not 'Prioress'. The term 'Superior' is a more general term, and not strictly Benedictine.
16   These words were spoken by Polding to the nuns of Stanbrook Abbey, prior to the departure of Magdalen le Clerc and Scholastica Gregory for the Australian mission in 1847.

bereft of strong Benedictine guidance and pastoral care.[17] While Dame Magdalen le Clerc and the community at Subiaco grieved for the loss of his monastic strength, the Benedictines of Sydney and the Senate of the University of Sydney, of which he was a member, 'experienced the loss of a Benedictine who brought to Sydney the finest traditions of Benedictine scholarship'.[18] Dame Magdalen le Clerc wrote of her grief to the Lady Abbess of Stanbrook:

> By this time, that is when I am writing these lines, you have received our mournful intelligence and you have joined your tears with ours, the source of mine is not yet dried up and never can I call to mind my saintly and deservedly beloved father without tears, so that I may truly call tears 'my daily bread', yet do not conclude that I am unhappy. I should indeed then prove myself a very unworthy Child of a Father whose characteristic virtue was conformity to divine will—his habitual motto keeps me from sinking 'God's holy will be done'; and with this I trudge on my now desolate path for may I not justly call it so, when the light of my steps and the staff of my weakness has been taken from me?[19]

1854 was a critical year for the Church of Sydney, and the Australian Benedictine missionary plan. Forster has described it as 'the clash of races, cultures and political ideologies […] which had their pivotal point in the Benedictine régime'.[20] This clash may have been brought on by the death of Bishop Davis.

The essence of the problem was that the Benedictine plan/dream/régime was a dysfunctional one. Notwithstanding that the first word

---

17 Davis was buried in the vault at the Subiaco Cemetery with the first of the foundresses—Sr Scholastica Gregory. A Mortuary Chapel was built over the vault in 1861. A list of donors was published in the *Freeman's Journal* (20 February 1861). In the six years before his death, Davis never saw the Diocese of Maitland to which he was appointed, since Polding was absent from Sydney for a number of months every year, visiting his vast Diocese, leaving Davis in charge at St Mary's and as Pastor of Subiaco.
18 Molony, *The Roman Mould*, 30. Molony is quoting Forster, 'Lyndhurst', 61–71.
19 Le Clerc, 'Letter to the Lady Abbess of Stanbrook Abbey, 24 May, 1854'. Letter 11 of the transcribed letters of Magdalen le Clerc.
20 Forster, 'Magdalen le Clerc', 288.

of the Benedictine Rule is *obsculta*, as the years went on there would appear a certain deafness to the real needs of Catholics in the colony and beyond. In addition, despite Polding's known concern for indigenous people in his area of responsibility, their needs were not fully considered or acted upon due to the overwhelming attitude of the colony and the socio-political culture of the times.

The male Benedictine community at St Mary's in Sydney was self-destructing, as an inexperienced Henry Gregory held the reins of authority, and governed through fear and suspicion. Polding was away on mission ministry and could be gone for up to six months, visiting all the Catholic families of the outback. Bishop Davis had spent six years in Sydney. O'Farrell focuses his readers on the diplomatic gifts of Davis, gifts which 'dampened the conflicts and resentment generated by Polding's strongly hierarchical and sometimes arbitrary ideas of how the monastic community should function'.[21] O'Farrell refers to the explosion of discontent which had been brewing since 1851. It was an 'anti-Gregory campaign within the monastery, and Polding's feeling that his own public popularity was waning, that prompted the Archbishop to go to Rome' with the intention of offering his resignation.[22] This scenario will be examined further in Chapter Eight.

Polding's return from Rome in 1856

Having been ordered to regularise the two monastic communities he had established in the Archdiocese of Sydney, upon his return Polding named Dame Magdalen le Clerc prioress, in the Benedictine tradition. However, he kept tight control over the women's community. In fact, written into the formula for Profession, were the words *immediata jurisdictione* in regard to Polding.[23] So tight was the authority of Pold-

---

21 O'Farrell, *The Catholic Church*, 90–91.
22 O'Farrell, *The Catholic Church*, 90.
23 Forster, 'Magdalen le Clerc', 284. This is also attested in the vow papers of the early nuns of the community. These documents are held in trust in the Abbatial Archives at Jamberoo Abbey, NSW. After 1982, with the election of the first Abbess, the vow papers changed to include a formula which acknowledged a pledge to live under the Rule and Constitutions of the community. It was, and still is, signed both by the Bishop and the Abbess.

ing that Dame Magdalen le Clerc had to ask his permission to write a letter to Stanbrook Abbey (during Advent), and receive a letter from the Stanbrook nuns (during Advent), given the circumstances of distance and the infrequency of the transportation of mail by ships sailing between England and Australia. Le Clerc informs Lady Abbess and the community of Stanbrook that his Grace has given a general dispensation for mail to be written and received during Advent.[24] This is an example of the modification of tradition which was known to Dame Magdalen le Clerc and Polding.

Forster notes that the extent of Polding's jurisdiction over the nuns was manifest in such details as the colour of a handkerchief. She quotes an unpublished source in possession of the Dominican nuns, recalling their visit to Subiaco in 1867: 'We could see them waving their white handkerchiefs until we were out of sight. It seems Dr. Polding will not allow any of the nuns in Sydney to use blue handkerchiefs, as they are too remarkable, so S. M. Joseph told us'.[25] This was the male-dominated Catholic Church of the Nineteenth Century. The women would have expected it to be this way, and the women of Subiaco would have expected to be subject to Polding's authority and the authority of those who came after him. There were other sisters in Sydney at this time. M. R. MacGinley notes The Sisters of Charity, The Sisters of the Good Samaritan founded by Polding in 1857, and the Marist Missionary Sisters.[26] All sisters would have been, at this time in history, under the authority of Polding.

Initially, the Subiaco School offered the basic curriculum: English, French, penmanship (writing), arithmetic, geography and the use of

---

24 In Monastic Communities and Religious communities of the 19th and 20th Centuries (until the time of the Second Vatican Council), letters were not written or received, nor were visits from family and friends permitted in the seasons of Lent or Advent. Today in the Benedictine Community of Jamberoo Abbey, these rules have been relaxed in some measure. A nun may occasionally visit her elderly parent if that parent is resident in a Nursing Home, or unable to travel to the abbey. Letters are written and received in Lent and Advent. Visits from family and friends are limited to ten per year.
25 Forster, 'Magdalen le Clerc', 323 n.36. 'Remarkable' is the language of the 19th Century. Drawing attention to oneself with a coloured handkerchief would have been against a spirit of humility.
26 MacGinley, *A Dynamic of Hope*, 343.

the globes, history, plain and ornamental needlework. The main subjects taught in all schools of the time were reading, writing, arithmetic, history, geography, and grammar. French, the use of the globes, and needlework were the three subjects added to the curriculum organised by the Denominational Schools Board.[27] At Subiaco, 'for board and a course of Education […] forty guineas per annum'[28] was the fee. In the case of two or more sisters in one family, a reduction was made. An extra five guineas per annum was added for washing.[29]

The religious life of the Subiaco School

For the pupils of Subiaco, the primary subject was Religious Instruction. As part of this overall 'religious' emphasis, the girls attended the major 'Day Hours' (of the Monastic Liturgy of the Hours), on Sundays and Solemnities, and daily Mass once they had a resident chaplain or when a priest stayed overnight. Pupils learned by heart the Gospel text for each Sunday of the school year.[30] Learning passages from the Sacred Scriptures by heart was a strong Benedictine tradition. When St Benedict wrote his Rule for Monasteries, it was woven into the fabric of the Scriptures. As part of *Lectio Divina*,[31] scriptures were learnt by heart if monks were illiterate, as was sometimes the case in the Sixth

---

27 Cf. the classes for girls to learn the skills of plaiting, sewing, and mending their own clothes offered by the network of 'Ragged Schools' (for poor children, whose parents couldn't afford school fees). Following the British Ragged Schools Union, these schools were introduced by Evangelicals independently in Hobart (1854), Melbourne (1859, by Hester Hornbrook), and Sydney (1862). Evangelista, 'From Squalor and Vice'.
28 Notes made in 1938 by Monsignor McGovern, and attested to in the chronicles kept by Sr Mary Mildred Smythe (JAA). MacGinley, *A Dynamic of Hope*, 79, notes that 'Subiaco's fee of forty guineas per annum was to be the normal figure for such convent boarding schools in colonial Australia and was a continuation of a then standard fee in the British Isles'.
29 Chronicles kept by Sr Mary Mildred Smythe (JAA). Mildred Smythe entered Subiaco Monastery on 15 August 1895. She died on 26 February 1931. She would have been free to keep chronicles after her solemn profession on 23 April 1903.
30 This was learned in English, even though the Gospel read at Mass was in Latin.
31 Rule of Benedict, Chapter 48.

Century AD.[32] Whether monks were illiterate or literate, part of their monastic day was to memorise the Sacred Scriptures and in particular the Psalter. In continuity of tradition, the Benedictine nuns of Subiaco taught the pupils to learn by heart the Gospel for each Sunday. A three-day retreat on return to school after the Christmas vacation was given, usually by Polding or a Benedictine monk from St Mary's. A three-day retreat was given before First Communion and before the girls received the Sacrament of Confirmation.

Subiaco School c. 1910

The 'call' bell was rung every morning at 6.30 a.m. The Headmistress called each girl individually. Then the Litany of Loreto was recited while dressing.[33] The Head Girl gave out the Litany and the other girls responded appropriately. The girls walked in procession to the school,

---

32   Cuthbert Butler, OSB, *Benedictine monachism*, 25, argued that the great majority of monks were recruited from the Italian peasantry or from the semi-barbarous Gothic invaders. John Chapman, *St. Benedict*, 189, restores a balance to the case by drawing attention to young men such as Maurus and Placid, from the Roman nobility, asserting that 'the majority of the monks were sons of aristocratic or middle-class *curiale,* and that Benedict's fame would have drawn to his monastery a larger percentage of the sons of important persons'.
33   The Litany of Loreto honours the Mother of God under various titles. Each title is responded to with the words: 'Pray for us'. For a brief history of this Litany, see Cross, 'Litany of Loreto', 813.

THE SUBIACO SCHOOL (1851–1854)

reciting the hymn *Ave Maris Stella* in English.[34] The girls then knelt for Morning Prayer and then sat for spiritual reading. Mass followed (when a Priest was available), before breakfast was taken in silence. The girls also took part in liturgical processions.[35] This is only a glimpse into the daily life of a pupil of the Subiaco School, and probably many denominational boarding schools of the Victorian era.

An expanding Curriculum

From its beginning, the Subiaco School, as advertised in the Prospectus, was a school for girls, or, as described formally, an 'Educational Establishment for Young Ladies'. Once the school had been established, the course of instruction became broader than that of National Schools. In fact, the Prospectus for 1859 listed: English (encompassing reading, the study of English literature and grammar), French, Drawing, Music, Penmanship, Italian, Epistolary Correspondence, Needlework of every description, Dancing, and Music. It is noted in most educational histories of this time that French, Drawing, and Music would guarantee a woman a secure position as a Governess or a Teacher, and therefore would bring her a stable wage. Professor Kathryn Hughes notes that the 1851 census taken in Britain revealed that 25,000 women earned their living teaching and caring for other women's children.[36] Many female readers, well into the Nineteenth and Twentieth Centuries, would have been familiar with Caroline Bingley's description in *Pride and Prejudice* of

> any young lady who considered herself accomplished: A woman must have a thorough knowledge of music, singing, drawing, dancing and the modern languages [...] and besides all this, she must possess a certain something in her air and manner of walking, the tone of her voice, her address and expression.[37]

---

34   The *Ave Maris Stella* is a popular Hymn to the Mother of God. The words date from the 9th Century and the author is unknown. The melody used at this time in the Subiaco School was Caspar Ett's melody from the *Cantica Sacra,* Munich, 1840.
35   E.g. the Annual Procession held on the Feast of *Corpus Christi* and the processions in honour of the Mother of God.
36   Hughes, 'The figure of the Governess'.
37   Austen, *Pride and Prejudice*, 85 .

The Catholic sodality of the children of Mary

All girls at the Subiaco school were children of Mary. This sodality is explained concisely and clearly by MacGinley in her history of the Dominican Sisters in eastern Australia. 'It was founded in France—part of the great Marian movements of the 19th century—specifically in response to the 1833 revelation of the miraculous medal to the Daughter of Charity, Catherine Laboré'.[38] In the Nineteenth Century alone, nine religious congregations who included the Mother of God in their title sent members to Australia: the Sisters of Mercy, the Marist Missionary Sisters, the Presentation Sisters of the Blessed Virgin Mary, Members of the Institute of the Blessed Virgin Mary, Our Lady of the Sacred Heart, Our Lady of the Missions, Members of the Little Company of Mary, the Sisters of Our Lady of Sion, and Our Lady of the Missions.

The sodality of the Children of Mary became part of the spiritual formation of girls in Catholic schools around the world. Although not part of the Benedictine tradition, the first Child of Mary ceremony in Australia was held at the Subiaco School. The candidate was Julia Marum, one of the first two pupils. The date for such a ceremony was always 21 November, 'a feast commemorated from early in the Eastern Church to mark the presentation, or special offering of the Virgin Mary by her parents in the Temple to a unique service of God'.[39] The one extant letter from this period (dated 25 July 1852),[40] written by a Subiaco School girl to her father, is headed 'Convent of the Presentation' and signed 'your loving daughter Emily, E de M.' (Enfant de Marie—Child of Mary).[41]

---

38   MacGinley, *Ancient Tradition*, 77.
39   MacGinley, *Ancient Tradition*, 77.
40   The letter is written in a script invented by Platt Rogers Spencer, and taught in schools across the English-speaking world of the time. It has also been used for the transcribed books dating from 1846 which are held in trust at the Jamberoo Abbey Heritage Centre.
41   The only Child of Mary Manual which survives in the JAA is written in French, and dates from 1849. The title, 'New Prayers for the Dedication of the Children of Mary' (Enfants de Marie), has the approval of the Cardinal Archbishop of Cambrai, and also contains a Liturgical Calendar, with dates for the major Solemnities and Sundays of the Church, from 1850–1882. The fact that the Archbishop of Cambrai has approved it could mean that it was taken to England by the Benedictines of Cambrai (later Stanbrook), and that it was given to Dame Magdalen to take to Australia. This is speculation.

Letter written by a pupil of Subiaco School to her father

Convent of the Presentation
July 25th, 1852

Dear Father

I have plenty of news to tell you in this letter which, I think, will interest you. We had a holiday on St Magdalen's day, and on the day after too, for we were too dissipated to settle down to lessons on nearly the last day of the week.

We went a long way out of the enclosure, to the tree which Brother Emilian[42] had discovered and chopped down for us, and which contains about five hundred weights of honey. We stayed all morning in the bush, and Emilian opened the tree for us. A boy was sent home for spoons and plates, and you may guess the rest. A bee stung Miss Connolly's tongue but as honey made it less painful it was soon well.

In the afternoon, those who were not in the Play went again to the tree to bring home some of the honey, and as they were returning, they met the two bishops who partook of it with a wooden spoon.

A bee got into the French Bishop's beard and there was some difficulty in getting him out again.

We had tea very early, and afterwards the French Play.

I told you about the dresses in my last letter, dear Father, but I omitted something, viz. my hat, which Sr M. Benedict trimmed beautifully for me. There was a variety in the songs

---

42 A Lay brother from St. Mary's in Sydney

that evening, dear Father, for we sang for Bishop Davis, the French ones. And for the French Bishop the Italian trio because it was asked for [...] The concert ended with a chorus in which the whole school joined, and when the two bishops [Dr Davis and the French Bishop] had blessed us and departed we danced till Sr M. Benedict was tired of playing for us. Mother Subprioress said that she was afraid we had not been able to enjoy ourselves on account of our anxiety for the Play, but the French Bishop would send for his Natives the next day to sing and dance for us.

The next day: In the afternoon we went to the community room, and the Natives stayed in the Blessed Virgin's Chapel while they sang. I never heard such beautiful singing in my life, dear Father, and I could have wished to listen to them forever.

[The letter goes on for another 140 words, ending with:]

Give my love to dear Mother, and ten kisses, and believe me dearest Father to be,
Your affectionate child,
Emily
Child of Mary

One reason for the importance of this sample of the Epistolary Correspondence as taught in the school is that the letter is written by Emily Heydon. Emily and her sister Catherine were both educated at Subiaco, and the Heydon sons were also educated by the Benedictines in Sydney. The father of these Benedictine educated children was journalist, printer and publisher Jabez King Heydon. Despite his grandfather being a supporter of John Wesley, after being strongly influenced by the Oxford Movement Jabez Heydon was received into the Catholic church in 1845 (as was his wife in 1866). Developing close relations with the Marist Fathers at Hunters Hill, Heydon became a Catholic lay leader in Sydney.[43] He was proprietor (1857–60) and editor (1858–60) of the *Freeman's Journal*, and responsible for much of the anti-Benedictine and anti-Polding journalism which fed the problems of the Archdiocese of Sydney in the late 1850s and into the 1860s. Those at the helm of most of the unrest at St Mary's monastery in Sydney wrote a letter to the Sacred Congregation of *Propaganda Fide*. Among the three grievances expressed, they petitioned 'for the removal of the Very Rev. Dr. Gregory, V.G. and Prior'. The women in initial formation at Subiaco had voiced praise of Henry Gregory when, after his sister's death in 1850, Sr Placida Burrows was to write of Abbot Gregory: 'He has watched over us all with tenderness and kind love of the best and most affectionate of fathers'.[44]

Victorian society and English Catholicism

The letter of Emily Heydon is also a comment on Victorian society of the 1850s, in that it is written to 'father', not 'father and mother'. Her mother is mentioned as the one from whom her father will obtain what she needs for sewing, and send it to her. This letter-writing arrangement reflects the status quo of women at the time. The image at the top the first page of her letter makes a statement about English Catholicism following the Emancipation Act of 1829. The sketched image is of the newly-built Chapel of St Cuthbert's, Ushaw, Durham. Established in 1568 for the English mission, the English College of Douai had been suppressed in the French Revolution (1793). Forced to leave France in 1795, some of its scholars settled temporarily at Crook Hall near Lanchester, northwest of Durham.[45] In 1804 Bishop William Gibson began to build at Ushaw Moor, four miles west of Durham. Designed by James Taylor, these buildings were opened as St Cuthbert's College in 1808. Designed by Augustus Welby Northmore Pugin and opened in 1847, this 'state of the art' Chapel born

---

43 See further Heydon, 'Heydon, Jabez King (1815–1885)'.
44 Sr Placida Burrows to the prioress at Princethorpe, 2 March, 1851 (JAA). This letter was obtained from the Princethorpe archives in the 1980s.
45 The Monastery of St Gregory's Douai in Flanders came to Downside in 1814 (Annual Entry in the Benedictine Yearbook, 93).

in the neo-monastic revival of the Nineteenth Century epitomised the College's steady expansion as it catered for both clerical and secular students in these new days of Catholic freedom.

The school expands

As the School at Subiaco expanded in both 1854 and 1859, the dowry[46] of Eliza Regan, who joined the community in March 1853, was sufficient to pay for the 'construction of a two-storey building for the school'.[47] Eliza (Sr Angela) was of Irish descent, and her father was a strong supporter of the Benedictine venture.[48] In 1859 another addition was built with the legacy of £2,300 which Dame Magdalen le Clerc received from her mother's estate. The expansion of the school proved to be of priority as the Benedictine nuns continued to listen to the needs of the colony. They gave a practical expression to the continuity of charism and tradition by adding to the school when the need was apparent. Their *obsculta* took on a structural expression. It is important to add here that these buildings were completed in the years when builders' labourers weren't easily available. The gold fever which began in 1851 brought an increase in population, but a loss of workers in most industries.[49]

For seven years, the Subiaco School was the only one of its kind in the colony, and therefore attracted girls from around the country, and from different regions and backgrounds. There were girls from South Australia, Victoria, Tasmania, and Queensland. There were Protestant as well as Catholic girls. Magdalen le Clerc wrote, in a letter to the Abbess and nuns at Stanbrook, that a Protestant lady has applied for three of her children to attend the Subiaco School.[50] The girls were accepted. Prendergast suggests that 'Protestant parents who sent their

---

46   A choir nun was expected to bring a dowry of five hundred pounds on her entrance day.
47   Malone, 'Obit List', 38.
48   It is of historical interest to note that in 1853, while the monastic community in Sydney was plagued by unrest, Subiaco seemed to progress and increase in numbers.
49   Phillips, et al., *New Ways*, 209.
50   le Clerc, 'Letter to the Lady Abbess of Stanbrook Abbey 14 March, 1853'. Letter No. 9 of the transcribed letters of Magdalen le Clerc.

daughters to the school saw the nuns as suitable models of feminine behaviour', or were 'attracted to the English ambience of the school'.[51] MacGinley offers a different view of the situation: 'Boarding schools in Australia [of which Subiaco was one], in a geographical environment very different from Europe, became a requirement of distance, not primarily a badge of social class'.[52]

Girls down by the Parramatta River, c. 1910

The Gabriel girls brought further variety to the school. These girls were the children of Charles Louis Gabriel, and Emma Rudder. Emma's father was the colonial founder of Kempsey, NSW, and her husband a pioneer doctor of Kempsey and the Macleay River district.[53] Their son was the famous 'black Doctor' of Gundagai and a professional photographer.[54] One of the three girls, Florence Eugenie, entered the Subiaco community in 1888, Australia's Centennial year.

There was a girl from the Sandwich Islands, and one from Samoa. The latter was Emma Coe, one of sixteen children of her father by

51 Prendergast, 'The Benedictine Schools', 71.
52 MacGinley, 'Irish Women', 63.
53 Rudder, *A Magnificent Failure*.
54 The term 'black doctor' comes from the Gabrielle ancestry traced back to the West Indies. Over 800 glass plate negatives of his are now in the National Library of Australia. For his life story, see MacDougall, *Belonging*.

various wives. Her father was Myndersee Coe, trader in Samoa and Special Commissioner of the U.S. President, Ulysses Grant. Her mother was Le'utu Taletatale, of the Malietoa family. According to her biographer, R. W. Robson, 'soon after her birth the Malietoa family, in solemn ceremony, named her Princess Tui Malietoa Coe, of the royal line'.[55] She came to the Subiaco School at the age of twelve, intelligent but restless under the monastic discipline.[56]

Emma Coe (1850–1913) as a school girl in the United States

Discipline

In the Rule of Benedict, there are twenty-two references to discipline. Chapter 63:9 states: 'Boys are to be disciplined in everything by everyone'. And in Chapter 30:

> Every age and level of understanding should receive appropriate treatment. Therefore, as often as boys and the young, or

---

55 Anonymous notes about Emma can be found on loose pages in Jamberoo Abbey Archives, in a file marked 'Subiaco School'. For her biography, see Robson, *Queen Emma*; and, for a novelised version, Dutton, *Queen Emma*. She was also the subject of a 1988 TV Miniseries.

56 Emma Coe is not a classic example of a colonial child who needed the education the Benedictines provided. She finished her education in the United States with family and was then initiated into her father's commercial concerns, going down in history as 'Queen Emma of the South Seas' (Prendergast, 'The Benedictine Schools', 70). Also noted in Forster and Prendergast, 'Alumnae Subiaco'.

those who cannot understand the seriousness of the penalty of excommunication, are guilty of misdeeds, they should be subjected to severe fasts or checked with sharp strokes so that they may be healed.⁵⁷

While there is no evidence of corporal punishment in the history of the Subiaco School, the very tight daily *horarium* outlined above (See p. 38) would, to some degree, have militated against unruly behaviour.

What began as a colonial need—education for young ladies—, grew into a larger venture with global contacts. The Benedictine nuns of Subiaco were attuned to the need for education in general. There is only one instance recorded where girls had to be sent away from the school. Dame Magdalen le Clerc, writing to Fr Therry, who, in his later years, had become a supporter of the Benedictine nuns, asks him to 'tell Mrs. Green and Mrs. Griffiths that the school is obliged to send home their girls, as they find they do not suit and are unable to work'.⁵⁸

Down by the Parramatta River, c. 1910

---

57 Fry, *RB 1980*, Chapter 23.
58 Le Clerc, Letter to Fr Therry (JAA, independent collection of letters written by Dame Magdalen le Clerc). This letter is also quoted by Prendergast in her article, 'The Benedictine Schools'.

Girls in drama class, c. 1910

1854 was an *annus horribilis* for Polding and his supporters. In March, Polding and Gregory hastily left Sydney for Rome. Their sudden departure was caused by a series of events: a public meeting at which the attendees expressed their grievances over the way in which the Vicar General (Henry Gregory) had such a strong influence on Polding; the discovery, reading, and publishing of private letters from Gregory to Polding; and the discontent of some of the laity towards the English Benedictines. Christopher Dowd describes Polding's reaction to all of this as one of belligerence. His intention in going to Rome was to remonstrate with Cardinal Fransoni[59] about the 'Roman practice of receiving complaints sent in against bishops by members of the lower clergy directly'.[60] All was not bleak. Polding had a small number of supporters, both in Europe, England, and Ireland.

---

59 Cardinal Giacomo Filippo Fransoni, 10/12/1775–20/04/1856, was a member of the Congregation of *Propaganda Fide* (the Propagation of the Faith).
60 Dowd, *Rome in Australia*.

View of Subiaco from Parramatta River, c. 1910

In 1856, Polding returned to Australia, having been told to 'regularise' or tidy up his monastic foundations of men and women. Upon his return, he also brought with him three nuns from Princethorpe Priory to help the struggling, over-worked Subiaco community. Chapter Six will argue that the birth of the Benedictine community of Subiaco near Parramatta was hampered rather than helped by the addition of these three nuns. The growth of the Australian foundation now experienced traditions and customs as forms of tyranny. The chapter will also acknowledge that because of the foresight and wisdom of one of the three nuns from Princethorpe, the financial situation at Subiaco was taken out of the control of the monks of St Mary's in Sydney and placed in the hands of the nuns of Subiaco.

CHAPTER SIX

The First Elected Prioress Walburge (Ruth Woods) Wallis (1864-1889)

*I*n the years 1856–1864, the Benedictine nuns of Subiaco settled into a new phase. Still living the *obsculta* of the Benedictine Rule, and still disposed and responsive to the call of God and the working of the Holy Spirit, the community experienced life under their first elected prioress.

Immediate concerns for the newly-elected prioress

In the first election of a prioress, approved by Polding, Sr Walburge Wallis was the successful candidate. Prioress Walburge (Ruth Woods) Wallis was in office from 1864 until her death in 1902. After her election, Polding appointed Dame Magdalen le Clerc both subprioress and novice-mistress. At the beginning of her term of office, she and the community were greatly supported by the Rev. Bede Sumner, a Benedictine monk of Sydney, who cleared the Subiaco community of debt in 1864.¹ The reality which continued to confront her and her community was the lack of suitable constitutions, a situation which had challenged them from the beginning. Another issue that troubled her was the ownership of the Subiaco property. Polding assured her that:

> he had made provision for Subiaco going to the nuns in his Will. There proved to be no Will and in spite of the Deed of Indenture made on 24 April, 1871, in favour of Ruth Woods Wallis, Jane Therry and a layman, Eyre Goulburn Ellis, the nuns did not get full title to the property [...] it remained a joint monastic-diocesan property until sold to the Fathers of the Sylvestrine Congregation in 1957.²

Archbishop John Bede Polding OSB, c. 1870

---

1   Charles Sumner was ordained a priest of the Catholic Church on 9 May 1836. His was the first ordination to the Roman Catholic priesthood in Australia. When Polding arrived in Sydney on 13 September 1835, there were three Deacons in his party: Sumner, Gregory (Scholastica Gregory's brother), and Spencer. Gregory was ordained to the priesthood on 17 March 1837. (Shanahan, *Out of Time*, 32). Sumner came from a wealthy English family, and had access to funds. There is no answer to why he had his own money, only that Polding must have allowed him to use the funds for the building of churches, or for other charitable enterprises, such as the community of Subiaco, who needed financial assistance.

2   Forster, 'Magdalen le Clerc', 324.

Polding and the community of Subiaco

During the first year of Wallis' office, Polding bent the 'rule' to allow a nun's family to visit during Lent.[3] These were the Melbourne Loughnans, the wealthy Catholic family of Isabella Loughnan, and important people for the contribution they brought to the building up of the Catholic Church at that time. Polding, in the same 'correspondence', mentions that Fr Austin Sheehy, in speaking with some of the younger nuns (novices), noted their dissatisfaction with the teaching of Magdalen le Clerc, and their desire to speak with Polding. He addresses the situation by saying that:

> It will never do for the members of a community, out of the time of [canonical] visitation, to solicit the interference of an authority external to that which governs the community, and for that authority to interfere, unless in a case of absolute necessity, which the present is not. The junior religious do not like M. Subprioress [Magdalen le Clerc] as their immediate superior. That is, I believe, the simple and plain fact. No one can instruct better, but if the instruction be received *malpre* [Latin: badly] little good can be produced.[4]

Polding assures the prioress that Magdalen le Clerc is well aware of the prejudice which the junior nuns have towards her, and advises the prioress to speak with her openly—that she will be 'prepared to co-operate with you in all that may be considered to the good of the community'.[5]

This episode brought the *obsculta* of Polding, of Dame Magdalen le Clerc, and of Ruth Woods Wallis together in strength and unity. There are examples of this kind of complaint which gained the sympathetic ear of many a chaplain in many a religious community. Ruth Woods

---

3   Both Advent and Lent at this time in Catholic Church history were penitential seasons. For enclosed nuns, this meant that visitors and the reception of letters were prohibited. Mail received was kept for Easter, or Christmas accordingly. The prioress also had the freedom to read mail received. As the person in charge of the community, she was responsible for announcing any news, such as the death of a parent, or sibling of one of her nuns.
4   Polding, 'Letter to Prioress Wallis, 5 March, 1864' (JAA, Box marked 'Mother Walburge Wallis, all correspondence and documents').
5   Polding, 'Letter to Prioress Wallis, 5 March, 1864'.

Wallis was already aware of what she would later describe as a 'confessional moan',[6] using the Sacrament of Reconciliation as a means of complaining about those in authority. Yet, at this time in history, there were no forums where individuals could air their grievances. This was the age of blind obedience. In Benedictine houses of the post-Vatican II era, Chapter Meetings have provided the forum where discussion, discernment, judgement, and policy-making can take place.

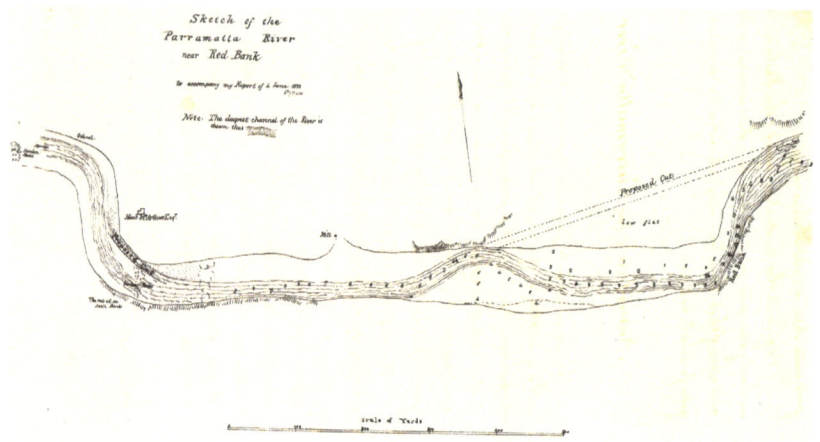

Sketch of Parramatta River, showing location of Subiaco, 1853

It is possible that the complaint of the younger nuns concerned the fact that Dame Magdalen used the spiritual writings of Fr Frederick Faber (of the Oratory). She wrote on 10 July 1860 to the abbess of Stanbrook, referring to the fact that 'His Grace is an unqualified admirer of Fr. Faber, and tells me to inculcate his spirit in the novices'. Then she adds: 'Who can raise our hearts to a closer union with God than that eminent spiritual master who seems to have been raised up by God to meet the exigencies of the present extraordinary age?'[7] Fr Faber's spiritual writings found a place in the guidance given to the novices of the 1860s and those who would follow in the decades

---

6   Prioress Wallis, 'Letter to the novices at Subiaco December 3, 1888'. The letter was written while Prioress Wallis was on her second tour of England, Continental Europe, and America.
7   Le Clerc, 'Letter to the Lady Abbess of Stanbrook Abbey, 10 July, 1860'. Letters of Magdalen le Clerc. Letter No. 10 in the collection of the Transcribed Letters of Magdalen le Clerc (JAA).

leading up to 1900. This was not monastic spirituality, and was not anchored in the Benedictine Rule. Frederick Faber of the Oratory also wrote hymns which appear in the hymnal used by the nuns of Subiaco in the Nineteenth and Twentieth Centuries up to the Second Vatican Council. These hymns were very markedly the fruits of Catholic piety. Faber's Hymns and other hymns of this historic period were used throughout the Catholic Church. As noted in Chapter One (p. 49), in July 1856 Polding had written a Pastoral Letter encouraging Catholics to sing hymns: 'get the books, read carefully and study the hymns, they are well worth it. You will find them the most exquisite voice of all you hold dear'.[8] The hymns he was referring to were those of the Dolman Hymnal which collected the best of popular spirituality of the Catholic Church. This hymnal itself was not used at Subiaco but the hymns were transcribed into music books and used both in the school and in the monastic community. The hymns continued in use until the 1950s. Originally these hymnals were the means whereby Catholics claimed what was uniquely theirs. They were expressions of the Catholic heart, especially the Catholic heart emerging into emancipation in England. As the world moved on, they became a fixed feature of Catholic prayer and ritual.

Canonical Visitation

The 1917 Code of Canon Law, Canon 513, refers to the Fourth Lateran Council (1215), to the Council of Vienne (1311–1313), and to the Council of Trent, as the foundation of the laws of canonical visitation of monasteries, both of men and women. Under canon 512, norm 1, 'the law gives full sway to the Ordinary (or the local Bishop) over two kinds of institutes: nuns with solemn vows, whose convents are subject either to the Ordinary himself, or immediately to the Holy See, and Diocesan Congregations of both sexes'.[9] The details of canonical visitation included examination of the interior of the house: cells, dormitories, other private areas. While conducting this examination,

---

8   Haines et al., *The Eye of Faith*, 234.
9   Augustine, *A Commentary*, Vol. III, 136.

the Ordinary was to 'wear his rochette and mantelletta, [and] be accompanied by two priests'.[10] The prioress was not included in the inspection. Individual members of the community must meet with the canonical visitor, and bring their issues to him. This is what Polding is referring to in the matter of the women who complained to Austin Sheehy outside the time of visitation.[11] It was also required that a canonical visitation be informed of the financial situation of a community, the growth, if any, in the number of monks or nuns, and the extent to which the discipline of the Benedictine Rule was maintained. In the Nineteenth Century, up until the arrival of Roger William Bede Vaughan as his coadjutor (December, 1873), Polding's annual canonical visitation was executed with a fatherly care and concern for the community he had established.

Archbishop Roger Bede Vaughan OSB (1834–1883), c. 1873

---

10   Augustine, *A Commentary*, Vol. III, 136.
11   The community of 2023 is a monastery *sui juris*, under the local Bishop. A canonical visitation takes place every six years. The abbess may request that the canonical visitor be a monk from another Benedictine Abbey. In the visitation of women's monastic communities, a woman is becoming the norm for the co-visitor, but as yet, not as the principal canonical visitor (Canonical document kept in the Abbess' files). The most recent document, *Cor Orans*, legislates that communities which are *sui juris* must join a federation. The Congregation for Religious has said 'no' to more than one monastery who asks to be excused from the legislation. With the availability of present day technology, Jamberoo Abbey is now considering joining the English Benedictine Congregation, attending meetings online.

Polding had lost both Sr Scholastica and Bishop Charles Davis—too young to die. He had rallied to energise his small flock, giving support and instilling confidence and courage. Some ventures were successful. Some weren't. He brought three nuns from Princethorpe Priory. They arrived in 1856, with strict conditions from their prioress. Polding adhered to the conditions and promised to uphold them. The nuns returned to Princethorpe in 1861, having exchanged nothing but convent and climate.[12]

Vaughan had a more rigid expectation of how monastic life should be lived. His formation as a Benedictine monk had been English. His experience of a canonical visitation with its accompanying hierarchical power would have been his model. The Catholic archbishops of Sydney who followed Vaughan took a different approach. The duration of the visitation was usually one day which included the celebration of Mass, the Liturgy of the Hours, and an inspection of the financial situation of the monastery. The Ledger begun in 1856 contains the signature of every Bishop or Archbishop who carried out a canonical visitation.

Obsculta: The Benedictine charism and tradition of hospitality

Hospitality is an important charism (among many), of Benedictine monasticism. For the nuns of Subiaco, 1871 saw the Benedictine charism and tradition of hospitality evidenced in the delicate matter of Mary MacKillop's excommunication from the Catholic Church.[13] Mary MacKillop had stayed at Subiaco on her way to Brisbane in December 1869. She wrote to her own mother of the 'Benedictines at Subiaco', saying that:

> Never for one moment [did we] imagine that such an ancient and dignified body would have given us the warm and truly beautiful welcome that this house did. The Rev. Mother [Walburge Wallis] and all her […] community received us with such love, and warmly commended our young work. The Rev.

---

12 Shanahan, *Out of Time*, 109.
13 Although the ex-communication of Mary MacKillop is not the topic of this book, I mention her in the spirit of hospitality that religious women showed each other during such tumultuous times.

Mother was overjoyed with the poverty and spirit of our Rule, and gave me much valuable advice.[14]

Sr Mary MacKillop (1842–1909) and Fr Julian Tenison Woods (1832–1889)

When the excommunication was formalised on September 21, 1871, the nuns of Subiaco were united in sympathy and joined in prayer for Mary MacKillop and her religious sisters. Mother Walburge Wallis wrote to Mary MacKillop:

> I [...] most warmly offer you, or any of you, or all of you, a home at Subiaco, whenever you find it our dear Lord's will to accept my invitation. I assure you that I should think Subiaco privileged to be allowed to shelter even one of St. Joseph's little violets.[15]

Hospitality was also shown to Fr Tenison Woods, who, with Mac-Killop, had co-founded the Sisters of St Joseph of the Sacred Heart at Penola, South Australia in 1866. In 1871, Fr. Woods gave a retreat to

---

14   Mary MacKillop, 'Letter to her Mother'. This Letter was obtained from the Archives of the Sisters of St Joseph, Sydney.
15   Collection of hand-written letters of Prioress Wallis. (JAA).

the nuns of Subiaco.[16] Polding later sent Woods to the monastery for rest when he was in the throes of a breakdown over his conflicting loyalties to his bishop and the sisters of St Joseph. In the *Life of Julian E. Tenison-Woods* by Fr George O'Neill, S.J., it is noted of Woods that 'He lay a helpless invalid under the shelter of the Benedictine nuns, to whose care the Benedictine Archbishop had sent him'.[17] The prioress [Walburge Wallis] wrote to Mary MacKillop that:

> Your Father is with us and is resting. He is weak, exhausted, and cannot write today. The Archbishop sent him to us; we are grateful ... and will do our best to help him to get strong.[18]

Woods later wrote to Mary MacKillop: 'The Rev. Mother here is still so kind. I am clothed and fed and everything done for nothing'.[19]

Hospitality had also been shown to the Marist Sisters who stayed at Subiaco for three months on their way to the Wallis Islands in 1859, and to the Auckland Sisters of Mercy on their way to New Zealand in January 1850. They stayed at Subiaco and were given half the house for their accommodation, while awaiting the final preparation of their sailing vessel. In August 1859 the Sisters of Mercy, on their way home to Bathurst, stayed at Subiaco for a week.[20]

In January 1850 the Marist bishop, Dr Battalian, brought a group of indigenous Papuan children to Subiaco. They formed a choir for the celebration of the Mass, and for years after, they renewed their visit

---

16 The movements of Tenison Woods from 1871 to 1889 are tabulated in Player, 'Julian Tenison Woods', 234–308, Appendix A. In the early 1870s, Woods numbered Angelo Ambrosoli, who Polding had appointed spiritual director to the Benedictine nuns at Subiaco, as one of his few friends; Player, 'Julian Tenison Woods', 219. He conducted 'retreats for Sisters and children' from October 4–9, 1871 (Woods to M. MacKillop, 10 October 1871, MSA; Birt, *Benedictine Pioneers*, II.367). He also stayed at Subiaco October 12–17 after making a hurried return when Dean Sumner lay dying in the care of the nuns (Woods to M. MacKillop 17 October 1871, MSA; Birt, *Benedictine Pioneers*, II.369), and again from October 27 to November 5, when he was sick for ten days (Woods to M. MacKillop, 5 November 1871, MSA). He was there again on November 22 (Woods to MacKillop, 22 November 1871, MSA), and back on 21 March 1872 to preach to the nuns (Woods to M. MacKillop, 19, 21 March 1872, MSA).
17 O'Neill, *Life*, 213.
18 O'Neill, *Life*, 213.
19 O'Neill, *Life*, 213.
20 Community Chronicles, 1849–1925.

annually on the Solemnity of the Epiphany.[21]

The manifestation of this Benedictine charism is one of the fruits of a lived *obsculta*. Listening to the immediate needs of the Sisters of Mercy or the Marist Sisters, or Mary MacKillop's newly formed congregation, was an act of solidarity with those who were also meeting the needs of the Catholic Church in Australia, or in the case of the Marist Sisters, the Wallis Islands.

Dom Bede Sumner OSB. c. 1860s

Until 1864, the Benedictine charism of hospitality, though manifest authentically, had been limited by the lack of a guesthouse.[22] Finally, the cottage on the Subiaco property, which had remained unused since the school was added to in 1859, was fitted out for guests. This restored the privacy of the cloister for the community, as guests had been staying in the front section of the Macarthur House, which had

---

21 Community Chronicles, 1850. Later in the 19th Century and in the early decades of the 20th Century, it was Bishop de Boismenu, M.S.C., also of Papua, who often visited Subiaco and stayed in the guesthouse. On one occasion, the Eucharistic Congress of 1928, he brought with him Thérèse Noblet, the superior of the Indigenous Sisters of Papua, and three Papuan boys.

22 Benedictine monasteries world-wide have Guest Houses for pilgrims and friends—all who come seeking peace and rest. Benedict taught that a monastery is never without guests or pilgrims. (Rule of Benedict 53:16.)

been adapted for this purpose. Bede Sumner, OSB, who retired to Subiaco, saw to other means of ensuring privacy, and executed these out of his own resources.[23]

Financial difficulties

At this time, the early 1870s, when hospitality was being generously practised, a Postulant's List, that is, what to bring if you are entering to become a choir nun, reveals both the serious financial situation of the community and the need to adapt the Rule of St Benedict to meet this situation (See pp.140–141).

> While some of its listed items were standard across religious congregations of the time, the bringing of a bed, mattress, bed linen, and furniture tells a different story. This was a change from Benedictine tradition in order to meet an immediate need, suggesting a lack of sufficient financial stability. The Rule of St Benedict, Chapter 58:24 and 25, stipulates that: if a candidate has any possessions, that person 'should either give them to the poor beforehand, or make a formal donation of them to the monastery, without keeping back a single thing [...] well aware that from that day he or she will not even have their own bodies at their disposal'.[24]

If a nun left before solemn profession, the items for the most part were returned to her, even up to the 1930s. Otherwise, because of the nature of solemn vows and the canonical law upholding such a sacred commitment within the Church, the items were not returned to a nun if she left after solemn profession. By the very nature of her profession, her 'goods' had already been 'donated' to the monastery.

---

23 Jamberoo Abbey Heritage Centre. Fr Bede Sumner was a good friend and benefactor to the community of Subiaco.
24 Fry, *RB 1980*: Chapter 58, verses 24 and 25.

A Postulant's List: what to bring when Entering the Monastery, 1871.

- Three black dresses to ankle, high neck, long sleeves with band
- Two yards of half-inch embroidery for cuffs and collar
- One and a half yards of black voile
- Three yards of black net
- Four yards of one-inch black ribbon
- Two black underskirts, usual under-wear
- Six pairs stockings
- One dozen handkerchiefs
- Two pairs nurses' shoes with rubber heels
- Two pairs black felt slippers
- Two pairs strong shoes
- Two pairs Blankets. Three pairs sheets, half dozen pillow slips
- Enamel jug and basin
- Bed and mattress
- One dozen mosquito nets
- One chair for cell
- One dozen unbleached calico for screens
- Stationery, stamps, pens, pencil, ink
- Work basket and fittings
- Tape: black and white
- Scissors—three pairs: needle-work, personal, and garden
- Hot water can: two gallons
- Broom (hair)
- Banister brush and dust pan. Soap, brushes etc.
- Boot polish outfit

Archbishop Roger Bede Vaughan

The last Benedictine Prelate, Roger Bede Vaughan, came to Sydney as Polding's Coadjutor in 1873. He was instructed by *Propaganda*, the Roman Congregation concerned with missionary countries, to report back to them on the state of the Benedictine mission in Sydney. The now old Archbishop, John Bede Polding, did not know of Vaughan's instructions from *Propaganda*.[25] Vaughan was highly regarded by the nuns of Subiaco, even though his canonical visitation of September 1875 found many things which were contrary to Benedictine monastic life. If a report of this visitation ever existed, it is apparently no longer extant, and the pages in the community chronicles referring to Vaughan's visit have been cut out. His solution to the situation was to advise Prioress Wallis to go to England, and in particular to Stanbrook Abbey, to learn how monastic life was lived there, and to imitate as much as possible Stanbrook's monastic practices. Perhaps this 'solution' to a less than satisfactory situation spells out the details which may have been in the missing pages from the community chronicles. Vaughan's solution can be assessed as the solution of a prelate who was both unfamiliar with and blinded to a new model of monasticism in a new world. Or, in

---

25 Kavenagh, 'The End of the Sydney Benedictines', 195–216.

fairness to Vaughan, the solution was the only one he knew. A return to England and all things English was his solution to what he judged as an unsatisfactory situation at Subiaco. Vaughan was under orders, obedient to a higher authority, and influenced by what he had found in Sydney—where Benedictine monasticism was in various stages of disintegration.

Vaughan also encouraged Wallis to find suitable constitutions for her monastery in Australia. A letter from Vaughan dated 2 March 1876[26] gives the prioress permission (which Vaughan sought from Polding), to make a journey to England. He conveys the concern of Polding that 'great care will be taken in the selection of the ship, and that something be known of the disposition of the captain—a matter of importance'.[27] Polding was a seasoned traveller, and had endured opposition from Captain Young of the *St Vincent* in 1847–1848 when his group of Benedictine nuns and monks, deacons, and priests were mocked on one occasion for praying on deck, and for the singing of hymns. Polding manifests, in this concern, the fatherly care of the abbot/bishop. He was overall in charge of the community until the election of Wallis in 1864. He was also the Archdiocesan Prelate to whom the community was subject.

- Half dozen black Cashmere (capes)
- Water can, rake, spade, garden gloves
- Half dozen galatea or Italian cloth for Aprons
- Books, small pictures (bookmark size—could be holy cards), music manuscript, two good exercise books
- Press (wardrobe)
- Table
- Tub and towels
- Two yards serge (for covering books)
- Missal
- Psalter
- Crucifix
- Warm shawl and rug
- Two mugs
- Umbrella
- Half dozen serviettes
- Two or three white quilts
- Half dozen dusters (hemmed)
- Strong Trunk. (Two purposes: to carry the above to the Monastery, and for storage in one's cell).

[NOTE: NO BIBLE]

In a spirit of obedience to Polding's concern, Prioress Walburge

---

26   Archbishop Roger Bede Vaughan, 'Letter to Prioress Wallis, 2 March, 1876'. (JAA, Archived in the box marked mother Walburge Wallis, all correspondence and documents). The letter head is St. John's College, University of Sydney, where Vaughan preferred to live.

27   Archbishop Roger Bede Vaughan, 'Letter to Prioress Wallis, 2 March, 1876'. (JAA)

Wallis travelled in civilian clothing, not a religious habit, to avoid any adverse response to her presence on a passenger ship.[28] The first part of the journey, taken on the *Colima*, a mail steamer[29] and less than adequate ship, was made safely to Kandavu, Fiji. Here many passengers met *The Granada* to take them on to their destinations.[30]

Journey of Prioress Wallis to England, 1876–1877.

A loosely printed record of Wallis' visit to Stanbrook survives in the archives of Jamberoo Abbey today, and notes that 'the nuns [of Stanbrook] tried to meet her needs by giving her copies of the Declarations, Rudiments [...] and a pattern for the monastic habit. She declared that she wanted to have everything they had to offer as the different climate and surroundings in Australia would permit'.[31] This, no doubt, was what Vaughan had advised, but was it just another impractical arrangement whereby traditions of the Old World were imposed on the New World?

It was the abbess of Stanbrook, Dame Gertrude D'Aurillac Dubois,[32] abbess from 1872 until 1897, whose wisdom prevented this from happening. She recommended the benefits of experiencing monastic life elsewhere, so Prioress Wallis then visited other monasteries as a listener and learner, before returning to Stanbrook for a second visit.[33] She went on to visit the Convent of Abbotsleigh, and the Monastery of Ramsgate, the Abbey of Beuron, Atherstone Priory, Teignmouth Abbey, and Minster-on-Thanet. Her visit to the Catholic Shrine at Lourdes was an added pleasure in addition to her real purpose. Overall, her pilgrimage would prevent tradition becoming a tyrant, as had been the

---

28   A friend, Mrs Heptonstall, was her companion.
29   The *Colima* was owned by the Pacific Mail Steamship Co. which carried mails for the U.S. between San Francisco, Japan, Hong Kong, Panama, Sydney, and New Zealand.
30   The *Colima* returned via New Zealand and was wrecked in Akaroa Harbour, having safely navigated the Cook Strait. It had been on its last run. The account of the demise of the *Colima* is in *The Argus* (Wednesday 5th April 1876), 5.
31   *Stanbrook Abbey Annals*, 1874–1878, 391.
32   Stanbrook Abbey, *Stanbrook Abbey Press*, 33.
33   All her letters written during this journey have survived and are held in trust in Jamberoo Abbey Archives.

case with the conditions which Madame du Chastelet placed on the three nuns who came from Princethorpe in 1856. However, a subject of deep concern was the fact that 'that Mother Walburge had no idea of enclosure'.[34] The abbess of Stanbrook had written letters of introduction for her to Ste Cécile at Solesmes and in turn the abbess of Ste Cécile wrote to Wallis, inviting her to spend some days within their cloister. After a visit to Solesmes, she went to Florence and Rome.

**Dame Gertrude d'Aurillac Dubois OSB
Abbess of Stanbrook Abbey 1872-1897**

In Italy Wallis stayed with an old Parramatta friend of the Australian community —Mrs Sconce, whose house was in Florence. With Mrs Sconce as companion, Wallis returned to England. Her friendship with Mrs Sconce meant that the abbess of Stanbrook could not receive her again into the Stanbrook Cloister: 'We treated her as we do a nun of an active order, letting her stay at the Lodge with Mrs. Sconce and visit us only in the parlour'.[35]

---

34 *Stanbrook Abbey Annals*, 392.
35 *Stanbrook Abbey Annals*, 392.

THE FIRST ELECTED PRIORESS

Changing times

New South Wales society of the 1870s was responding to the 'trumpet of science and rationalism' which saw that 'religion decayed steadily throughout the second half of the 19th century'.[36] Statistics reveal that by the end of the 1870s attendance at church in New South Wales was by only twenty percent of the population, and these were mainly Anglican or Roman Catholic. Henry Norbert Birt, OSB, in a table which shows the progress made during the ten years from 1873–1883, names the figure for Catholics as being 12,633 (country districts), and 32,195 in city and suburbs. By 1883, the Catholic population was, in country districts, 21,784 and in city and suburbs, 56,732. The total population was 317,819.[37] In the 1870s, 'about half of Australia's Catholics had been born in Ireland'.[38]

The number of Catholic girls who attended the school at Subiaco remained steady, rising from seventeen in 1870 to thirty in 1877. Was this because of a decade of economic stability? Or was it because of the demands of a law such as the Catholic Bishop of Bathurst had declared in 1870: 'the sacraments would be withheld from parents who sent their children to public schools'?[39] Vocations to the community in the 1870s remained steady. Three lay sisters entered the community in the 1870s. Margaret Gallagher, born in Ireland in 1832, came to Australia and went into domestic service before asking to be admitted at Subiaco. Margaret Carroll entered to be a lay sister. She was Australian, born of Irish parents. Sara Parkinson, an ex-pupil of the Subiaco School, entered in 1878, to be a choir nun. Sarah Catherine Emblem entered to be a lay sister in August 1879. She is remembered as Sr Patrick Emblem. She was born at Hartley, New South Wales, in 1855.

The 1870s also saw major changes in education, not just in New South Wales, but throughout Australia. Referring to the education of girls, Fogarty notes that by 1879, the days of 'mere accomplishments

---

36 Cannon, *Australia*, 86.
37 Statistics found in Birt, *Benedictine Pioneers*, Vol. II., 460–461.
38 O'Farrell, *The Catholic Church*, 238.
39 Clark, *A History of Australia IV*, 279.

were over'.⁴⁰ This affected the Subiaco School, an Educational Establishment for Young Ladies, which now had to face up to 'popular demand for examination results',⁴¹ and a standard of education with matriculation exams set by the University of Sydney. Fogarty claims that there was resistance to these changes by the nuns of Subiaco, and yet there are archival documents to the contrary. Their school after all had been founded on the *obsculta* of the Benedictine Rule, a 'listening' to the need for education in the colony of New South Wales. When the school opened in 1851, university education for girls was unheard of. In reality, education for girls was up to parents who could afford it. MacGinley explores another dimension at play in this matter of education:

> The Benedictine concept of enclosure came to be seen as restrictive for contemporary girl boarders now competing with boys in public examinations. The Benedictine nuns also had their reservations about these examinations as inducing undue concentration on a narrow field of study to the neglect of a broader culture.⁴²

The *Freeman's Journal* of 10 January 1891 notes that 'the University Course is adhered to in the Convent school [of Subiaco], so that the pupils may matriculate if they desire'. This would indicate that the nuns were attuned to the challenge before them. In the 'Alumnae Subiaco', there is mention of a pupil called Dorothy Waite, who was one of the first candidates for the Intermediate exam. She achieved an unsatisfactory result, because, it is asserted, the nuns were unfamiliar with examination requisites.⁴³ Emily Heydon, also a pupil of Subiaco, did gain her certificate to teach with the national schools and apart from her work there she taught at Subiaco and with the Marist Sisters at Woolwich, showing considerable talent as an educator. There are other instances like this, and also examples of girls achieving well in

---

40 Fogarty, *Catholic Education in Australia*, Vol. II, 380. He supports his statement with a reference to *The Education of Our Girls,* by Teresa Magner, Austral Light, 1 July, 1907, and *Higher Education for Women*, Loreto Eucalyptus Blossoms, 1886, 7.
41 Fogarty, *Catholic Education*, Vol. II, 380.
42 MacGinley, *A Dynamic of Hope,* 92.
43 Forster and Prendergast, 'Subiaco Alumnae', entry under Mary Cook.

the Intermediate exams. At Subiaco, there were highly educated nuns, governesses, and at least one male teacher for the 'Botany' class.

From a positive angle, Vaughan's presence in Sydney manifested a more authentic spirit of the Benedictine *obsculta*, a listening to the needs of the 'rapidly growing colony', to the 'impracticability' of 'Polding's Benedictine aspirations [...] and a clear perception of the role which the [new teaching congregations] were to play in the forthcoming educational struggle'.[44] Vaughan admitted that Sydney had been 'a little sleepy in matters of education [...] only thirty-four Catholic schools existed when he arrived in 1873; [...] by 1879, he had added another twenty'.[45]

After Polding's death in 1877, when Vaughan succeeded Polding as the Catholic Archbishop of Sydney, he suppressed Lyndhurst and secularised the monks. He brought the Jesuits and Marists to Sydney. In 1868, the Irish Christian Brothers returned to Australia, but would not come to Sydney while a Benedictine Prelate was Archbishop.[46] It was rumoured that Vaughan would also suppress Subiaco, but this never eventuated. Perhaps a school the size of Subiaco, with just eighteen pupils in 1879, was a non-issue in regard to the direction which Catholic education was taking.

1879 was a crucial year for New South Wales. MacGinley sums up the effects of the Joint Pastoral Letter of the bishops of New South Wales, led by Vaughan. It was the 'strong statement [which] challenged the secularising forces at work [in Australian education] and decisively launched Australia's comprehensive Catholic school system',[47] in view of the forthcoming Education Act of 1880. New South Wales was prepared. Increasingly, teaching Congregations of men and women were needed in the Archdiocese of Sydney. Vaughan's main

---

44 Fogarty, *Catholic Education*, Vol. I, 246.
45 Fogarty, *Catholic Education*, Vol. I, 249.
46 Fogarty, *Catholic Education*, Vol. I, 249. The Irish Christian Brothers had lost much respect for Polding when they first came to Sydney in 1842, with conditions laid down by their then Superior General of their Order. Their conditions were not met, and during Polding's absence, Gregory produced 'a rescript which Polding received from Rome, setting up a separate Institute of the Sisters of Charity in Australia. It was then that the Irish Christian Brothers decided to leave, in order [...] that no document could reach them from Rome to upset their intentions, or change their identity'.
47 MacGinley, *A Dynamic of Hope*, 180.

antagonist was Henry Parkes, who wanted a 'common national education for all, not only wanting to provide education for all children, but that all children attend common national schools'.[48]

Wallis returns to Australia

Prioress Wallis returned to Australia on 19 July 1877. She was absent for Polding's death. While abroad she did not obtain suitable constitutions, but she did gain innumerable practical ways to enrich the community in Australia. She was attuned to trends in church architecture, with a view to building the first monastic church at Subiaco, to sacred and classical music, and the nature of monastic communities—their customs, their spirit of simplicity, and dedication. She noted, in the churches she visited, what sacred music was in use, and that the 'Exercises of St. Gertrud the Great'[49] were used in monasteries and religious houses of women. She lamented the lack of 'awareness' of affairs of church and state, and commented that many of the houses she visited seemed to be too closed off from the real world. She expresses relief that this was not so at Subiaco. And this continued to be a significant difference between the old countries and the emerging new country, Australia. Awareness of social justice in the Nineteenth Century, with love and compassion towards the needy, has always been the reality for those who take 'the Gospel for their guide'.[50]

Her most enriching encounter, and one which would have a lasting influence on Subiaco, was a meeting with Maurus and Placid Wolter of Beuron.[51] The two brothers had established the Abbey of Beuron in 1865 in the ancient Abbey of St Martin of Beuron, a former Augustinian monastery situated on the banks of the Danube on Hohenzollern

---

48 Michael Adams, 'Paper delivered to the Australian Catholic Historical Society in June, 1972', 31. (JAA)
49 Gertrud the Great was one of three mystics of the Convent of Helfta in Germany. A fourth mystic, Mechtild of Magdeburg, lived at this Convent. She was a lay Dominican. Lewis and Lewis, *Gertrud the Great*, 'Introduction', 2.
50 Fry, *RB 1980*, Prologue: v.21.
51 The brothers (Rudolph and Ernst) were named after Maurus and Placid, two young disciples of St Benedict. Their story is written in Gregory the Great, *Life and Miracles of St. Benedict* (Zimmerman, 1949).

land, with Maurus the first abbot. This was a result of the generosity of Princess Katharina von Hohenzollern-Sigmaringen, who had been greatly assisted by Maurus after encountering him in 1859, and persuaded by the two brothers of the need for the restoration of monastic life in Germany. Before taking possession of this abbey, the two brothers went to Solesmes, the heart of the neo-monastic revival of the Nineteenth Century, where they studied under Abbot Prosper Guéranger, adopting the customs of Solesmes before taking up the challenge in their new monastery, and subsequently continuing close links with Solesmes. When the Abbey of Beuron was closed by the Prussian Government in December 1875, Maurus Wolter moved to Volders in Austria with most of the monks, and Princess von Hohenzollern managed the buildings and lands during their absence until the monks could return in 1887.

In the 1876–77 encounter with Prioress Wallis, Maurus Wolter shared about Beuron's Monastic School of Art and Illuminations, the importance of plain chant, and the establishment by Beuron of a school of sculpture and painting. He spoke to her of vestment making, and in particular the art of painting on vestments, with the Italian Dominican painter, Fra Angelico being the choice for beauty, rich colouring, and harmony of tone. Wallis learned that Beuron was a school of music, art, illumination, and academic study. One piece of Maurus' personal advice to her was noted in one of the letters she wrote home to the community at Subiaco:

> Keep up the Divine Office [...] don't expect in the Spring the fruits of the Autumn. It is a good sign to be slow. See how many rings around the oak tree, how slow its growth and how strong and beautiful after many years. Cultivate great zeal for the Office. Make it a study. Use plain chant. Other Music may edify. Plain Chant converts.[52]

---

52   This sharing with its historical perspective and story-like delivery echoes what took place between Abbot Maurus Wolter and Prioress Wallis, when she visited Beuron. She then writes it in a long letter to the nuns of Subiaco. Plain chant is closely one with the human breath, and rests the mind and the body, especially when the Latin words accompany it. Even in English, the repetition of words, and harmonies day after day allows the word of God to penetrate the heart. 'Listen with ear of the heart' is the way Benedictine monks and nuns are converted. Other music does edify, but the repetition of the Sacred Scriptures chanted, converts the heart.

Another and much deeper listening is the *obsculta* of plain chant, the music that converts, that rests the spirit, while at the same time embracing all of humanity, and holding them in prayer.

In the late 1870s, after Wallis returned to Australia, it was Archbishop Vaughan who suggested to the nuns of Subiaco that their monastery and school be made more accessible. Vaughan was concerned that with a small parcel of land having been sold off in 1871 (because of financial difficulties), access to Subiaco might be an obstacle for travellers. Until this time, the main access to Subiaco was via water. Girls coming to school from interstate or the northern districts of New South Wales came by steam ship to Sydney and then on to Subiaco via the Parramatta River.[53] In a letter dated 28 November 1882 Vaughan mentions that he is told:

> in the plan for the sale of your 90 acres, that no provision is made for any road to the convent from Parramatta […] If it is the case, I advise you to arrange for some carriage way to the convent which, though late, no doubt could still be done. It would be a great mistake to block yourselves out from all access except by water.[54]

This action on the part of Vaughan is one of consolidation, rather than repression. He wants Subiaco to be accessible, and thus part of the Catholic community of Sydney and its surrounding countryside.[55]

The first Sydney rail line to Parramatta during the 1850s was

---

53 This is verified in the community chronicles and in the 'Alumnae' compiled by Prendergast and Forster. One governess, Arabella Naughton, was drowned in 1854 on her way home when the coastal steamer was wrecked. In information obtained by Marie Forster, it is thought that Arabella was promised in marriage to the Australian Poet, Henry Kendall. One source says she was a Subiaco pupil, who on leaving school was sent to an exclusive dressmaker to become equipped for earning a living. A relative of Arabella Naughton is of the opinion that girls like Arabella were sent to Subiaco as one would be sent to a 'Finishing School'. (Private source—Jamberoo Abbey Archives).

54 'Collection of Letters written by Roger Bede Vaughan to the Prioress and community of *"Subiaco"'* (JAA). These letters are kept in a file which contains letters from all Bishops, Archbishops, and Cardinals from the time of Polding, until the community's departure from Pennant Hills in December 1957.

55 The distance from the Parramatta Railway Station to Subiaco was three miles by coach or horse, depending on the elements: rain, floods, etc. It is interesting to note that the death notice for Sr Mary Joseph (Margaret) Diamond, in the *Sydney Evening News* 24 October 1888, still identifies the Benedictine Convent of Subiaco as being on the Parramatta River.

used mostly by the wealthy of the colony.[56] If visitors to Subiaco took a train to Parramatta, there was then the problem of how to get to Subiaco. Horse and carriage would have been the norm. When Archbishop Vaughan visited Subiaco, he rode his own horse. So, rail travel wasn't preferable. Victoria Road was not constructed until 1887, and a rail connection to Clyde and Carlingford was not installed until the 1890s.[57] It is noted by Cannon[58] that most working-men [and women in domestic service or menial work] tended to live near [or in] their places of employment.[59] This was certainly the case with those employed as workmen, parlour maids and domestic servants at Subiaco. It would not have been affordable for them to travel to work. A small number of such employees lived on the property, in the old Macarthur cottage. There were also rooms in another building called 'The Lodge'. And those dealing with girls in the Boarding School had a room in the girls' dormitory.

Wallis was back in Australia one year when Magdalen le Clerc died (28 March 1878), at the age of 80. Her heroism and fidelity to the Benedictine tradition was admirable. She had always been delegated to second place, from the day the foundation was established, at first sharing equal authority with Jane Gregory, with Polding overall in charge. She was appointed by Polding as superior when Jane died in 1850. It wasn't until 1864, after Wallis was elected, that le Clerc was appointed by Polding to the offices of sub-prioress and novice mistress. From the beginning of her arrival in the colony of New South Wales, she had embraced the role of a Benedictine missionary, and given herself to all that this meant.

---

56   A one-way fare from Sydney to Parramatta first class was four shillings. It was reduced by a quarter in the 1860s and dropped more as the century went on.
57   Rydalmere files, Local Studies and Family History Library, Parramatta City Council.
58   Cannon, *Australia*, 46.
59   Cannon, *Australia*, 63.

DEATH OF THE MOTHER SUPERIOR OF SUBIACO.

The Roman Catholic community in this colony will learn with deep regret the death of Mother Mary Magdalen Le Clerc, Superior of Subiaco Convent, which took place on Thursday morning at ten o'clock. The venerable Mother was in her eightieth year; she had been sixty-four years a nun, and was thirty years ago one of the founders of the Subiaco Convent and the important educational establishment connected with it, of both of which she afterwards remained the head. Notwithstanding her advanced age the deceased enjoyed excellent health until about three weeks ago, when she was afflicted with the illness which resulted in the termination of her long and exemplary life. She passed away very peacefully; and, indeed, did not seem to suffer much at any period of her illness. Her remains were interred at Subiaco cemetery yesterday morning at eleven o'clock. We believe we are right in stating that the memory of the deceased will be revered far beyond her own community; to the poor, of whatever denomination, she was a practical friend; and her Christian example and ability went far towards obtaining for Subiaco school the prestige that it has long enjoyed as the leading educational institution of its class in the colonies.

Obituary: Magdalen (Constantia) le Clerc, *Cumberland Mercury*, 30 March 1878

In the year of le Clerc's death, 1878, there were twenty-four pupils in the school. In addition to the work carried out by lay sisters, six female servants were also employed. When the number of pupils decreased in 1879, the number of servants dropped to four. Women continued to apply to join the community. In April 1881 Margaret O'Grady entered the community. She was a gifted teacher. Tuberculosis claimed her life, just a few months after her profession. She was twenty-five years of age. Bridget O'Sullivan, born in Ireland, entered in 1885, to be a lay sister. Mary Ellen Hishon entered the community in 1888, to be a choir nun. She died from tuberculosis in 1894. Esther Parkinson, a teacher and musician, entered in 1885 to be a choir nun. Florence Eugenie Gabriel, daughter of Dr Charles Louis Gabriel, entered the community in 1888 to be a choir nun. Mary Anne Hay entered in 1886, to be a choir nun.[60] Maria Rose Fairland, an English woman, entered in 1883, to be a choir nun. In the school, she taught Algebra and Arithmetic. Catherine Connolly entered in 1880, to be a lay sister. Catherine, born in Ireland, emigrated to Australia and worked in domestic service before asking to join the Subiaco community. Agnes Egan, an Australian, educated by the Good Samaritan Sisters in Wollongong, entered in 1887.

Sr Gertrude McLachlan

Following upon the death of le Clerc, Wallis was faced with a conflict situation, for which she asked for help from Archbishop Vaughan. Sr Gertrude (Teresa) McLachlan absented herself from the monastery for a period of time (no record as to how long), without the permission of her prioress.[61] Then she made the decision to depart from the monastery, demanding that her dowry be returned to her because her vows were not solemn vows. There was no question over her vows. Her vow paper, signed by Archbishop Polding on the day of her Solemn Monastic Profession, states 'solemn vows'.[62]

The following letter is an example of Vaughan's manner of dealing with a situation involving a nun or a monk of the archdiocese of Sydney. Polding had dealt with the situation of Evangelista Donovan in the 1850s, and revealed a compassionate and pastoral care rather than a dismissive manner. Polding had carried out a discernment process, which involved listening and facilitating, long before 'discernment' entered into the language of religious institutions. Vaughan's letter begins with the brief acknowledgement that he had received Sr Gertrude's letter, and had intended to deal with it at the next visitation.

---

60 Sr Philomena (Mary Ann Hay) had a brother, José, who became a conservationist. He contributed to the decision to declare the Blue Mountains of New South Wales a National Park.
61 Her actions were in conflict with Chapter 67 of the Benedictine Rule which specifically states that a nun may not absent herself from the community at any time without the permission of the abbess (in this case the prioress).
62 Solemn Vows were those taken by monastic and contemplative orders. Simple vows were those taken by women and men in the active apostolate of the Church.

To Sister M. Gertrude

I received your long letter some time ago, and intended to deal with it at the Visitation in October. Now, I hear of the talk and the scandalous step you took the other day. There will be a question of your Solemn Profession at the time of Visitation, and it is my duty to tell you that unless an entire change is made in your conduct, and unless the Superior can convince me that you are a fit subject for Solemn Vows of Religion, it will be my painful duty to declare you unfit for Religious life, and to free the community from the presence of one who has given such terrible scandal.

In any case your probation will have to be prolonged and you will have to learn many lessons which you have not learned as yet.

That Almighty God may open your eyes before it is too late. And save you from yourself—is the earnest prayer of yours faithfully in Christ.

Roger Bede, Archbishop of Sydney. September 20th, 1881.[63]

In 1883, Bishop Torreggiani,[64] 'following a Supreme Court Writ on behalf of Miss McLachlan to recover the five hundred pounds from the nuns on the grounds that it was hers, because her vows were not solemn, declared "[…] your Profession is a solemn one"'.[65] He wrote a letter from Woollahra in Sydney on 19 September 1883, informing Prioress Wallis of the conclusion he had reached:

---

63 Archbishop Roger Bede Vaughan, 'Letter to Prioress Walburge Wallis, September 20, 1881'. The letter to Sr Gertrude McLachlan was enclosed with the letter to Prioress Wallis.
64 In Vaughan's absence, Bishop Torreggiani was placed in charge of the Archdiocese of Sydney, and therefore of the nuns of Subiaco. His signature appears on some Vow Papers, as the one who presided at Solemn Monastic Professions.
65 Forster, 'Magdalen le Clerc', 330.

> I have carefully studied your difficulty regarding your Religious Professions, and I find in Theology that although an alteration was made by the late Pope Pius IX in 1857, affecting the Professions of Religious men in general and Religious Women in France and Belgium in particular [...] your Order is still in the same position now as it was before. That is, your Profession is a Solemn one and does not require to be preceded by a Simple Profession. [...] this is the same for nuns in Ireland, England and in any other part of the world, where the nuns have been in the habit of making their Solemn Professions and taking their Solemn Vows at once after their novitiate. The exception to this is France and Belgium where vows are only Simple Vows on account of Political disturbances.[66]

Was it possible that Sr Gertrude McLachlan was simply a woman who had grown up with the changes of the Nineteenth Century, a century that had 'witnessed massive changes in thinking about women's role in society [...] women's education, employment opportunities, marriage, sexuality, psychology and the right to vote'?[67] Her understanding of women's rights may have clashed seriously with the Rule of Benedict. Her behaviour would have been unacceptable in Vaughan's understanding of monastic life. Vaughan was English, and a male cleric in Victorian England where the intellect of women was 'not for invention or creation, but in sweet ordering, arrangement and decision'.[68]

In 1883 Archbishop Vaughan returned to England for a visit, during which time his sudden death occurred. This was the end of ecclesiastical jurisdiction in Sydney by Benedictines, which was to have a negative effect on the nuns of Subiaco for the next two decades.

The next chapter will examine the impact of Cardinal Moran on the Subiaco community—both the negatives and the positives: the call for a greater listening (*obsculta*), patience, and discernment, while misunderstanding between the cardinal and the prioress dominates.

---

66   Bishop Torreggiani, 'Letter to Prioress Walburge Wallis, 19 September, 1883'. (JAA: 'Mother Walburge Wallis, all letters and documents').
67   Phegley, *Courtship and Marriage,* 34.
68   Hughes, *The Victorian Governess,* 147.

CHAPTER SEVEN

Continuing the Wallis years (1889–1902)

This chapter will follow the demands of the *obsculta* of the Benedictine Rule on Wallis and her community as they sought to move forward, still seeking suitable constitutions against a background of ecclesiastical disapproval from Vaughan's successor, Patrick Francis Moran, and a foreground of a colony which was emerging into a nation. Wallis' second voyage to England and her exposure to the neo-monastic revival of the Nineteenth Century will provide a strong focus, as will the 'ban' which Cardinal Moran placed over the Subiaco community.

The arrival of Archbishop Patrick Francis Moran into a climate of rationalism and science

The Irish Archbishop Patrick Francis Moran arrived in 1884 to take over the Roman Catholic Church of the Archdiocese of Sydney. This was a triumph for Irish Catholicism, and gave great hope to the majority of Catholics who were Irish, and to the Irish Clergy, who had longed for a reprieve from Benedictinism, and English Benedictinism in particular.

Archbishop Patrick Francis Moran, c. 1880s

It was in 1883, the year of Vaughan's death, that the debates of 'science *versus* religion' were exercising strong influence in certain church communities of eastern Australia. This was typical of the Enlightenment Era generally. In 1883 a leading Victorian judge, George Higginbotham, said that:

> the intellects of the great majority of educated and thinking laymen at this day lie wholly outside the influence of the intellectual teaching of the Christian clergy [...] [there is] a growing and profound distrust of all church systems of religious and moral belief.[1]

Higginbotham was considered to be 'the greatest legal figure in Australia at that time', and had 'shocked a congregation of the Scots Presbyterian Church in Melbourne by telling them that they were living through the death throes of Christianity as they knew it because science had shown it to be false'.[2]

---

1   Cannon, *Australia*, 86.
2   Higginbotham, *Science and Religion*, 52–53.

This statement is aligned closely with the fact that at the end of the 1870s, as already noted, only twenty percent of the population attended church services, mostly Anglican or Catholic. It was a time of new discoveries in science. Pope Leo XIII wrote an encyclical at the end of 1878, in which he addressed 'the organized tendency of the masses towards atheism', the cause of which, as Clark suggests, was 'technical progress [… along with] the philosophy of secularisation, and materialism'.[3] Indeed,

> never was science so arrogant as when Leo XIII began to recommend to Catholics the study of sound philosophy. Scientists everywhere were proclaiming the victory of science over religion, when Leo declared that there could be no question of victory where there was no conflict.[4]

In spite of the trends towards secularism, statistics reveal that during Vaughan's time in Sydney the Catholic population increased from 32,195 in 1873, to 56,732 in 1883.[5] Irish immigration and population increase were factors in the 1883 statistics. O'Farrell draws attention to the fact that by the time of Vaughan's death (1883), Sydney had 102 Catholic Schools, with 12,500 of 15,200 Catholic school children as pupils.[6] The total population in Sydney, suburbs of Sydney, and in country districts on the fringe of Sydney at this time was 317,819. The monastery of Subiaco was still considered as 'country'.

Subiaco–1870s and 1880s

While the numbers of Catholics in the colony continued to increase during the 1880s, this did not equate to greater attendance at church on a Sunday. In the case of the monastery and school of Subiaco, their fidelity to the church and Catholic teachings remained steadfast within the confines of the cloister, where through the 1870s and 1880s

---

3   Clark, *A History of Australia*, IV.284.
4   Wynne, *Great Encyclicals*, 4, as quoted by Fremantle, *Papal Encyclicals*, 156.
5   Birt, *Benedictine Pioneers*, I.461.
6   O'Farrell, *The Catholic Church*, 180.

lived ten choir nuns, three lay sisters, and an increase from fifteen to thirty pupils.[7] It could be argued that the stable number of pupils in the 1870s and 1880s was the result of the positive economic climate of these decades. The 1860s had seen a fall in economic growth and financial security, similar to the fall in the 1840s that forced Hannibal Macarthur first to mortgage, and then to sell his colonial mansion that became the home of the Benedictine nuns. The 1890s would face another, more serious economic downturn. Having been part of the district known as Parramatta since 1791, in 1886, the subdivision of Rydalmere was created by Thomas O'Neill, from Rydal in the English Lake District.[8] In 1889 Rydalmere was incorporated into the new municipality of Dundas. From this time through to 1949, the Benedictine nuns were therefore identified as living in Rydalmere and not 'near Parramatta'. By the 1890s, rail connection to Clyde and Carlingford was in place. Rydalmere, however, remained semi-rural into the Twentieth Century. The most notable landmarks for many years were Subiaco, in the grand house built by Hannibal Macarthur on 'the Vineyard', and the Rydalmere Hospital for the Insane, which in 1888 took over premises in which the Female Orphan School had operated since 1813.[9]

---

7   Numbers recorded in the annual Ledger which Scholastica McCarthy (from Princethorpe) set in place in 1856. (JAA)
8   Parramatta was the name the Burramattagul people gave to the fertile ground at the headwaters of the river that fed the Harbour. In 1791, this name was adopted by Governor Phillip. (Dictionary of Sydney, 'Rydalmere').
9   See University of Western Sydney, 'Female Orphan School'.

Dundas – Ermington and Rydalmere. Parish of Field of Mars (1885–1890)

The 'single catechism'

The Plenary Council called by Moran in 1885 launched a 'single catechism' which was 'made mandatory for Australia'.[10] This compulsory catechism, taught to the children in Catholic schools, of which there were 102 in 1883, would surely have had an influence on attendance at Sunday Mass.[11] Campion quotes the inspector of schools in the Sydney Archdiocese as reporting that:

> in general the Catechism is well known by heart, and as it contains in a small compass a large amount of instruction, well calculated to guide people in their duty through life, any child who learns and understands it must derive much benefit from it.[12]

Catholic children would surely have communicated this 'large amount of instruction' to their parents. This may have accounted for the ongoing increase in attendance at church on a Sunday. The pupils of the Subiaco School learned the Catechism by heart and were examined on its contents. It appeared to be a strong safeguard against scientific and rational philosophies—at least for Catholics. It is worth noting that the first woman to embark upon scientific studies at the University of Sydney was a member of the Anglican Church—Fanny Elizabeth Hunt. She graduated with a Bachelor of Science Degree in 1888.[13] It wasn't expected that the pupils of Subiaco would be any more than good wives, homemakers, governesses, or nuns in other religious congregations of the time, or in the Subiaco community. What was of the utmost concern was that their Catholic faith would be grounded, and that Victorian etiquette would be well-practised.

---

10 Campion, *Australian Catholics,* 146.
11 The number of Catholic schools in Sydney in 1883 is quoted in Birt, *Benedictine Pioneers,* insert, as 108. Both Campion and O'Farrell have the number 102. Birt's statistics are less reliable. They were based on the numbers sent back to England, and in particular by the English Benedictines. Campion and O'Farrell have access to research material, with statistics which were unavailable to Birt.
12 Campion, *Australian Catholics,* 146.
13 Bygott and Cable, *Pioneer Women,* 41.

Focus for Catholics and Anglicans

In regard to country-dwelling Roman Catholics, O'Farrell gives a positive aspect, quoting the Catholic Bishops in their report of 1885, saying that their flock was numerous 'wherever the hours are long, the climate merciless, the labour unskilled, the comforts few and the remuneration small'.[14] Reasons for this would surely have been the faith of the country people, relying on God for a successful harvest, or for rain in time of drought. It was a different lifestyle, and one where faith in God was, for the most part, not in question.

In the Anglican Church, the 1880s saw the work of Bishop Barry, who 'pressed upon all church people the need to take full advantage of the rights of visiting and teaching in state schools'.[15] It is also noted that 'more than any other denomination, the Church of England in Sydney made great efforts in the 1880s to cultivate this link'.[16] As in the case of Catholics, so the children of the Anglican Church would also have passed on their knowledge of Catechesis to their parents. In the case of both Anglican and Catholic Churches, education of children in the Christian faith was paramount to survival.

The Public Instruction Act of 1880 had, in section seven, required government schools to include 'General Religious Teaching' as part of the curriculum. Under section seventeen, visiting clergymen or other accredited religious teachers could give religious instruction in a public school. Under section eighteen, parents could object to their children attending a class of religious instruction given by a clergyman or accredited religious teachers. The New South Wales Catholic Bishops' Joint Pastoral Letter of 1879[17] had stated that Catholics must send their children to Catholic schools, unless given special dispensation by their parish priest. This would surely have accounted for the fact that Catholic children were in Catholic schools, not public schools, and therefore the need for clergymen or those trained for religious instruction was not a primary issue.

---

14   O' Farrell, *Documents*, Vol. II, 21.
15   Judd and Cable, *Sydney Anglicans,* 130.
16   Judd and Cable, *Sydney Anglicans,* 130.
17   O'Farrell, *The Catholic Church,* 185–222; Southerwood, *Time-line,* 67; Fogarty, *Catholic Education,* Vol. I, 250–251. Archbishop Vaughan, 'Lenten Pastoral', *Freeman's Journal,* 10 February 1883, 18.

Vaughan's Canonical Visitation

At Subiaco in 1883 Archbishop Vaughan carried out a Canonical Visitation. At this visitation, he made a definite commitment to assist the nuns in their need to obtain suitable Constitutions to guide them forward into their future in Australia. He was also displeased with the situation at Subiaco, finding that it lacked monastic authenticity, compared with English monastic communities.[18] With Vaughan's sudden death in England, the nuns of Subiaco were left in the same predicament which had characterised their history so far—no suitable constitutions. Constitutions are the road map—the practical interpretation and application of the Rule—in this case, the Rule of Benedict.

Wallis continues the search for constitutions

In the light of Vaughan's death, Prioress Wallis asked, and received permission from, Cardinal Moran, her Canonical Superior,[19] to make another journey to England and Europe, in search of suitable constitutions for her community. This time, Eliza Merewether (Mother Justina) travelled with her. This voyage and its pilgrimages took place from 1888–89. Besides renewing contact with the Archbishop of Birmingham, William Bernard Ullathorne (formerly the Vicar General of Australia), and a visit to the widow of Augustus Northmore Welby Pugin, the significant event was their arrival in Beuron, in January 1889. The Archabbot had just drawn up constitutions for a convent of Benedictine nuns about to be founded in Prague. He offered these to Prioress Wallis when he heard of her difficulties. The Princethorpe

---

18 Vaughan himself knew one kind of monasticism: English. In order to be authentic, one had to copy what was being lived at Stanbrook and other English monasteries of women.

19 The Monastery of Subiaco was a monastery *sui juris* (of one's own right or competency) under the Local Ordinary, whoever that might be in the Archdiocese of Sydney. With the trials of the 1890s, it was expressed (in one letter only), that the nuns wished not to be in this situation, i.e. under the jurisdiction of the Sydney bishops. It appears that this letter was never sent to Moran.

Constitutions were still in use at Subiaco.[20] The new constitutions were accepted, with the understanding that they would be modified and amended to suit Australian conditions.[21] While the constitutions resembled those of St Peter's Abbey, Solesmes, and of the Abbey of Ste Cécile, birth places of the Nineteenth Century neo-monastic revival, they were also improved and simplified. As was the custom, they began with the word *obsculta*—the call to 'listen'.

Mother Justina (Eliza) Merewether, c. 1910

20 Behind the Princethorpe Constitutions was a prioress and community rigidly attached to every word and command in regard to monastic life. Gardens and outdoor shrines, extra prayers, devotions multiplied (Marie Forster) did not come easily to an Australian monastic community. Magdalen le Clerc, 'Letter to the Lady Abbess of Stanbrook Abbey, January 23, 1861' says that Mother Subprioress' (Scholastica Macarthy) ideas of perfection are far too exalted for Infant Establishments, nor is she a person altogether calculated for government.
21 Prioress Wallis, 'Letter to Sr Mary Placid Loughnan, February 2, 1889'. (JAA, archived in the box marked 'Mother Walburge Wallis, all letters and documents'.) This letter was written from Beuron.

Moran's response to the Beuronese Constitutions.

On returning to Australia, Prioress Wallis endured a period of illness. The long sea voyage and the pilgrimage she had undertaken in England and Europe had caused a great fatigue. She was fifty-seven years old. The constitutions she brought home were to be adopted at once, but Moran, on reading through the document, began to make difficulties. Most of these were justified. He questioned that the nuns would be under the authority of the Abbot of the Beuron Congregation. No such person lived in Australia.[22] He did not approve of the severity of the fasting, and the lack of communal recreation on the Fridays of Lent. He questioned the Liturgical Calendar as being that of Germany not of Australia. He noted: 'The feasts of obligation are those of Germany, not of Australia'.[23] The saints Moran is referring to appear in the context of Declaration 1: *Ausculta O Fili* (Listen O Son).

> Albeit the most holy Father Benedict addresses himself to monks alone, his Rule has for centuries served as a code for nuns, so that they are as rightfully named the daughters of the venerable patriarch as the monks who follow his Institute are styled his sons. It was by living as daughters of St. Benedict that St. Scholastica, St. Walburge, St. Hildegarde, St. Gertrude, St. Mechtilde, and so many other holy Virgins adorned the Church by their wonderful sanctity.[24]

---

22 The tyranny of distance was still a reality at this time in history, and visitation of a monastery in Australia by a German abbot would have been difficult on a yearly basis, or more, should a situation arise which required a second or even third canonical visitation.
23 Cardinal Patrick Francis Moran, 'Letter to Mother Walburge Wallis, 1889' (no date); Moran Letters M.201 (SAA).
24 The names have been Anglicised. The extract is Declaration No. 1 of the Beuronese Constitutions.

Liturgy

In the list of first and second class feasts (Figure 6), St Scholastica and the Passing of St Benedict are ranked as First Class Feasts. St Maurus, a young disciple of St Benedict, is ranked as a Second Class Feast. A second reference to the German Benedictine women is found in Chapter 73, 'This Little Rule Written for Beginners':

> It is therefore just and fitting that the sisters should make it their life-long study, to learn, relish and practise this Holy Rule. And they may rest assured that, if they fulfil it faithfully and with a 'dilated heart',[25] they will, in the world to come, enjoy the society of their Divine Bridegroom for all eternity, and be by Him associated to the glorious Choirs of the Saints of our Order, amongst whom shine pre-eminently our Holy Mother Scholastica, St. Walburge, St. Hildegarde, St. Mechtilde and St. Gertrude.[26]

Apart from St Scholastica, whose feast is noted in the Roman calendar as 10 February and therefore appears in the Roman Missal which was in use across the Catholic Church from 1858 until 1921, the Benedictine male and female saints were celebrated only in Benedictine monasteries and therefore would have been listed in the Monastic Breviaries used by monks and nuns of the time. The Roman Breviary would have been used by Cardinal Moran and other bishops and priests of the Nineteenth Century.[27]

---

25 This word is used in the way Paul uses it in 2 Corinthians 6:13: 'Widen your hearts', as opposed to being restricted and restrained. The word also appears in the Prologue to the Rule of Benedict, v.49: 'We shall run on the path of God's commandments, our hearts overflowing with the inexpressible delight of love'.
26 Beuronese Constitutions, declaration no. 73.
27 The only source for this information is both the Roman Breviary and the Monastic Breviary.

Duplicia Prime Classis (Double First Class):
Nativitas Domini (The Nativity of the Lord).

Epiphania Domini (Epiphany of the Lord).

Pascha Resurrectionis cum tribus antecedent, et duobus seq. (Pasch. of the Resurrection, with three days before, and two days following).

Ascensio Domini (The Ascension of the Lord).

Pentecostes sum duobus seq. diebus. (Pentecost with two days following).

Festum Corporis Christi (Feast of Corpus Christi). This is a simple translation for a simple title. Over the last 10 to 15 years, the *Ordo* has given the title as 'The Most Holy Body and Blood of Christ'.

Assumpto B. Mariae Virginis (Assumption of the Blessed Virgin Mary).

Nativitas S. Joannis Baptistae (Birth of St. John the Baptist).

Fest. SS. Apost. Petri et Pauli (Feast of Saints Peter and Paul, Apostles).

Natale SS.P.N. Benedicti (The Passing of Our Holy Father, St. Benedict).

Festum Omnium Sanctorum (Feast of all Saints).

Dedicatio propriae ecclesiae (Anniversary of the Dedication of a Church Proper to each community).

Duplicia Secunde Classis (Double Second Class Feasts)
Festum SS. Trinitatis (Feast of the Holy Trinity).

Circumcisionis Domini (Circumcision of the Lord). This feast is no longer celebrated in the Catholic Church.

Inventionis S. Crucis (The Finding of the Holy Cross). This feast is no longer celebrated in the Catholic Church.

SS. Nominis Jesu (Feast of the Holy Name of Jesus). This feast is no longer celebrated in the Catholic Church.

Pretiosiss Sanguinis D.N.J.C. (The Precious Blood of Our Lord Jesus Christ). This feast is no longer celebrated in the Catholic Church.

The Blessed Virgin Mary:
Conceptionis (Conception), *Purificationis* (Purification), *Annuntiationis* (Annunciation), *Visitationis* (Visitation), *Nativitatis* (Nativity).

Dedicat S. Michaelis Archangel (Feast of the Dedication of St. Michael the Archangel).

S. Joseph Sponsi B.M.V. (St. Joseph, Spouse of the Blessed Virgin Mary).

Patriocinii ejusdem S. Joseph (St. Joseph, Protector of the Blessed Mother and Child—a free translation!).

Natalitia undecim Apostolorum (The Birth of the Eleven Apostles) (Minus Judas).

Festa Evangelistarum (Feasts of the Evangelists – Matthew, Mark, Luke and John).

Festum Omnium Sanctorum. Ord. A.A.P.N (Feast of all Saints of the Benedictine Order).

S. Stephani Protomart (St Stephen, First Martyr).

SS. Innocentium (Feast of the Holy Innocents).

S. Laurentii Martyr (St Laurence, Martyr).

S. Mauri Abbatis (St Maurus, Abbot).

S. Scholasticae, Virgin (St Scholastica, Virgin).

Commem. Solemnis SS. P.N. (Solemn Commemoration of all Souls of the Benedictine Order).

Fest. SS. Placidi et Socior, Martyrum (Feast of St Placid and Companions, Martyrs)

DOMINICAE MAJORES, dividuntur in duas Classes
Dominica
Prime Classis

Prima Advent (First Sunday of Advent).

Prima Quadrag. (First of Quadragesima). *In Albis.*

Passionis (Passion Sunday).

Palmarum (Palm Sunday).

Paschae (Easter Sunday).

In Albis.

Pentecostes (Pentecost Sunday).

Trinitatis (Trinity Sunday)

Dominica

Secunde Classis

Secunda, Tertia, Quarta Adventus (Second, Third and Fourth Sundays of Advent)

Septuagesimae, Sexagesima, and *Quinquagesimae.*

Secunda, Tertia and *Quarta Quadragesimae.*

DUPLICIA MAJORA PER ANNUM

Fst. Transfigurationis Dni (The Transfiguration of the Lord).

Exaltatienis S. Crucis (The Exaltation of the Holy Cross).

S.S. Cordis Jesu (The Sacred Heart of Jesus).

Duplicia Majora Per Annus: Blessed Virgin Mary

Dispensationes

Septem Dolorum (The seven sorrows of the Virgin Mary).

Carmeli (Our Lady of Mt. Carmel).

SS. Nominis (The Holy Name of Mary).

De Mercede (The Motherhood of Mary).

Iterum VII Dolorum (Second Feast of the Seven Sorrows of the Bl. Virgin Mary).

SS. Rosarii (Feast of the Holy Rosary).

Praesentationis (Feast of the Presentation of the Lord).

Expectationis (The expectancy, waiting, for the birth of the Child).

Apparit. S. Michaelis Archaelis Archang (The Appearance, apparition, of the Archangel Michael).

Figure 6: Liturgical Classification of Feasts.

Wine

From his comment on German women saints, Moran moved on to the issue of wine. He thought that the measure of daily wine (in accordance with the Rule of St Benedict) was not suitable for nuns. Wine was a part of the midday and evening meals in European monasteries of monks and nuns. More than one monastery planted vineyards and made wine as a means of income.[28] Cardinal Moran was Irish. Wine wasn't the drink of the Irish or the English at this time.[29] The nuns changed this declaration in the light of his objection. They wrote: 'Wine not being the ordinary drink of the country, the contents of this chapter are inapplicable'[30] (Chapter 40:1).

Lay sisters

Moran also questioned the Office for Lay Sisters, suggesting that they would be better praying the Rosary, with a few additional prayers. The following is the excerpt from the Beuronese Constitutions that Moran thought would be better changed:

> The lay sisters will go to the Church each morning at 5.00 o'clock, to make half an hour's meditation. They shall assist daily at Mass, make a visit to the Blessed Sacrament, be present at the examination of conscience after Compline, the Chapter of faults, Vespers on Sundays and Festivals, Benediction of the Blessed Sacrament, clothings,[31] professions, and on all other solemn occasions which concern the whole Family. When

---

28   Those monasteries with vineyards suffered in the 1860s and 1870s from the phylloxera outbreak which destroyed the vines at their roots. Australia also suffered as they watched thousands of acres of vines die, due to drought.
29   Although, the Subiaco land was known as 'the Vineyard', because its original grant holder, Philip Schaeffer, had planted vines, it was John Macarthur, uncle of its subsequent owner, Hannibal Macarthur, who is credited as the first to cultivate a commercial vineyard and winery in Australia. The industry developed slowly, beginning to make an international impact by the 1870s. It was by no means the primary alcoholic beverage of Australians: cf. Molony, *Penguin Bicentennial History*, 172–174.
30   Beuronese Constitutions, Chapter 40:1, as altered by the community of Subiaco.
31   The reception, by a postulant, of the Monastic Habit. At this time, monastic clothings were presided over by the Archbishop, or his delegate.

not prevented by the labours imposed on them, they must say the entire Rosary daily[32]—it must never be omitted without permission, which will only be given in a case of absolute necessity—but in this, as in all other spiritual exercises, they must remember that manual labour is their principal obligation and the object of their institution, consequently to be preferred whenever the Superior judges it necessary. However, that all may be able to take part in the different pious exercises, the lay sisters should charitably help each other in their work. In saying their Rosary, the lay sisters should unite with the intentions of Holy Church, according to the Feast and should honour the Mysteries which she honours by her several Canonical Hours.

In the Subiaco revised copy of the Beuronese Constitutions, lay sisters are still placed in Chapter 57 of the Rule of Benedict, and called the trades people or a separate body from the choir nuns, 'the intention being to furnish hands for servile work'.[33] It is emphasised that these sisters are not properly nuns, but are true religious and form a part of the monastic family. No one is to be admitted to be a lay sister without a true vocation to the religious life. There is to be sufficient probation as regards her disposition, perseverance, bodily, and spiritual qualifications. Her stages of initiation are spelt out, and a member from the choir nuns is to be overall in charge of lay sisters. A protective policy is built in as to their place in the monastery, and it looks to a peaceful life alongside the nuns in solemn vows.

The period of probation

Added to the objections already discussed, Moran saw that the time of probation ought to be made definite, with the freedom to prolong it in exceptional cases.[34] Moran was within his rights to question this norm. Different time spans for initial formation could and did at times lead to unrest among sisters who were made to wait longer while their

---

32   The fifteen decades of the Rosary.
33   *Constitutions*, Chapter 57, Declaration 1.
34   Probation refers to the time of initial formation required of women joining the community.

companions in the novitiate went ahead of them. There is the example of Margaret Macklin, who came to Australia as a young Irish girl and worked as a domestic servant on a cattle station in Queensland. She entered Subiaco in the early 1890s, received the habit in October 1894, before the 'ban' imposed by Moran, and was not professed until May 1916 because of uncertainty about her suitability.[35] She thus lived neither as a lay sister nor an oblate, as is noted in her obituary, but as someone who was not given the stability granted to the other nuns in community. She is described as 'a sort of oblate, helping the guest-mistress in her work at the cottage'.[36] As time progressed, an institution called 'regular oblates' emerged. These women lived inside the cloister, doing menial work but with the freedom to leave the enclosure to see family or friends.[37]

The Chapter of Faults

Moran questioned the confession of interior faults at Chapter.[38] He saw that only the confession of 'exterior violations of the Rule' were suitable in Chapter.[39]

---

35 She was professed at sixty-one years of age.
36 Malone, 'Obit List', 35–80.
37 A number of Benedictine monasteries have 'Regular Oblates', an institution which has been successful. Jamberoo Abbey does not have regular oblates. The experiment was tried and found wanting. 2018 was given over to four women living in a retreat cottage and attending the Liturgy of the Hours, and other work. It was an experiment that was successful both for community and for women concerned, although it has not been repeated to date.
38 Chapter of Faults, as it was known in monastic life, was a formal gathering, either daily, or weekly (according to the tradition of the community). It was a ritual with prayers and the reading of the Holy Rule. At this Chapter of Faults, a nun would have to confess failings which had disrupted the peace and prayer of the monastery during that day. This could have been the breaking of a dish at meal times, due to a lack of mindfulness, or talking in places of silence. Faults which occurred during the Liturgy of the Hours were dealt with after that particular 'Hour', when a nun knelt in the middle of the monastic choir, and stayed there until the prioress told her to rise.
39 The formal assembly of nuns in solemn vows.

Housework

Moran thought sweeping the house once a week would not suit the Australian climate, nor would the daily Mass time (9.00 a.m.) be suitable to the Australian climate.[40]

The reading of mail

Moran also questioned the reading of letters. He insisted that the superior did not have the right to read outgoing or incoming mail to or from the Archbishop. The revised paragraph was to read: 'The superior will read all letters written to or by the sisters except those to or from His Grace the Archbishop (or other ecclesiastical superior), which are to be sent and delivered unopened'. The Benedictine Rule does not sanction the reading of letters. Chapter 54, entitled 'Letters or gifts for monks', states: 'In no circumstances is a monk allowed, unless the abbot says he may, to exchange letters, blessed tokens or small gifts of any kind, with his parents or anyone else, or with a fellow monk'.[41]

Chapter 24 of the Rule of Benedict—dealing with small faults

Chapter 24 posed a problem for Moran. The chapter is entitled: 'Of small faults' (*In levioribus culpis*). In the matter of small faults, Moran advised that 'the superior's sense of justice and discretion' must be the deciding factor. Automatic excommunication from the common table, or punishment by making a nun sit alone in the centre of the refectory at mealtime, or further still making the culprit eat at a later time— these punishments were thought, by Moran, to outweigh the nature of the fault. In this whole matter, he asks that each case be judged for itself, and that the rigidity of Chapter 24 be modified.

---

40 Malone, 'Cardinal Moran', 66.
41 Fry, *RB 1980*, 54:1.

The Beuronese Constitutions are shelved

Even though Moran asked that the prioress and her council consider the issues he had raised, there is no written record of their response to him. The adoption of the Beuronese Constitutions was shelved because of two issues which estranged the Subiaco community from the Archdiocese of Sydney. These two issues will now be discussed.

Benedictine patience

The 1890s was the era of Benedictine patience—the call to share through patience in the sufferings of Christ (RB80 Prologue, v.50).

After Prioress Wallis returned from Europe in 1889, Moran made his annual canonical visit to the community. During this visitation, it became evident, according to one source, that 'someone had been making mischief and from His Eminence's words we gathered that he had been influenced by a certain cleric who was unfriendly towards the community'.[42] This was probably Austin Sheehy, a priest who had shown hostility towards Prioress Wallis and the community since the 1860s.[43] He was an ex-Benedictine monk, Vicar General under Polding, and in the late 1860s 'it had become intensely important to Polding that Sheehy be made a bishop, coadjutor to himself'.[44] As it eventuated, Sheehy never became a bishop, because the Irish bishops stood against the proposal.[45] In 1867, Polding declared in a letter that Fr Austin Sheehy

---

42   Smythe Chronicles (JAA). Sr. Mildred Smythe kept a book, quite independent of the Community Chronicles. Probably no one else knew of her doing this. In the Community Chronicles, the pages relating to the 1890s have been cut out of the book, so there is no record by the chronicler of community events. A further source of information for this period is the detailed recount provided by Sr Justina Merewether in the impassioned letter written by the Subiaco Community Councillors (Mary Austin Marum, Mary Scholastica Therry, Mary Justina Merewether, Mary Ignatius Harnett, Theresa M. Parkinson, Claire Gabriel) to Cardinal Moran on 2 November 1901, which receives attention below.
43   As already noted above (p. 131), Austin Sheehy took the part of the novices against Magdalen le Clerc in 1864, and reported to Polding on the matter. Sheehy was raised to the status of 'archpriest' by Moran.
44   O'Farrell, *The Catholic Church*, 199.
45   At the last moment, Polding received a letter from the Vatican asking him to defer Sheehy's consecration.

has been accused not of mere negligence [...] but actually of having connived at the apostasies of some monks, including of course, the wretched Anselm's case[46] [...] a nasty insinuation is made, that Mother Scholastica [Mother General of the Good Shepherd Sisters—later the Good Samaritans] was seen coming out of his room. And this miserable unnamed calumniator's story is preferred to my testimony.[47]

Moran appointed Sheehy as Extraordinary Confessor to the nuns of Subiaco on two occasions, though Prioress Wallis begged him not to do this.[48] The community objected, based on their experience of the 1860s. Sheehy himself asked for leave not to take on this appointment. Moran may not have known the history of Sheehy's interference in the appointment of Magdalen le Clerc as novice mistress, and the episode which led to Polding's active intervention.

The Cardinal withdraws

At this time in Sydney there were the Sisters of Charity, the Sisters of the Good Samaritan founded by Polding, the Marist Missionary Sisters, the Sisters of the Sacred Heart Society, the Poor Clares, the Little Company of Mary, who founded Mt St Margaret's Hospital at Ryde, the Discalced Carmelites, and the Sisters of Our Lady of the Sacred Heart.[49] All these communities of religious women were under Cardinal Moran's ecclesiastical jurisdiction in his position as Cardinal Archbishop of Sydney.

---

46   This refers to the fact that Anselm Curtis, a monk of Lyndhurst, left the monastic life after becoming involved with a woman. See further, Livingston, 'Anselm Curtis'.
47   Polding to Henry Gregory, 24 August, 1867, *The Letters of John Bede Polding, Vol. 3,* 274. This letter is also quoted in Birt, *Benedictine Pioneers,* II.329.
48   Subiaco Community Councillors to Cardinal Moran, 2 November, 1901; noting the correction in Justina Merewether to Cardinal Moran, 4 November 1901: 'Fr. Austin Sheehy was sent twice as extraordinary [confessor], not for two years'. An Extraordinary Confessor is a Catholic priest who comes to administer the Sacrament of Reconciliation a few times each year, and thus provides an alternative to the regular priest-confessor.
49   MacGinley, *A Dynamic of Hope,* 343.

After the canonical visit in 1889, when Prioress Wallis first returned from Europe, the Cardinal did not visit Subiaco for eleven years. If the Cardinal didn't visit a monastic or another religious community, that community was targeted as being non-acceptable. A maze of turmoil dominated these years. The Beuronese Constitutions were just one issue. After Moran's critique of the document, the nuns waited for an opportunity to speak with him about implementing them with the modifications he had suggested. That opportunity never came. In 1893, Dr Joseph Higgins was sent by Moran to carry out the annual Canonical Visitation, which occurred just before Moran left for Rome.[50] The nuns sent messages through him to the Cardinal. They never received a reply.

At the time of the visitation, Dr Higgins gave the nuns what they considered an 'incomprehensible' message—that Moran did not visit Subiaco because he was 'displeased at Mother Prioress's continued illness'.[51] This strange message was as close as Moran could get to stating outright what his problem was. Only much later would it be revealed that a Catholic priest was responsible for malicious gossip about Wallis. Slander, calumny, and detraction all but destroyed her. Moran believed the accusatory gossip that Prioress Wallis was sleeping in the cottage with a man. This was the first rumour. She therefore became pregnant. And then a Protestant[52] medical doctor whispered in Moran's ear that 'one of your nuns has had a medical procedure which looks to me like an abortion'.[53] This was the gossip which led to the false accusations focused on Wallis and her community, placing them under a ban, which announced to the Catholic Church that the nuns were being punished—officially punished by the hierarchical institution.

---

50   Dr Joseph Higgins was ordained as Auxiliary Bishop of Sydney on 31 March 1889 and served in that post until he he was assigned to the Diocese of Ballarat on 3 March 1905. His 1893 visitation on behalf of the cardinal is mentioned by Justina Merewether's detailed recount of events in Subiaco Community Councillors to Cardinal Moran, 2 November 1901.
51   Subiaco Community Councillors to Cardinal Moran, 2 November, 1901.
52   The use of 'Protestant' to describe the doctor places the terrible accusation as that which a Catholic doctor would not make.
53   Subiaco Community Councillors to Cardinal Moran, 2 November 1901; Cardinal Moran to the nuns, 5 November 1901.

Sr Evangelista Bridge

The next issue, also integrated into the sufferings of the 1890s, was that of Sr Evangelista Bridge. Mentally ill, her presence in the community was a source of communal upheaval. The nuns asked the Cardinal, in a letter dated 7 February 1895,[54] if this nun could be removed from the premises. The Cardinal's response was to obtain full, accurate, and unprejudiced information about the case, by appointing a special commission of enquiry, consisting of the Very Rev. Aubrey, SM, and the Very Rev. Slattery, OSF, to investigate all matters connected with the well-being of the monastery, the observance of rules, and the peace of the community. As the ecclesiastical head of the Catholic Church in the Archdiocese of Sydney, the Cardinal had the right to do this. He was the higher superior of the Benedictine nuns of Subiaco. However, the fact that he sought accurate and unprejudiced information about the overall well-being of the monastery presented a new challenge to the *obsculta* of the Benedictine life. With purity of heart at the core of monastic living, could the nuns speak honestly, aware of the prejudice against them which may or may not have taken hold of others?

Evangelista (Elvina McIntyre) Bridge had been professed on 3 December 1889. The community chronicles record that her mind 'gave way soon after Profession' and that her mind and its twisted thoughts were responsible for a lot of the gossip which surrounded the events of this time. As Sr Justina Merewether later recounted:

> Sr. M. Evangelista Bridge said in the noviceship that when M. Prioress was in England and Europe she was tracked everywhere by your eminence, that at each place she went to, you had someone "to shadow her". M. Prioress did not, and does not believe this, neither do we, but it shows that malicious reports must have been spread. Much harm was done by that poor sister's tongue (though personally we consider she was irresponsible). Your eminence would not believe the statements we sent you at three visitations and the letters as to her state

---

54 Prioress and Council of Subiaco, 'Letter to Cardinal Patrick Francis Moran, 7 February, 1895'. (JAA, Box marked 'Prioress Walburge Wallis, all Letters and documents'.)

of mind for about five years, but that we were right has been proved by the trouble she has since given to other communities – and that she had no real grievance here is shown by the petitions she has sent to be allowed to return.[55]

After enduring five years of her destructive behaviour, with threats of suicide, fabrications of events which never took place, and outbursts of abnormal excitability, insubordination, and contempt for the Benedictine Rule and customs of the house, she was eventually admitted to Mt St Margaret's Hospital at Ryde which had been opened in the early 1890s on Victoria Road.[56]

Mt St Margaret's Hospital, Ryde. Founded by the Little Company of Mary sisters, specializing in psychiatric nursing.

---

55 Justina Merewether to Cardinal Moran, 4 November 1901. There is no documentation regarding the nature of Elvina McIntyre Bridge's mental illness, apart from the Community Chronicles and letters written to the Cardinal by the prioress and her council. The mental illness may have been schizophrenia, or bipolar disorder. Whatever the nature of the illness, it would have been difficult for her to live within a monastery, disrupting community life and prayer, as expressly noted here.

56 St Margaret's became a hospital for dementia patients, geriatric patients, private female patients, and psychogeriatric patients.

Her brother, Fr Bridge, who was also responsible for some of the slander against Prioress Wallis,[57] said that the community at Subiaco worked underhandedly, and would soon have no members, and that all priests spoke against them: 'If we sent his sister away, it was only another nail in Subiaco's coffin'.[58] Once again, this kind of verbal mud-slinging has surely been a not so welcoming feature of the Catholic Church through the ages, and certainly a feature of the Catholic Church of Australia in the Nineteenth Century. The accusations against Bishop O'Mahony of Armidale, and Mary MacKillop, foundress of the Sisters of St Joseph, would be two more in a long list.[59]

In November 1901, three letters were written to the cardinal within a six day period revealing the nature of the calumnious information against the prioress and the injustice caused to the enclosed women's community at Subiaco.[60]

The longest of these letters, consisting of approximately 1600 words, is dated 2 November. It was signed by the Community Council, consisting of six senior nuns: Sisters Mary Austin, Scholastica, Justina, Ignatius, Theresa, and Clare. As her contribution to the November 2 letter, Justina Merewether penned an explanation in the most minute detail of the Prioress's activies over a decade. It was written, they said, without the approval or knowledge of the prioress. Perhaps such disobedience freed their tongues and pens even further. This letter is remarkable for its rage, and from the nun's perspective the sending of it could only prolong the cold war, which had begun after the Prioress returned from Europe in 1889 with a new set of Constitutions. Subsequently, the cardinal's attitude to Subiaco

---

57 Subiaco Community Council to Cardinal Moran, 2 November, 1901. In this letter, it is relayed that the Fr Kerwick told the guest mistress at Subiaco that Fr Bridge said at a dinner table with other priests that Mother Prioress did not stay in the monastery, but she had a room in the cottage next to the priest.

58 Justina Merewether to Cardinal Moran, 4 November 1901. See also Prioress and Council of Subiaco Monastery, 'Letter to Cardinal Patrick Francis Moran', 2 November 1901.

59 See Duffy, 'O'Mahony, Timothy (1825–1892)'; Farrell, 'Archbishop Vaughan'; and Thorpe, 'MacKillop, Mary Helen (1842–1909)'.

60 Copies of these letters were obtained from St Mary's Archdiocesan Archives on 17 March 1987, and are now archived in the Jamberoo Abbey Archive, in the box marked 'Prioress Walburge Wallis, all letters and documents'.

effectively prevented the community from receiving vocations, and holding ceremonies of Clothing or the taking of Vows.

From the letter, it seems that the nuns had finally heard from the Cardinal himself the reasons behind his not visiting them for more than eleven years—'the awful calumny against our beloved and venerated mother, which we heard of for the first time from you'. Merewether refers to the cryptic remark of Dr Higgins during his 1893 visitation that 'the cardinal is displeased at Mother Prioress's continuing illness'.[61] The nuns had thought the unspoken accusation—the reason for the withdrawal of his support as indicated by him not conducting the visitation of 1893 personally—was that the 'incomprehensible' message from Dr Higgins might have been a euphemism for drinking: 'We denied this indignantly you may remember and begged you would come to see us as soon as you returned from Rome'.[62] However, despite such pleas, the Cardinal had never returned to Subiaco, and maintained a cryptic silence, refusing to answer any of the prioress' letters, although responding to some letters from individuals in the community—'our superior slighted in every possible way'.[63] Now, the nuns say, they find the accusation is of an affair, and an abortion. This letter from the women of the Subiaco monastery therefore issues a cry for justice for their prioress against accusations which they know are groundless.

They had already known that the hostile Fr Bridge had said at a dinner table with other priests that Mother Prioress did not stay in the monastery, but had a room in the cottage next to the priest. They could hardly believe the Cardinal would have taken that seriously. But they had not heard that someone had told the Cardinal of a comment made by a Protestant doctor that the prioress had had an abortion, 'the most disgraceful accusation that could be brought against a woman has been made against a person consecrated to God'.[64] Eleven years of public and shaming silence—all based on a reported whisper

---

61 Justina Merewether to Cardinal Moran, 4 November 1901.
62 Subiaco Community Councillors to Cardinal Moran, 2 November, 1901.
63 Subiaco Community Councillors to Cardinal Moran, 2 November 1901.
64 Subiaco Community Councillors to Cardinal Moran, 2 November 1901.

from a 'Protestant doctor'—a man the nuns had difficulty believing actually existed. They feared the enemy was much closer to home: 'We strongly suspect that a priest is hidden behind the doctor'.[65] For, as noted by Sr Justina in her follow up letter two days later, 'Our most bitter enemies have been and are, priests'.[66]

But the main person in their sights is the Cardinal himself, the willing believer of slander: 'You made no investigation, no enquiry'.[67]

> Since your Eminence ceased to visit us, bishops and priests seemed to consider we are under a ban [...] the School and the Noviceship have suffered [...] what a burden we have had to bear, though we did not know it was all because somebody said that somebody else had spoken evil against our mother. No further proof! No further investigation![68]

The community challenged him to come out of hiding, 'to inform the bishops and priests of the country that the slanderous accusations have been made against the prioress of Subiaco', and that the cardinal had investigated them and that they are utterly false and groundless.

> We do not wish this matter hushed up, but made as public as possible [...] It has struck us that the approaching synod would be a good opportunity for our natural protector to set things right—does not your Eminence think so too?[69]

Reflecting on the circumstances of the nuns' lengthy letter of appeal, the second letter, written by Sr Justina Merewether and sent the day after the first, tells of how the nuns' state of mind at the time led to some errors that needed correcting.

> My Lord Cardinal, though we delayed writing to you for a few days, we were anxious that you should get our letter (sent yesterday), and there were so many interruptions when writing, that

---

65 Subiaco Community Councillors to Cardinal Moran, 2 November 1901.
66 Justina Merewether to Cardinal Moran, 4 November 1901.
67 Subiaco Community Councillors to Cardinal Moran, 2 November 1901.
68 Subiaco Community Councillors to Cardinal Moran, 2 November 1901.
69 Subiaco Community Councillors to Cardinal Moran, 2 November 1901.

> I find I left two errors which should have been corrected, for which I only am to blame, and which I now hasten to rectify.[70]

As she corrected several errors in detail, Sr Justina added a further memory that becomes pertinent alongside the recent revelations.

> Another incident which evidently bears on the late painful revelation I take this opportunity of relating. Some years ago we were informed by a friend that a young man told his mother that a priest, after Mass and in his vestments, had in his presence said something about M. Prioress so bad that he would not tell his mother what it was, but remarked that only the priest had "his things" on he would have kicked him. The young man had at that time never seen M. Prioress. When he did so, later on, the same person told us he said he felt as if he could knock that priest down. We know that this same priest and others have spoken much against Subiaco, and we have been frequently told that postulants and pupils have been kept away by priests.

On November 5, the Cardinal's reply to the nuns' letter of the 2nd arrived. However, the Chapter members found his reply to their energetic and lengthy letter requesting an investigation to clear their Mother Prioress's name quite insufficient for what was required. Moran replied only briefly, claiming that Higgins' mysterious accusation against the prioress 'referred to the statement made by the Protestant Doctor: "One of your nuns has been very ill, I am told; from all that I have heard it is very like a case of an abortion"'.[71] Declaring he had 'never learned who the doctor was. It is all now, apparently, past and forgotten', Moran blithely, if somewhat convolutedly, finally asserted that 'the fact that the rumour took no hold on an unfriendly public is sufficient proof that it had no solid foundation'.[72]

---

70 Justina Merewether to Cardinal Moran, 4 November 1901.
71 Cardinal Moran to the nuns, 5 November 1901.
72 Cardinal Moran to the nuns, 5 November 1901.

Even if this remark shows that Moran may have at last come to a better opinion of the matter, his curt reply made no reference to his own serious breach of relationship with the community, despite the nuns' letters showing how deeply wounded they were by the one who should have been their protector. Even if Moran now dismisses the matter with a mere wave of the hand, assured that 'the rumour took no hold on an unfriendly public', this was in complete contradiction to their own painful experience across the previous decade. Yet, despite the nuns' clearly articulated grievances, this unempathetic memo from their ecclesiastical superior contained no suggestion of any apology that the rumours had actually taken hold of him.

The six members of the Council swiftly responded with the same direct language they had found the freedom to use on November 2:

> You said that what you had to say would be painful to yourself and painful to us – that the Prioress had some years ago asked permission to go to Sydney to the Carmelites, that a Catholic gentleman had told you in confidence that one of your nuns was very ill, and that a protestant doctor had said from what he had heard of the illness it was very like a case of abortion. We asked why your Eminence did not speak to M. Prioress's doctors, and did not come to Subiaco to investigate. You said you thought it better to await the course of events. You did not say that it might not be M. Prioress who was alluded to. On the contrary, you repeated more than once that this report was the only reason for your remaining away for so many years. Remembering these facts we cannot understand how the rumour could be said to refer to an indefinite nun in an indefinite convent, still less, why, such being the case, Subiaco should be chosen for special punishment.[73]

---

73 Subiaco Community Councillors to Cardinal Moran, 6 November 1901.

Moran and Dill Macky

During the 1890s, Moran was embroiled in his own scandals. Sectarianism was 'endemic'. Stuart Macintyre sums up the scandal as follows:

> The fire [was] fuelled by public disputation, most notably in the protracted conflict in Sydney between Cardinal Moran and the Rev. William Dill Macky, minister of the Scots Church and grand chaplain of the Loyal Orange Lodge. Beginning in the mid-1890s, when Moran made frequent bigoted remarks against Protestant missionaries, it came to a head in 1900 with the Coningham case (or as Protestants would have it, the O'Haran case). Coningham was an Australian Cricketer who had toured with the Australian team to England in 1893. O'Haran was the private secretary to Moran. Coningham brought a law suit against O'Haran, for adultery with his wife […] It attracted enormous media coverage, and 5000 people waited outside the courthouse for the first trial. O'Haran was eventually cleared but the sectarian bitterness had taken a hold on the society of the closing years of the 19th century, and lingered well into the 20th century.[74]

The way O'Farrell sums up the situation challenges the historian to a deeper reality than that of surface bitterness and tensions:

> The activities of O'Haran's champions, no less than those of his opponents, point to the existence of an ugly and unprincipled religious underworld in which the labels Catholic and Protestant had no real religious meaning, but denoted merely rival politico-social power factions.[75]

There is but one reference to the O'Haran/Coningham case in the collection of letters written to Moran by Mother Justina Merewether and the Councillors of the Subiaco community. Perhaps it would be prudent to relegate the demise of Prioress Wallis and her nuns to

---

74 Macintyre, *The Oxford History of Australia,* 4.66.
75 O'Farrell, *The Catholic Church,* 275. See also Nairn, 'Coningham, Arthur (1863–1939)', and D'Arcy, 'O'Haran, Denis Francis (1854–1931)'.

O'Farrell's 'ugly and unprincipled religious underworld', but one not of politico-social power factions, but of the politico-power factions within a religion as dominant as the Roman Catholic Church.

The effects of the 'ban'

The nuns of Subiaco, embroiled in their own scandalous affair, were anxious that the Prioress be cleared of the accusation and its effects which had gone on for years. This scandal and the controversy surrounding Evangelista Bridge, contributed to the suffering of the last decade of the Nineteenth Century, made worse by the fact that Moran and the clergy of Sydney believed that the Subiaco community wanted to separate from the Archdiocese.[76] The nuns maintained that vocations were affected and the numbers in the school were diminished. The vocation issue was a reality, because the Cardinal forbade any Clothing Ceremonies[77] or Religious Professions to be carried out while the nuns were under his 'ban'. Honora Hennessy entered to be a lay sister in 1894. She was clothed in the monastic habit in 1901. Frances Pechy entered in 1894 to be a lay sister. She was clothed in the monastic habit in 1901. Lucy Smythe entered in 1895, to be a choir nun and remained a postulant until October 1901, when the 'ban' was lifted.[78] Margaret Macklin entered Subiaco in the early 1890s, before the 'ban' and was clothed in the monastic habit in 1894. All these women remained in monastic life, and were not deterred by the 'ban'.

---

76 It is written down in one letter that the nuns did want to separate from the Archbishops of Sydney.
77 The reception of the monastic habit.
78 The time of postulancy was usually nine months to a year, but longer in the case of uncertainty.

Hildebrand de Hemptinne (1849–1913), first Abbot Primate of the Benedictine Confederation, c. 1890s

As a desperate measure following the exchange of letters with Cardinal Moran in November 1901, the nuns sought the help of Rome-based Hildebrand de Hemptinne, the first Abbot Primate of the Benedictine Confederation. Founded in 1883, the Confederation is not a governing body, but a source of appeal. In response to the letters from the nuns of Subiaco, in 1902 the Abbot Primate wrote to Cardinal Moran from Sant'Anselmo (the Headquarters of the Benedictine Confederation):[79]

> The community [of 'Subiaco'] feel it deeply that you abstain, my Lord Cardinal, during several years, from calling at the monastery […] they wrote several letters to me […] it struck my mind that you, my dear Lord Cardinal, might be pleased to give comfort to a dying religious superioress [Walburge Wallis] and to her community, and that you might choose to do it (sic) by addressing me a few lines to that effect. Allow me to say, my dear Lord Cardinal, that I would consider such a condescension, as a personal favour to me, for which I would ever be grateful. Venerating the Sacred purple and asking your blessing

---

79 Hildebrand de Hemptinne to Cardinal Moran, 12 April, 1902. (JAA)

for all at St Anselm's I beg to remain of Your Eminence, the humble and devoted servant in Christ,

+Hildebrand de Hemptinne, Abbot Primate, OSB.

One of the hurtful remarks the nuns had previously heard as if from the cardinal, was that he would not even come to Subiaco for Prioress Wallis's funeral.[80] Whether or not they had relayed this to Abbot Hildebrand, against this background the visit he proposed to Moran, asking the cardinal to visit the prioress who was dying to bring comfort to her and her community, would have no doubt helped to heal some deep wounds. But as it turned out, presumably in God's providence, Moran would not attend the funeral, for when the Prioress died, he was on an extended trip in Europe, visiting Ireland and Rome.[81] Six months after she was buried, Cardinal Moran and his private secretary Dr O'Haran came to Subiaco for the Profession of one choir nun and two lay sisters on 23 April, 1903. From this, one could conclude that the estrangement period was over—even if Prioress Wallis was not around to experience the rapprochement.

The economy of the 1890s

To say that the numbers in the school were affected by the 'ban' does not present a realistic picture. In 1890, there were nineteen girls in the school. Eight of these did not pay school fees. From 1891 until 1904 the numbers were down, mostly nine or ten. Sixteen were enrolled for 1895, but only ten were paying school fees. This tells a different story, one which is surely linked to the financial depression of the 1890s which saw a maritime strike lasting two months:

> the transport and shipment of wool […] shorn by non-union labour was arriving at the wharves, and in a matter of days,

---

80   Sr Justina Merewether to Cardinal Moran, 4 November 1901: 'And it is about three years instead of two since Fr. Kerwick said your Eminence would not even come for M. Prioress's funeral'.
81   Cardinal Moran left Sydney on 3 March 1902 and returned to Sydney on 6 December, *Sydney Morning Herald*, 4 March and 8 December 1902. Prioress Wallis died on 11 October.

marine officers, seamen, wharf labourers and coal lumpers all had gone on strike, to prevent the loading of 'black' wool.[82]

Were the nuns of Subiaco aware of the financial depression and its effects on Australia at large, or were their own troubles the main focus during this the last decade of the Nineteenth Century? Because of the structure of the Catholic Church in that period, a church governed by a male hierarchy, the nuns, it is fair to say, would have been fairly desperate to remain on friendly terms with that male hierarchy. This would have been their focus.

However, the close of the Nineteenth Century brought drought, falling wool prices, unemployment, and domestic hardship. Brian Matthews notes that the summers of the early 1890s brought a drought that was the worst in living memory. It was felt mostly by the farmers and graziers of western New South Wales. Matthews quotes Henry Lawson, who wrote in a letter to his aunt: 'You can have no idea of the horrors of the country out here. Men tramp and beg and live like dogs'.[83] During the depression of the 1890s, men were out of work, and 'at a loose end in the cities, or in the widespread metropolis of the great scrubs, as Lawson called the bush, where men "on the wallaby" and "humpin' bluey" trudged from station to station'.[84] Under these conditions affecting wider society, education also suffered. This would have had an impact on the school at Subiaco. As recovery came in the early years of the Twentieth Century, pastoralists were able to resume educating their children at boarding school with a view to perhaps sending them to Oxford or Cambridge.

Chloe

There was one indigenous girl educated at Subiaco in the 1890s. She bore the name 'Chloe'. Dr Prendergast notes that Chloe was a protégé of the Hurleys of 'Hurleyville', Cootamundra. According to the 'Alumnae Subiaco', Margaret Hurley, one of their daughters, had been a pupil

---

82   Molony, *Penguin Bicentennial History*, 168.
83   Matthews, *Federation*, 28.
84   Matthews, *Federation*, 26.

at Subiaco in the 1850s, and another paper referred to by Prendergast says that she was a novice in the Benedictine Community of Subiaco.⁸⁵ Margaret (1842–1916) gave the Subiaco community another connection with the Wicklow chief, Michael Dwyer, and his compatriots, since her mother Mary was the fifth daughter of his lieutenant, Mr. Hugh 'Vesty' Byrne.⁸⁶

Registration Number	15796
Date of Death	9 NOV 1898
Place of Death	SUBIACO CONVENT, RYDALMERE, ERMINGTON MUNICIPALITY
Name	CHLOE MARY HURLEY NORTH
Occupation	AN ABORIGINAL, DOMESTIC SERVANT
Sex	FEMALE
Age	12
Cause of Death	TUBERCULOSIS, DROPSY
Duration	UNKNOWN, 14 DAYS
Medical Attendant	W.S. BROWN, 8 NOV 1898
Father	UNKNOWN PARENTS
Father's Occupation	
Mother - Maiden Name	
Informant	PATRICK KERWICK, HOUSEHOLDER, THE CONVENT, SUBIACO, RYDALMERE; REGISTERED 12 NOV 1898, RYDE
When Buried	10 NOV 1898
Where	PRIVATE CEMETERY, SUBIACO CONVENT GROUNDS
Undertaker	E.A. SPARKS
Minister	PATRICK KERWICK, PRIEST
Religion	ROMAN CATHOLIC
Witnesses	THOMAS WILLIAMS, CHARLES MICHAEL
Where born	NORMANTON, QUEENSLAND
Time in Colony/State	10 YEARS IN N.S. WALES
Place Married	NOT MARRIED

Death Certificate of Chloe North

85 Those who entered and left before their profession of vows are not recorded in any archival documents. Now and then, a name appears in letters—a name of someone who is expected to enter. Margaret Hurley's name is not recorded in the community's history, but in a private source quoted by Ann Prendergast; see Prendergast 'Benedictine Schools', p. 78 n.10. Information about Margaret Hurley as a Novice at Subiaco is taken from [Author], 'The family of Hugh and Sarah Byrne'. Sr Marie Gregory (Forster and Prendergast, 'Alumnae Subiaco') places Margaret Hurley as a pupil of the Subiaco School.
86 https://australianroyalty.net.au/tree/purnellmccord.ged/individual/I40622/Margaret-Hurley; https://australianroyalty.net.au/tree/purnellmccord.ged/individual/I69269/Mary-Byrne; https://australianroyalty.net.au/tree/purnellmccord.ged/individual/I54648/Hugh-Byrne.

Although born in Normanton, in far north Queensland on the Gulf of Carpentaria, Chloe most probably came from amongst the Aboriginal people who worked as stockmen, cooks, and domestics at 'Hurleyville', now sent to be educated at Subiaco. A small fragment of a letter written by Prioress Wallis during this period mentions Chloe.[87] Wallis writes of her compassion for the plight of the indigenous children, stating that they are victims, and certainly not culpable for the state in which they find themselves. As a disciple of Benedict, a person who lived Benedictine values, and a 'listener' to the needs of God's people, Wallis expresses hope that the Jesuits, who established St Ignatius' College Riverview in 1880 after being brought to Sydney by Vaughan in 1878, would educate indigenous boys. Letters were written by the pupils to Prioress Walburge Wallis during her absence in 1888–89, and she praised Chloe for the improvement in her writing and spelling. Chloe died at Subiaco on 9 November 1898, aged twelve years. Since there is no date of birth for Chloe, only the place of birth, it is likely that she was older than twelve. Her death certificate bears the name 'Chloe Mary Hurley North (An Aboriginal)', and it is noted in the records that she was at Subiaco School in the 1890s.

In the decade of the 1880s, the colonial Government of New South Wales, along with other colonies 'instituted compulsory education for children of school age. All parents, of whatever racial or ethnic background, were required to enrol their children'.[88] This remarkable legislation may be what prompted Margaret Hurley to send Chloe to Subiaco for an education. The interesting piece of information on her death certificate is that she was a 'domestic servant' at Subiaco. It was not unusual for Aboriginal, or white girls aged ten to twelve, to take employment as domestic servants. Did Chloe then work as a domestic servant for a year or two? This information is not documented in the Abbey Archives. After her death from tuberculosis, she was buried with the nuns in the Subiaco cemetery within the enclosure of the monastery. Prior to her death, she had been visited by Dr W. S. Brown,

---

87 This letter has no date. It may have been written when Prioress Wallis was in hospital at some point, or away convalescing.
88 Fletcher, *Clean, Clad and Courteous*.

and cared for by the nuns.[89] This was another example of the spirit of the Benedictine monasticism which exhorts monastics to 'prefer nothing to the love of Christ', and to see Christ in everyone.[90]

It is noteworthy to compare this Christological charism with the views of seemingly misguided Christians such as Sir George Grey, with his 'jagged edge of ruthless rhetoric: the strongholds of murder and superstition are cleansed, and the Gospel is preached amongst ignorant and savage men. The ruder languages disappear successively, and the tongue of England alone is heard'.[91] Blainey illustrates that 'the journals of many explorers breathe the confidence that they are instruments of God',[92] by referring to the words of John Lote Stokes R.N., Lieutenant on *The Beagle* on its survey of the Northern Australian coastline, following its previous and more famous voyage carrying Charles Darwin (1833–36). Some weeks after naming Port Darwin after his former shipmate, Stokes left a note in a bottle on 'Indian Hill' along the Victoria River. His journal entry (October 21, 1839) expresses his delight in his role as its explorer:

> I would fain hope that ere the sand of my life-glass has run out, other feet than mine will have trod these distant banks; that colonization will, ere many years have passed, have extended itself in this quarter; that cities and hamlets will have risen on the banks of the new-found river, that commerce will have directed her track thither, and that smoke may rise from Christian hearths where now alone the prowling heathen lights his fire.

89 Note in a Community Chronicle kept by an individual nun (JAA); cf. Death Certificate.
90 As one might expect, the names of Chloe's parents are entered as 'unknown' on the death certificate. The same certificate notes that she was 10 years in New South Wales. This piece of information is unreliable. It was oral tradition which told of her living with the Hurley family on their land at Cootamundra. The interest Margaret Hurley took in this child is a mixture of oral tradition and community memory. The one fact is that she attended the Subiaco school, died there in 1898, and was buried in the Nuns' cemetery—as was a girl called Laura Edwards and a servant called Catherine Gogarty who came to Australia on "The Elizabeth", one of the most 'foul' ships to sail with its human cargo.
91 These words of George Grey are quoted by Blainey, *A Land Half Won*, 97. 'Explorer, governor, and politician [...], Grey argued that the only way of saving Native [sic] people from extinction was to wean them from their tribal customs by bringing them under British Rule, making them Christian, educating their children in boarding schools, and employing the adults among the white settlers', [*ADB*], 'Grey, Sir George (1812–1898)'.
92 Blainey, *A Land Half Won*, 97.

> There is an inevitable tendency in man to create; and there is nothing which he contemplates with so much complacency as the work of his own hands. To civilize the world, to subdue the wilderness, is the proudest achievement to which he can look forward; and to share in this great work by opening new fields of enterprise, and leading, as it were, the van of civilisation, fills the heart with inexpressible delight.[93]

To the ear of a later day, such words entangle the Christian mission with the spirit of imperialism.

In their avowedly feminist history of Australia published in 1994, Patricia Grimshaw, Marilyn Lake, Ann McGrath and Marian Quartly offer a challenging new approach, writing of social Darwinism and its effects on the White Australia Policy, and the association of 'whiteness' with racial purity. By the middle of the 1890s it was believed that the indigenous peoples had been defeated. Grimshaw et al, refer to the words of C. H. Pearson in *National Life and Character: a Forecast*, published in 1893:

> Australia is an unexampled instance of a great continent that has been left for the first civilised people that found it to take and occupy. The natives have died out as we approached; there have been no complications with foreign powers […] we know that coloured and white labour cannot exist side by side […] we are guarding the last part of the world, in which the higher races can live and increase freely, for the higher civilisation.[94]

With such views being expressed at the time, to take an Aboriginal girl into the Subiaco School in the 1890s, or for the Hurley family to be concerned about her education, was a radical step.

Also present in the Subiaco School was a child referred to as the 'Little Chinese girl'. Nothing is known of her, since she was there for such a brief period. Oral tradition says 'under a week'. The historians assert correctly that

---

93 Stokes, *Discoveries in Australia*, 2.46. For Stokes, see Bolton, 'Stokes, John Lort (1812–1885)'.
94 Grimshaw et al., *Creating A Nation*, 177–178. Citing Pearson, *National Life and Character*, 16.

from the time of the gold-rushes, white colonists had demonstrated their concern for preserving the new southern lands for their own stock, not only by their ruthless dispossession of Aborigines, but by their hostility to Asian immigrants, notably the Chinese.[95]

Was the Chinese girl who came to Subiaco to be educated, placed there for safety? The Lambing Flat Riots of 1860–61 (near present-day Young) illustrate how the temporary shelters of a gold field may have become a most dangerous place for a small girl. However, nothing is known of this child in archival documents pertaining to the Subiaco School, except for some handwritten notes saying she was only at the school for a week. After missing her too much, her father had come and taken her back home.

The Boer War and Australian federation

The Boer War and Australian federation dominated history at the end of the 1890s. While pastors of various Sydney churches accompanied Australians to South Africa, Francis Timoney, the parish priest of Mosman, was the only one of Moran's priests to volunteer. He was aged forty-two when he accompanied the New South Wales Citizens Bushmen Regiment, the Third Contingent to land in Portuguese East Africa. The *Freeman's Journal*, in an article entitled 'Looking Backwards, Our Catholic Life of Long Ago', comments on Moran's attitude to the Boer War, citing Melbourne's *The Age* of February 1900:[96]

> Moran has frequently stated his views in public as well as in private [...] he did not hesitate to challenge the accepted fact that the war had been undertaken to redress the grievances of the Outlanders in South Africa. 'I look forward', said the Cardinal, 'to the happiest results flowing from the war so far as religion is concerned. When the work of the British Army is crowned with

---

95   Grimshaw et al., *Creating A Nation*, 178.
96   *Freeman's Journal*, 10 June, 1926.

success, the whole of South Africa will be thrown open and will be as free as Canada and Australia'.

It was Fr Timoney who wrote to him of the hideous crimes being committed by British and Australian soldiers.[97] A private letter, written to Moran in 1900, described the atrocities of corpses being dismembered, and equally horrible actions in the name of War. Agnes Macready, an Irish woman who went as a nurse and a journalist with Moran's blessing, two weeks into the War wrote frequently to the *Catholic Press* of the horrors of the Boer War. In the Subiaco community only one nun, Sr Mary Clare (Florence Eugenie) Gabriel, had close relatives who went to this war. Archibald and Wilfred Rudder were both Troopers in the New South Wales Citizens' Bushmen Contingent. Lindsay Ernest Rudder was in the New South Wales Imperial Bushman's Contingent, and received the Queen's South Africa Medal for bravery.[98] All three men (from Kempsey) were her first cousins.

Apart from the news of war coming via priests, visitors, letters (only a few survive), and Agnes Macready's articles, there was not the means of communication which the nuns would later have during the First and Second World Wars, with the advent of the wireless and access to newspapers. Their attitude to those who fought in the Boer War is the same as that expressed concerning later wars: all people, on both sides of the fighting, need prayer. It is not written anywhere in archival documents that the Benedictine nuns of Subiaco believed that war was acceptable, or that one country should exert military power over another. There are no written notes which indicate that the women of Subiaco supported Moran's views on the Boer War. War of any kind was contrary to the spirit of the Benedictine Rule and its maxim to 'let peace be your quest and aim'.[99] Into this quest for peace came the prayer of reparation, as an instrument of healing.

---

97 Fr Timoney founded the *Catholic Press*, and was its Boer War correspondent. He died in London on 8 December 1901. Johnston, 'Francis Timoney'.
98 Murray, *Official Records*, 80, 105. *Australian Town and Country Journal*, 17 February 1900, 23.
99 Fry, *RB 1980*, Prologue, v.17.

The Prayer of Reparation

Written into the history of the Benedictine community of Subiaco is their desire for 'Perpetual Adoration of the Blessed Sacrament' in reparation for the harm done by the British penal system which coloured the beginnings of the Australian nation in images of human degradation, despair, and death.[100] This spirit of reverence for convicts as persons created in the image and likeness of God began with Polding and the early Benedictine monks and priests who first came to the shores of New South Wales. Their ministry to convicts is well-documented, as is the ministry of other Churches and Mission Centres of Nineteenth Century Australia.[101]

Nuns during Adoration

---

100 The prayer of reparation (repairing, or restoring), is not part of the Benedictine tradition. The two foundations of prayer in the Benedictine tradition are the Liturgy of the Hours and *Lectio Divina*.
101 Breward, *A History*, 75–133.

While in Europe in 1877, Prioress Wallis, in a private audience with Pope Pius IX, had requested that he grant the privilege of 'perpetual adoration'. The Pope, in his wisdom, showed concern because of the paucity of numbers[102] to support both 'perpetual adoration' and a school simultaneously. In a compromise, he allowed this prayer to take place between the end of Mass and the beginning of Benediction[103] in the evening, on all Fridays, Sundays, and days of First and Second Class Feasts (see Figure 6, pp. 166–167)—and on January 26 which was called at this time the annual Anniversary of the Foundation of the Colony. The nuns believed, under the leadership of Prioress Wallis, that their vocation, 'apart from the ordinary Benedictine life [daily-ness] and their commitment to the school [was] to make reparation for the sins of Australia'.[104]

There was an acute awareness of the circumstances of the birth of the colony of New South Wales, and the horrors of transportation. The prayer of 'reparation' is a prayer of 'sacrifice', not a prayer of words. It situates a person in the presence of God within the chapel, and carries with it the notion that however one feels, one gives oneself to this prayer in remembrance of those who suffered the humiliation of the British penal system. William Ullathorne, who is remembered for his intervention in the transportation of convicts to NSW with a pamphlet condemning the system,[105] continued to communicate with the nuns of Subiaco, and in particular with Mother Justina Merewether.

---

102 Fifteen choir nuns, and nine lay sisters.
103 Cross, 'Benediction of the Blessed Sacrament', 156.
104 Community Chronicles, 1878.
105 Ullathorne, *The Horrors of Transportation*.

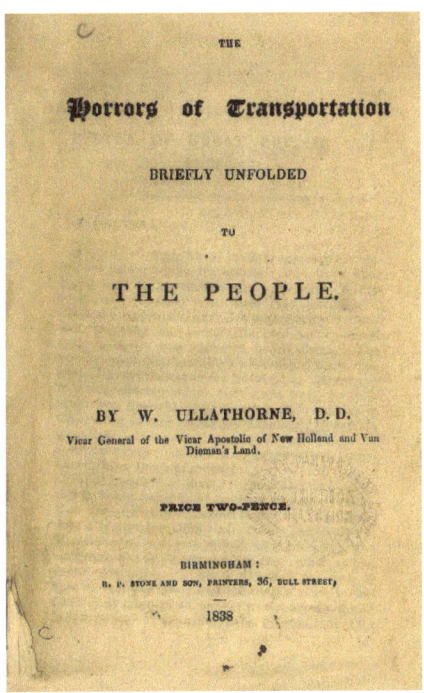

W. Ullathorne, *The Horrors of Transportation* (1838)

Polding shared his own experiences of the wretchedness of those human beings to whom he ministered, and Magdalen le Clerc, while she lived, kept the memory of that first year (1848) alive—the year when she found herself teaching the poor and the old, and witnessing the long hours Polding and others spent in the confessional at St Mary's. The Sisters of Charity kept close ties with the women of Subiaco and there are instances of their sharing experiences of the 'Female Factory' at Parramatta. Perhaps a constant reminder in the Subiaco community was Sr Dominic (Margaret) Fitzpatrick, the daughter of two Irish convicts who had gained their ticket of leave, having served their sentences with hard labour.[106]

---

106 This example has already been noted above (p. 104).

Federation

Alongside the Boer War, the second event which affected both Australia and the rest of the world in the 1890s was Federation. The years leading up to this event were years in which the average Australian working man was preoccupied in finding work, or seeking ways in which to care for and feed his family. Matthews states that,

> Depression, drought and hardship, strikes and pickets, though not uniformly biting across the vast Continent, were a mighty distraction from the fluctuating intensity of discussions about federation.[107]

Cahill notes that Henry Parkes, in his old age, acknowledged the importance of Cardinal Moran as 'one very prominent Federationist', who was 'not a career politician'.[108] The issue for Moran was about protecting the civil rights of Catholics and therefore he put himself forward as a candidate for election. Because of this, it is recorded that fifty-five percent of the population of New South Wales voted—they bothered to vote—compared with for example thirty percent in Tasmania. The *Freeman's Journal* noted that Moran 'made Federation a burning political question'.[109] Botsman emphasises the reality that 'eighty-four percent of the people could not or did not vote in the federal referendums of the late 1890s'.[110] Included in the non-voters were women and indigenous people. Like other women in New South Wales, the women of Subiaco were not permitted a voice in the referendums. The first state in Australia to grant women the right to vote was South Australia (18 December 1894), but in New South Wales, women were not granted the right to vote and to stand for Parliament until 1902.

---

107 Matthews, *Federation*, 30.
108 Cahill, 'Cardinal Moran', 3.
109 *Freeman's Journal*, 11 June 1898.
110 Botsman, *The Great Constitutional Swindle*, 3, XII, and 52—Table 1: The Federation Referendum Results, quoted in Cahill's Article on 'Cardinal Moran'.

Pictorial Souvenir of the Federation of Australia, 1 January 1901

On the evening of the inauguration of the Commonwealth of Australia, Moran was dealt a blow from the Governor General who informed him that preference was being given to the Anglican Archbishop of Sydney in all official public ceremonies for 1 January 1901. In the light of this, Moran said he could not accept this 'without compromising the civil rights of Australian Catholics [...] so Federation began with an official Catholic boycott of the events of New Year's Day, 1901'.[111] The absence of Moran from the processions and celebrations of the inauguration of Australia as a nation was surely the culmination of sectarian bitterness which had not only characterised much of his leadership, but would continue to plague society well into the Twentieth Century, up to the Second Vatican Council of the 1960s. And yet the Benedictine School of Subiaco had always taken Protestant girls and educated them. Looking back on her school days at Subiaco, Rhoda Williams (at Subiaco from the age of five) comments:

---

111 Cahill, 'Cardinal Moran', 10.

There was never any bigotry at the school. There was quite a spirit of ecumenism (as is said nowadays). Quite a goodly proportion of pupils were non-Catholics. The non-Catholic girls attended Catechism and Christian Doctrine classes. While remaining non-Catholics all their lives, they returned at intervals to visit the nuns and their old school.[112]

Two significant documents issued by Pope Leo XIII

The year 1900 was a significant one for the Benedictine women of Subiaco and for Religious Congregations (Orders) across the world. Two significant documents were issued by Pope Leo XIII. The first of these was *Conditae a Christo*, of 8 December 1900. This document of Canonical Legislation

> gave clear recognition to simple-vow institutes as genuinely religious and […] outlined with clarity their operating relationship with local bishops. In particular, it made clear that the internal authority to govern the institute belonged to its own officials and not to the bishops.[113]

The second document of canonical legislation was entitled: *Normae secundum quas. S. Congregatio Episcoporum et Regularium procedure solet in approbandis novis Institutis votorum simplicium.*[114] These norms situated the Government of the General Chapter of the Institute as the central body, to be convened regularly, with the 'responsibility for electing superiors-general and their councillors'.[115]

Already present in New South Wales in 1900 were the Sisters of

---

112 Notes made by Rhoda (Sr Mary Fidelis) Williams, in her older age (JAA). She was sent to Subiaco School from the age of five, following the death of her mother. She was the niece of the Gabriel girls who attended the School in the 1870s. After her school years, Rhoda entered the Subiaco community. Her aunt, Sr Mary Clare Gabriel, died in 1910.
113 MacGinley, *A Dynamic of Hope,* 275.
114 Sacred Congregation for Religious, 'Norms according to which the Sacred Congregation of Bishops and Regulars is accustomed to proceed, in the approbation of new Institutes of Simple Vows'.
115 Sacred Congregation for Religious, 'Norms according to which the Sacred Congregation of Bishops and Regulars is accustomed to proceed'.

Charity, the Sisters of Mercy, the Good Samaritan Sisters (founded by Polding in 1857), the Sisters of St Joseph, The Ursuline Sisters, and the Teaching Poor Clares.[116] There were also other groups of Religious Sisters who were nurses and missionaries. Some of the notes in the chronicles of Subiaco reveal an awareness of the rise of the teaching orders of women, and portend that the school at Subiaco will not remain as a functioning educational institution. In the spirit of *obsculta*, the excerpt from the chronicles reveals a community tuned into changing times. This written record of the community's history shows that the nuns of Subiaco were accepting not just of the teaching orders, but saw their coming as being the work of the Holy Spirit in the Church of Australia.

The end of an era–death of Prioress Wallis

Prioress Walburge Wallis died on 11 October 1902. The *Freeman's Journal* spoke of her many years of 'indifferent health', with 'her infirmities only [increasing] with the lapse of years'. Despite her cheerful readiness to assist wherever she was able, she had endured the last seven years in great pain, sufficient to give her life 'the dignity of a martyrdom', before suffering 'a severe paralytic stroke' in January 1901, 'from the effects of which she did not fully recover'.[117]

The community had requested Philip Anderson to write her obituary for publication in *The Tablet*. An Anglican clergyman, after Anderson became impoverished following his conversion to Catholicism, Wallis took his daughter Elizabeth, aged three, as a boarder at Subiaco without the usual school fees. Elizabeth was at Subiaco until she was seventeen years of age. Anderson and Wallis had become good friends.

---

116 The history of the Poor Clare Sisters of Waverley, Sydney, and the history of the Dominican Sisters who came to Maitland in 1867, have both been written by M. R. MacGinley. MacGinley, *A Lamp Lit*; MacGinley, *Ancient Tradition*.
117 'Death of the Mother Prioress, Subiaco', *Freeman's Journal*, 18 October 1902.

Death of a Benedictine Prioress

A special correspondent writes to us from Sydney, New South Wales: The Community of Benedictine Nuns established for upwards of fifty years at Subiaco on the Parramatta River, New South Wales, sustained a severe loss in the death of the Prioress on the 11th October, in her 71st year. Mother Mary Walburge was daughter of the late captain Stanhope Wallis, R.N. She arrived in Australia from England in 1853, with a view to becoming a Benedictine Nun at Subiaco. Accordingly, she entered the monastery in March of that year and was clothed in the religious habit the following August. In June, 1856, she was professed, both ceremonies being conducted by the Most Rev. Dr. Polding, OSB, first Archbishop of Sydney. Her remarkable personality appears to have made itself felt from the first, for in January, 1864, she was elected Prioress of Subiaco, and her tenure of this important office ended only with her life. She filled it for nearly thirty-nine years. Owing to the fame Subiaco maintained—as it does still—as a high school for ladies, the late Mother Prioress was widely known even outside of her Order; and wherever she was known she was beloved and revered. With rare skill and administrative ability, deep and sincere piety, and almost monumental learning, she administered the affairs of Subiaco for more than a generation. As to which of the many scintillating virtues that adorned a singularly brilliant character shone out most brightly in the Mother Prioress, opinions might differ; though probably next after her genuine devotion to religion—and its outcome, surely—were her great charity and benevolence, and her ceaseless consideration for others. Avoiding mere fulsome platitudes, it is strictly true to say that the Mother Prioress of Subiaco was an exceptionally gifted woman, even for a Prioress of an Order which is so famed for learning, and which has given so many shining lights to the Church, as the Benedictines. Often of late she suffered acutely. Surgical skill appeared at first successful in operating; but in the commencement of this year paralysis set in. Beloved by a vast circle of friends far more in number than usually falls to one of three score and ten even, and more than beloved by her Community, the good Prioress was called away, fortified by the Church's rites, and surrounded by the nuns of Subiaco. The obsequies were celebrated on Oct. 13th. The last remaining Benedictine priest in the archdiocese, the Venerable Dr. Augustine Sheehy, Archpriest, sang the Requiem Mass, the final Absolutions being given and the last prayers said by his Grace the Coadjutor Archbishop of Sydney, Most Rev. Dr. Kelly. The remains of the Prioress rest in a vault or crypt beneath the cemetery chapel at Subiaco, where many members of the Benedictine Community who predeceased their "mother" lie around her. So indissolubly is the name of Mother Mary Walburge associated with Subiaco that the place itself is her monument, and as such it will ever be deemed, especially by those to whom in times of trouble it proved a very haven of refuge, and its Prioress a tower of strength and consolation. R.I.P.

Obituary: Prioress Walburge (Ruth Woods) Wallis

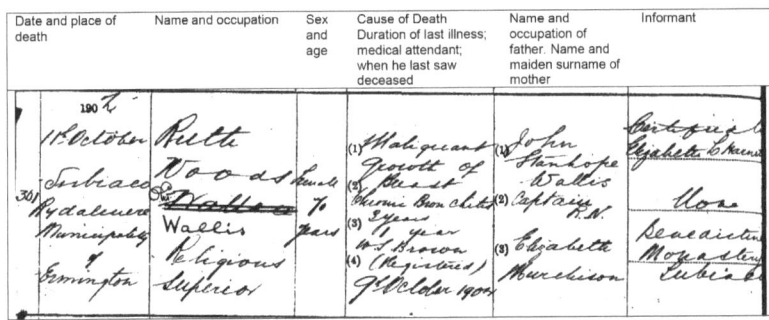

Death Certificate. Ruth Woods Wallis

In the letter written to Moran dated 2 November 1901, the senior nuns of the community quoted the Prioress as saying: 'I have been accused of drunkenness, adultery, and murder: what more could be said of me?'[118] Her death certificate states the cause of death as 'Malignant growth of breast', with three years of 'chronic bronchitis' perhaps indicative of further complications. (p. 201) She had advanced breast cancer and had already faced surgery in 1899, which was deemed successful.[119] Then a second surgical procedure was necessary in 1901. This was carried out by her doctors, 'Dr McCormick, assisted by Dr Brown and Dr Craige', at the Subiaco monastery.[120] One letter, written on 16 July 1901 to Moran, refers to the fact that he may misunderstand the reason for Sr Justina Merewether and the Community Councillors writing to him, rather than the Prioress herself. They explain that she cannot use her hand because of the damage to her arm from both the cancer and the effects of surgery.[121] Ironically, Archpriest Austin Sheehy was the main celebrant at her funeral. Before she died, Moran's Coadjutor, Archbishop Michael Kelly, was also present and performed the Last Rites.

Chapter Eight will focus on the term of office of Elizabeth Louisa Harnett, successor to Ruth Woods Wallis. Her years as prioress will be presented within the context of the *obsculta* within the following components:

1. Some historical details of her family in relation to the colonial history of New South Wales, and therefore to the Benedictine nuns of Subiaco.
2. The implementation of the Beuronese Constitutions.

The community of that time understood that the implementation of the Beuronese Constitutions was their major goal and one which Prioress Wallis couldn't fulfil in her lifetime.

---

118 Subiaco Community Councillors to Cardinal Moran, 2 November 1901.
119 This surgery was performed at Subiaco and supervised by Mother Joseph O'Regan, LCM, and Nurse Agnes Hill.
120 Sr Justina Merewether to Cardinal Moran, 4 November 1901.
121 Subiaco Community Councillors to Cardinal Moran, 16 July 1901.

CHAPTER EIGHT

Prioress Ignatius (Louisa) Harnett 1902–1915

*E*lizabeth Louisa Harnett was thoroughly formed in the Benedictine Rule and its many charisms and traditions, having embraced the *obsculta* of the Benedictine Rule since her entry into the Subiaco Monastery in 1867. She was born in New South Wales in 1840 to the Surgeon Patrick Harnett and his wife, Margaret Louisa Murray. Patrick and Louisa, both from Ireland, met on the ship H.M.S. *Sophia*, which arrived in Sydney on 16 July 1832. They were married at St Mary's in Sydney. From 1832 until 1839 the couple spent time on Norfolk Island, where Patrick was the doctor. One of their children was born on Norfolk Island. Patrick Harnett was the assistant surgeon to Kinnear Robertson in 1839 and then Colonial Surgeon until September 1844, when he (Patrick) died suddenly 'by the visitation of God' at the age of 34.[1] Louisa Murray was a first cousin of Sir Terence Aubrey Murray who was already politically active in the colony when she arrived. In fact, it is probable that his presence in the colony may have been one of the reasons for her emigrating to Australia.[2]

---

1   Watson, *History of the Sydney Hospital*; *Morning Chronicle*, 18 September 1844.
2   Sir Terence Aubrey Murray was the elected Speaker of the Legislative Assembly in 1860, and in 1862 he was appointed to a seat in the Upper House, and elected President of the Council; Bartley, *Australian Pioneers*, 95–97.

Louisa Harnett (nee Murray) c. 1870s
Mother of Prioress Ignatius Harnett OSB
Unfortunately, a picture of Prioress Harnett does not exist

Elizabeth Louisa Harnett, who would become the second elected prioress at Subiaco, was born on 8 June 1842 in Sydney. She was two years old when her father died. Her brother John, born on Norfolk Island, was later educated by the Benedictine monks at Lyndhurst College. He received a scholarship for his first year at the University of Sydney, the first colonial university in the British Empire. In the examinations of 1854 he obtained first class honours in Chemistry and Experimental Physics.[3] Elizabeth was educated by the nuns at Subiaco, and thus became a student of Benedictine principles, values, tradition, and customs—all within the broader institution of the Catholic Church. She entered the Subiaco community on 3 March 1867 and

---

3   Most research on the Harnett family was carried out by Marie Forster, OSB, working closely with Sr Peter Damian McKinlay, SGS. In a letter dated 19 September 1996, Tim Robinson, acting University Archivist, supplied the details of John Harnett's academic achievement from the register entry for Michaelmas Term 1853 (University of Sydney).

made her profession of Benedictine vows at the end of 1869. During her early years as a Benedictine nun she worked in the Subiaco School, and was later appointed novice mistress. Her election as prioress took place on 8 December 1902, approximately two months after the death of Prioress Wallis.[4]

The focus of Prioress Harnett's leadership

Prioress Harnett saw her task as that of continuing and consolidating the work of Prioress Wallis. She took up office when the community was at its lowest ebb financially, but at the same time she inherited a united and stable community.[5] Her term of office reflected a more literal interpretation of the *obsculta* of the Benedictine Rule. Declaration 1 of the Beuronese Constitutions sums up the focus of her years and the years of those in the community at this time:

> The sisters must do their utmost to acquire the Regular or Monastic Spirit, which the Prologue and many chapters of the Holy Rule set before us as in a mirror. As the Spirit is the essence of the monastic life, we declare that all the Holy Patriarch has commanded is to be literally observed as regards the spirit, so that even though we may differ from other Communities in our exterior mode of life, we must not deviate from the Spirit of St. Benedict's Rule.[6]

Following years of personal and communal upheaval, Prioress Harnett's years in office saw a period of stability. This enabled the prioress to focus on two projects: the implementing of the Beuronese Constitutions with the modifications suggested by Moran, and the building of a monastic church at Subiaco. Both had been the desires of Prioress Wallis in her lifetime. In the spirit of *obsculta*, Prioress Harnett recognised that Moran's thirteen modifications (see above pp. 164–172) were right for Australia.

---

4   Canonical Records of Elections. (JAA)
5   Community Chronicles—quoted in Malone,'Obit List', (28), 35–80; and (29), 47–71.
6   Beuronese Constitutions, Declaration 3, on the Prologue to the Rule of Benedict.

The Beuronese Constitutions were implemented on the Benedictine Feast of Sts Maurus and Placid, 15 January 1903.[7] The community found the impact of the Constitutions to be minimal. First, the choir nuns were called 'Dames', the English title for nuns.[8] The purpose of this title was to differentiate between choir nuns and lay sisters. 'Dom' was the masculine equivalent for monks. Secondly, the Hour of Vespers was recited later in the afternoon than it had been. One could well ask why, after fifteen years of waiting, the impact of the Constitutions would be as minimal as it turned out to be. The answer is found in the fact that the community had already been growing into the Beuronese Constitutions after the thirteen modifications Moran had requested in the early 1890s. Despite his lack of communication with them over the matter, and despite his lack of visitation for eleven years, the community had implemented his suggestions. Two of the modifications concerned lay sisters, whose vocation was to do the servile work of the community.

On 23 April 1903 Cardinal Moran and his private secretary, Dr O'Haran, presided at the profession of one choir nun, Lucy Smythe, and two lay sisters, Honora Hennessy and Frances Pechy.[9] This may indicate that the relationship between the Cardinal and the Subiaco community was a more positive one than it had been in the 1890s. These nuns were the first to be clothed in the monastic habit after the 'ban' was lifted.

---

7   St Maurus appears in the Roman Missal, but not the boy Placid. Both are acknowledged in the Benedictine supplement of the time. For the stories which capture the relationship of both boys with Benedict, see Pope Gregory the Great, *Life and Miracles, Book Two*, Chapters 6 and 7, 19–22.
8   Some of the nuns in the English Benedictine Congregation still retain this title: 'Dame', or 'Lady'.
9   Lucy Smythe was professed at the end of her novitiate, and thus did not make the Temporary Profession, whereby a simple profession is made prior to a period of preparation for solemn profession (see Vermeersch, 'Religious Profession'). Originating with the order of Ignatius of Loyola, Temporary Profession has now become universal practice. Although it was made a requirement by the 1902 Decree of Pope Leo XIII (see pp. 231–232 below), the fact that Moran presided without questioning the 'time' element may point to the fact that he hadn't yet read this document.

Post-Federation vocations

The first two choir nuns who entered after Federation were Australian women.

The first to enter was Hilda May Brady. She was born at Wangaratta, Victoria, to Dr Francis Brady (born in Dublin) the Medical Superintendent at the Wangaratta Hospital, and Mary Moreton (born in Wanyarra, Victoria), a Registered Nurse. When Hilda's father died in 1886, the family moved to Port Pirie, South Australia. This was a significant move for Hilda Brady, who was then educated by the Good Samaritan Sisters, the first congregation of religious women in Australia, founded by Polding and Mother Scholastica, of the Sisters of Charity, in 1857 under the Benedictine Rule. In 1890, the first foundation outside of Sydney had been established at Port Pirie.[10]

Hilda was trained in vocal skills by the Rev. John Henry Norton. Press suggested that Norton was 'able to realize [his] dream of training children's choirs, first in Adelaide, and then in Petersburg'.[11] It is also noted that as musical daughters of families went to join convents, he wrote heartfelt recommendations to their superiors: Mary Fitzpatrick, to the Good Samaritan Sisters in 1893, and Hilda Brady.[12] Of the latter, he wrote to Prioress Harnett that Hilda was 'accomplished, obedient and humble, clever at singing and music [… and] he had trained her to sing a *prima donella* at their concerts'.[13] She was one of the most accomplished musicians in the history of the Subiaco community and accomplished in the day-to-day execution of the music of the liturgy.

Hilda left her home and the Parish of St Anacletus, Petersburg, South Australia,[14] and entered the Benedictine community of Subiaco on 23 April 1904.[15] She became Sr Mary Joseph Brady. She was formed in the Benedictine tradition by Justina Merewether, who was her novice

---

10   Walsh, *The Good Sams*, 142, 154–55.
11   Press, *John Henry Norton*, 90.
12   Press, *John Henry Norton*, 91.
13   Press, *John Henry Norton*, 90–91.
14   Changed to Peterborough during World War I, when German place names in Australia were Anglicised or changed.
15   Bishop Norton made one visit to Subiaco, to see his past pupil: 25 October 1921. (Subiaco Chronicles)

mistress, and Mother Justina, in turn, had been formed by Magdalen le Clerc. These connections assured continuity of charism, tradition, and monastic discipline. Mary Joseph Brady taught in the school at Subiaco, served as organist, and was found to have natural gifts of spiritual counselling. Thus, in an unofficial capacity, she helped pupils who were burdened by the ordinary trials affecting children and teenagers.

Within a year of her entry, a second Australian woman, Mary Agnes Doyle from Sydney, entered the community on 11 January 1905. Her roots were Benedictine. Her father, John Benedict Doyle had attended St Mary's Cathedral when the Benedictine monks were there. He had been an altar boy and served the Masses of Polding both at St Mary's and in the Sydney suburbs. He witnessed the destruction of the Cathedral by fire in 1865.[16]

St Mary's Cathedral today
The architecture is typical of the Gothic Revival of the 19th century.

---

16   Information about Mary Agnes Doyle derives from 'The Doyle Family History', researched over 25 years by her nephew Peter Doyle, Ireland, now deceased (unpublished). Some oral history was also recorded by the Chronicler after Mary Agnes Doyle entered the community of Subiaco. John Benedict Doyle's obituary was found in the archive box with all letters, papers, and certificates pertaining to Sr Mary Hildegarde Doyle.

John Doyle was, for many years, the assistant conductor of music at St Mary's Cathedral, and on the death of Albert Delany, he became the choirmaster. He was forty years in church music and facilitated the execution of ceremonies for the Eucharistic Congress of 1928. All of this 'grass roots' Catholicism was passed on to his daughter. Mary Agnes Doyle was born in 1885. Her mother was Norah Mary Gunning, born in Victoria. Mary Agnes became the first Australian woman born of Australian parents to respond to the call to monastic life in the Subiaco community, and for this reason hers was a significant vocation following Federation.

Both women, Hilda and Mary Agnes, were 'cradle' Catholics and in Mary Agnes' case, the Benedictine tradition was part of her family story. At the time of her entry to the Benedictine community of Subiaco, Mary Agnes was working as a pupil-teacher, and her father was headmaster of a Sydney public school. As a nun of the Subiaco community, she worked in the School, teaching the younger children, and in the role of sports' mistress. Sport in schools became more popular and competitive after Federation.

Both women also became immersed in the early missionary spirit of the community, which began by providing education for the young ladies of the colony. Both Mary Agnes Doyle and Hilda May Brady made profession of Benedictine vows on 23 January 1907. Prior to their profession of Benedictine vows, the nuns of Subiaco were given the opportunity to incorporate more fully into their monastic living, one of the foundations of the neo-monastic revival—the 'Plain Chant which converts'.[17] A student from Rome had visited Sydney, who had studied plain chant under Monsignor Antonio Rella, conductor of the Sistine Choir. Her name appears in the community chronicles as Miss Wallington. She was an English woman, who had joined a convent of nuns in Rome. The convent had been disbanded for reasons not given in the Subiaco chronicles. Miss Wallington saw in Subiaco the monastic home she had lost. In 1903–04, she entered the community and stayed for two years. While there, she trained the nuns, and

---

17 Prioress Wallis, to the Subiaco community, 20 June 1876. From Stanbrook Abbey she writes about the visit she received from the Abbot of Beuron.

particularly the musicians of the house, in the art of plain chant. She departed for England when her father died and her mother was in need of her care. Before her departure, Prioress Harnett asked her who would be best qualified to take over the monastic choir, and keep up the tradition which was established. Miss Wallington named Sr Mary Joseph (Hilda) Brady. When Monsignor Antonio Rella visited Subiaco in 1922, he complimented the prioress, by this time, Mother Mary Joseph Brady, on the monastic choir. He was not aware that one of his own students had made a significant contribution from 1904–1906.[18]

Other women who entered during Mother Ignatius Harnett's term of office were: Clotilde de Castella, from a Swiss immigrant family;[19] Honora Sugrue, born in Cork, Ireland; Elsie Bradshaw, whose father was born in Ireland and mother in Pymble, NSW; Agnes Ruby Muschialli, who entered in 1908; Mary Magdalene Bryant in 1910, whose father was a past pupil of Lyndhurst Academy, and herself a past pupil of the Subiaco School; Mary Walsh, who entered in 1909, born in Ireland; and Margaret Kelly, who entered during this period as a lay sister, also born in Ireland.[20]

The building of a monastic church at Subiaco

The second major focus for Prioress Harnett during her term of office was the building of the first monastic church. (See p. 212). This project was carried out between 1908 and 1910. With the financial assistance of the community friends of that time, and of past pupils of the school, enough money had been raised for the laying of the

---

18 Miss Wallington's story was reported in the Jamberoo community's post-Pentecost 2022 newsletter *Pax*. Monsignor Rella was in Australia in April 1922, with his choir, giving concerts in Sydney, Melbourne, Adelaide, and Hobart, and generally encouraging church choirs. The Subiaco chronicles have recorded this visit and the fact that he was visiting other Catholic church choirs and giving performances of sacred music. Byrne, 'Sacred or Profane', recorded the visit of Monsignor Rella and the Sistine Choir.
19 Prendergast, 'The Benedictine Schools', 72, notes that Clotilde may have been educated at Subiaco.
20 Margaret Kelly became Sr Mary Bridget, and was the great aunt of Fr Michael Kelly, OSB, who is a monk of St Benedict's Monastery, Arcadia, also elected, since 2010, Abbot President of the Sylvestrine Benedictine Congregation.

foundation stone of the church, on 25 October 1908. Bishop Olier, SM, who had been consecrated Bishop of Tonga by Moran in 1904,[21] took the Cardinal's place on this occasion, who was suffering from a cold.[22] Although not present on that occasion, Moran visited Subiaco again in November, for the Golden Jubilee of a choir nun and lay sister, when he also presided at a profession. The new monastic church was opened on 1 February 1910. The community chronicles show that Archbishop Kelly, Moran's successor, was the one involved in this ceremony, and those that followed over the next few months. The altar was not consecrated until 17 June of the same year. When the foundations stone of the chapel was laid, the *Catholic Press* noted that

> for 60 years the Benedictine Nuns [...] have imparted higher education to Australian girls in their monastery at Subiaco on the banks of the Parramatta River. [...] For some time after its establishment Subiaco was the only high school for Catholic ladies in Australia, and in those days no girl was considered fully educated unless she had been under the tutelage of the Benedictine Nuns. Pupils came to Subiaco from every part of the continent, as well as from Tasmania and New Zealand. Hence Mother Walburge's former charges are scattered over the Commonwealth and beyond.[23]

Despite this glorious history, by 1910, the educational landscape was very different. Catholics made up only 19.4 percent of the population of New South Wales.[24] The Subiaco School had eighteen pupils, four of whom were unpaying. MacGinley notes that the 'years around 1910 constituted a watershed in the development of education in Australia', and that by 1910, 'there were over 200 convent schools in Australia providing post-elementary education'.[25]

---

21 See his obituary, *New Zealand Tablet*, 12 October 1911. https://paperspast.natlib.govt.nz/periodicals/NZT19111012.2.52.
22 *Catholic Press*, 29 October 1908.
23 *Catholic Press*, 29 October 1908.
24 O'Farrell, *The Catholic Church*, 371.
25 MacGinley, *A Dynamic of Hope,* 277–278, referring to Orth, *The Approbation of Religious Institutes*, 71–72 and 85–91.

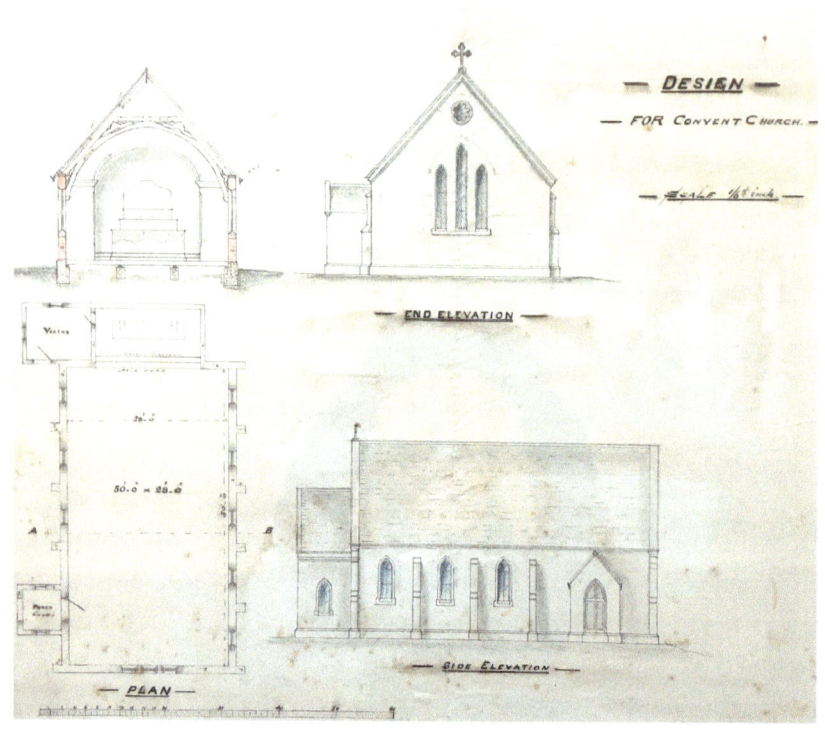

The Plans for the Monastic Church

The Monastic Church, opened 1910

As mentioned above (p. 199), the Benedictine nuns were fully aware of the situation and the chronicles provide several indications that the end of 'education' as part of their Benedictine tradition was in sight. Their *obsculta* from the 1850s onwards, which led them to meet a need for Catholic education in the colony, would soon give way to the challenge of another call: monastic life without a school and therefore without a substantial income.

Archbishop Michael Kelly c. early 1900s

In 1911, Cardinal Moran died, and Archbishop Michael Kelly succeeded him. After the declaration of World War I on 4 August 1914, Archbishop Kelly wrote a Pastoral Letter dated 13 August. In this letter he asked religious communities of his Archdiocese that, after the midday meal and the evening meal, the Antiphon *Sub Tuum Praesidium* with Versicle and Prayer to the Mother of God might be said:[26]

> We place ourselves in your keeping, holy Mother of God. Do not refuse the prayer of your children in distress. But deliver us from all danger, ever Virgin, glorious and blessed.

26 Freeman, 'Two Hundred Years of Devotion', 43–46.

With origins in the very early Christian communities of Egypt and dating from the year AD 250, this is probably the oldest known prayer that calls upon the Mother of God, and is used in both the Roman Catholic and Eastern Orthodox religions. In union with the other religious communities of Sydney, the nuns of Subiaco prayed this prayer.

The death of Prioress Ignatius Harnett

Prioress Harnett died on 23 April 1915, one year into the First World War. The numbers in the Subiaco School during the war years were about seventeen or eighteen, with from two to four unpaying. The building of the church, the situation in the school, and the cost of living during the war years (as noted explicitly in the community ledger) led to serious financial difficulties. When the Prioress died in 1915, the total amount in the bank account was £50. Aware of this and of the cost of living from 1914 onwards, the Missionaries of the Sacred Heart priests from Kensington gave one or more annual retreats to the nuns free of the usual payment. Of nineteen pupils attending the Subiaco School in 1919, only two were paying the full fee of forty-five guineas. In 1920, there were fifteen pupils and in 1921, only seven. Again, some could not afford the full fee. The Rule of St Benedict, Chapter 58, although dealing with artisans and craftsmen of the monastery, presents the issue of avarice:

> The evil of avarice must have no part in establishing prices, which should, therefore, always be a little lower than people outside the monastery are able to set, so that in all things, God may be glorified. (1 Peter 4:11)[27]

Generosity, being one of many significant Benedictine values, is first manifest in the number of 'unpaying' pupils taken by the nuns to be educated.[28] It is also recorded in the community chronicles that often

---

27 Fry, *RB 1980*, Chapter 57:7–9.
28 The same is attested to by numerous girls who attended convent schools throughout the 20th Century and who couldn't afford the full fee. The nuns came to a suitable 'arrangement' with their parents, or—as is the case of the post-World War I years, after a generation of men had been annihilated or maimed for life—an arrangement with the mother of the household.

the price of a vestment, rochet, or dalmatic would be lowered because the recipient cleric was struggling to meet the full cost. Following the death of Prioress Harnett, one of the two Australian women who had entered after Federation was elected: Hilda May Brady (Sr Mary Joseph).

1915 Buick C Series hearse.
Northern New South Wales, c. 1930.

At Prioress Harnett's funeral in 1915, the nuns witnessed for the first time the use of a motorised hearse.[29] Despite the war, this was a time of great change. The First World War facilitated a more common use of the motor car, not just for emergency vehicles but for the wealthy. In the case of Subiaco, the motor car saved more than one life of a nun who was seriously ill. The same was true of the telephone. Though it was war time, and finances were tight, the generosity of the mother of the prioress enabled such innovations as the installation of electric light throughout the house and the introduction of the telephone, which made communication so much easier between the monastery of Subiaco and St Mary's Cathedral. However, at this time there was no wireless. War news was slow to filter through to the monastery. The nuns relied on family visitors and priests to bring them up to date with the terrible reality of the First World War.

---

29 The first motorised hearse in Sydney was operated by W. N. Bull in 1914, a company with close links to the Catholic Church.

Chapter Nine will examine the years 1915–1945, from the election of Prioress Mary Joseph Brady until her resignation in 1945. It will cover the short period when industrialisation affected the community negatively, forcing them to relocate, when Prioress Brady led the community of Subiaco. The most significant Catholic Church event, the 1917 Code of Canon Law, will also be closely examined. Added to this will be the impact of international events which changed the world—from 1929 with the crash of Wall Street, through the years of the Great Depression, and then World War II. In the light of these wider factors, the response of the nuns of Subiaco in listening to the work of the Holy Spirit, and discerning the way forward to a future that was relevant for Australia, will also be assessed in some detail.

CHAPTER NINE

Prioress Mary Joseph (Hilda) Brady 1915-1945

The 1917 Code of Canon Law

The first major Catholic Church event to present a challenge to Prioress Brady and the community at Subiaco was the promulgation of the 1917 Code of Canon Law. The Benedictine *obsculta* was challenged beyond the norms of the Benedictine Rule. The new Code called for obedience to the Catholic Church in ways that hadn't been experienced up to this point. The reason for this is that this Code brought together in one document the 'separate collections [of Church Law] which had been reproduced without any, or at least without a sufficient attempt to reduce them to uniformity and do away with those enactments which, in the course of centuries, had become obsolete or had been superseded by later legislation'.[1] The new Code embodied the essential understandings of the 1901 legislation. This chapter will begin with a discussion of the national and international events of the time, in order to then examine the way the *obsculta* of the Benedictine Rule, and the listening to the promptings of the Holy Spirit, inspired a community prepared for commitment to suffering humanity.

---

1   Papi, *Religious Profession*, VII.

Prioress Mary Joseph (Hilda May Brady), c. 1915

National and international events

When the Catholic Church launched this new Code of Canon Law in 1917, Australia was in the throes of the conscription debate, and the First World War was raging. Already 38.7 percent of the male population of Australia had enlisted to fight in the Great War, as it came to be called. This percentage amounted to 420,000 men.[2] At this time in Australian history, it was not common for women to go out to work. Thus women on the home front cared for their children, or, if single, worked on the farms and in factories to support the war effort. In addition, 2286 women went to war as nurses or assistant nurses, ambulance drivers, and medical supervisors.[3] They worked in Burma, India, Egypt, Greece, Italy, France, and England. Things were changing for women. The First World War contributed to the idea of the professional working woman, who had been slowly emerging since the beginning of the Twentieth Century.

2   Engwerda, *Conscription*; Lewis, *Our War*.
3   Oppenheimer, 'Australian women and war'.

Catholic Church and the conscription debate

Archbishop Kelly of Sydney supported conscription, but the public 'position of the Catholic Hierarchy was one of neutrality'.[4] The position of the Catholic hierarchy was influenced by the former sectarian bitterness of the 1890s. It had subsided a little after Federation, but was 'inflamed […] again', with the result that 'for years after the war the catholic church would not participate in public commemorations of Anzac Day'.[5] The Easter Uprising in Ireland in 1916, which was suppressed by the British, affected the working-class Catholics of Australia, who saw 'pro-conscription' as supporting the British Empire, and this, in the end, is what swayed the Catholic hierarchy towards neutrality in 1917.[6] In the light of this background, the first significant mention of Anzac Day in the Subiaco Chronicles is in 1933. It is described as a day which is observed by the people of Australia as a holiday 'when services are held in all the churches, including St Mary's Basilica, for the Soldiers who fell in the Great War (1914–1918) […] and] special wreaths are placed on the Soldiers' memorial'.[7]

Extant letters and the records of the Chronicles show that the community of Subiaco was attuned to national events, such as the re-surfacing of sectarian bitterness, the conscription debate, the slaughter of Australians at Gallipoli, and trench warfare on the Western Front. The first response of the nuns to all of this was prayer. Added to prayer as the first response went the practical response to the poor. Of the pupils who attended the Subiaco School, through the First World War, some did not pay.[8] By 1919, out of nineteen pupils attending the school, only three could afford to pay their fees. The nuns educated them in a spirit of Benedictine Christology:

> Great care is to be shown in receiving poor people and pilgrims, because in them more particularly Christ is received; our very awe of the rich guarantees them special respect.[9]

4   Beaumont, *Australia's War*, 55.
5   Beaumont, *Australia's War*, 56.
6   The greater percentage of the Catholic hierarchy was of Irish descent.
7   Subiaco Chronicles, April, 1933.
8   The numerical details are in the Subiaco Ledger, begun in 1856 by Sr Scholastica McCarthy, one of the Princethorpe nuns.
9   Rule of Benedict, Chapter 53:15

Some families could not afford to pay because the father, who was the bread-winner of the family, did not return home from the battlefields, or had returned home injured to subsequently die. The Benedictines of Subiaco were certainly not the only religious order to educate children free of charge. While a few congregations are known to have done this, it is probable that all religious heard the call of Christ to look after the poorer families in their midst. This was the case for the Presentation Sisters, founded by Nano Nagle in 1775 and coming to 'the ends of the earth' in Australia in 1866, for whom an option for the poor was always to the forefront.[10]

Ad Normam Canonis[11]

The 1917 Code of Canon Law was followed in 1918 by the papal document *Ad Normam Canonis*, requiring the revision of older constitutions in the light of the Code. It is difficult to comprehend that during a war which was one of the deadliest conflicts in the history of the world, with 70 million deaths, Canon Law would be the priority of the Congregation for Religious. It appears to be in contrast to the focus of Pope Benedict XV:

> [O]n turning a fearful glance on the blood-stained battlefields, [we] felt the anguish of a father who sees his homestead devastated and in ruins before the fury of the hurricane. And thinking with unspeakable regret of our young sons, who were being mown down by death in thousands, we opened our heart, enlarged by the charity of Christ, to all the crushing sorrow of the mothers, and of the wives made widows before their time, and to all the inconsolable laments of the little ones, too early bereft of a father's care.[12]

Because of these changes in Canon Law, the Beuronese Constitutions, practised at Subiaco since 1908, also had to be revised. This work was

---

10 https://www.smc.tas.edu.au/about/history/the-presentation-sisters/.
11 Canonical norms, or norms of Canon Law resulting from the 1917 Code.
12 Fremantle, *The Papal Encyclicals*, 216.

carried out by Romanus Rios, OSB, of New Norcia Abbey, Western Australia. He began his work on 26 January 1919, translating the English into Latin.[13] In the meantime, Cardinal Moran's adaptations had been applied to the document, under the leadership of Prioress Harnett, who listened and responded to Moran's advice.[14] The end product of the work done by Romanus Rios was: 'Constitutions of the Holy Rule of our Glorious Father St Benedict, with approbation, slight additions and changes made by the Holy See—October 1922'. The Constitutions had been submitted to the Sacred Congregation for Religious by Michael Kelly, Archbishop of Sydney. The end product is signed by C. Cardinal Laurenti, and Abbot Maurus M. Serafini, OSB, Secretary of the Congregation.

The laws of fasting

The Subiaco community was affected by the 1917 Code in another area of monastic living. The new Code, it is noted in the community chronicles, brings a simplification of the laws of fasting and abstinence (Canons 1250 and 1254).[15] From 1917 there were three kinds of days: days of abstinence, fast days, and days of both fast and abstinence. Fast and abstinence was the rule for Ash Wednesday, Fridays, and Saturdays in Lent. The same (fast and abstinence) applied to the Vigil of Pentecost, Assumption, All Saints, and Christmas.[16] Fasting, according to the Rule of Benedict, is as follows:

> From Pentecost until 13th September, the monks fast until mid-afternoon on Wednesday and Friday, unless they are working in the fields or the summer heat is oppressive. From 13th September to the beginning of Lent, they take their meal in the

---

13 It was thirty years to the day since Prioress Wallis had first translated the same document from German into English.

14 It appears that Prioress Harnett was obedient to Moran's adaptations in order to have the Beuronese Constitutions introduced in the Subiaco community. She didn't have the adverse conditions which dominated Prioress Wallis in the 1890s.

15 A simplification for Catholics, but additional laws for the Benedictine women of Subiaco.

16 With more intricate detail, this aspect of the 1917 Code can be found in Fortescue, 'Some Notes on Fasting', 304.

mid-afternoon. From the beginning of Lent to Easter they eat towards the evening. (RB80, 41).

The revised Constitutions, approved in 1922, specified that:

> Besides the Ecclesiastical fasting days which, according to the practice of the present day [1917 Code], include all the weekdays of Lent, the Ember days, the Fridays of Advent, the Vigils of Christmas, Whit Sunday, the Assumption, and All Saints, the fast of the Rule [of Benedict] is to be observed on each Friday from 13 September until Lent (except from Christmas Day, till after the Octave of the Epiphany, during which time there is no Regular fast). In Advent, Wednesday is also added—moreover the Vigils of our Holy Mother Scholastica, the Solemn Commemoration of our Holy Father St Benedict, and the Purification of the Blessed Virgin Mary, the Titular Patroness of the Monastery. The occurrence of a Feast on any of these days dispenses from the Regular fast.[17]

The nuns had responded in a spirit of *obsculta* (listening with the ear of the heart and responding in obedience) to the ecclesiastical fasting which was added to the already ascetic fasting laid down in the Benedictine Rule.

Closure of the School

The 1917 Code brought with it a further change in lifestyle, in that it made impossible the continuation of the girl's school at Subiaco. The change concerned the solemn vows of Benedictine nuns. On 18 April 1920 the community of Subiaco assembled under the leadership of Prioress Brady to discuss certain details about enclosure and the

---

17 Note in RB80, Chapter 14 Declaration 1. In the wider Church only Fridays were days of abstinence. The Benedictine community of the present observes abstinence from meat on Wednesdays and Fridays, even if those days are Feast Days. The period from 14 September until Lent of the following year, with its exceptions, is still observed with only one meal on a Friday, taken towards evening. Saturdays of Lent are not fast days. Holy Saturday is an optional fast day.

solemnity of their vows. Two episodes concerning solemn vows have already been noted in the cases of Elvina Macintyre Bridge and Teresa McLachlan (pp. 145–6 and 122–4). A third episode concerned Dame Mary Ethelreda (Margaret) Searson, who left the community in 1917. After she petitioned the Holy See for a dispensation from her vows, the Apostolic Delegate to Australia, Dr Bartolomeo Cattaneo, questioned the request, and the nature of her vows.[18]

After this episode, the Prioress and her council sent letters to the Roman authorities.[19] Were their vows solemn or simple? Archbishop Kelly, on his way to Rome with these letters and the revised Constitutions, wrote to the Prioress from Colombo, asking if the nuns were in favour of papal enclosure, should this be one of the conditions of solemn vows. The nuns knew what this meant. Their easy natural enclosure, bounded by the Parramatta River, banks of high trees and a creek, securing all sides of the property, would not be sufficient for Rome. They knew that Rome would order what they called the 'canonical wall'. They asked themselves: 'Are we prepared to sacrifice our freedom and erect grilles and other physical structures necessitated by papal enclosure?'[20]

Their answer was in the affirmative.[21] They were prepared to accept whatever conditions were laid down by canon and monastic law for the privilege of solemn vows. The nuns were of the opinion that their vows had always been solemn and Rome confirmed this. Papal enclosure and an apostolate of teaching were incompatible. The school, with its last seven pupils, closed at the end of 1921.

18 Margaret Searson left the community at 3.15 p.m. on 6 September 1917, after suffering depression and manifesting a disregard for authority, along with episodes of rebellion. In fairness to this nun, many of the community felt that her ill-health was the cause of her problems. There is an indication that she may have had breast cancer, with secondaries (Community Chronicles).
19 The Congregation for Religious in Rome.
20 Records of the Chapter meetings on the issue of papal enclosure.
21 The result of the vote on this issue was not unanimous. There was a minority who did not favour papal enclosure. Francis Merewether's daughter Eliza was one such person, born in Australia, with a broader understanding of monastic life in a vast country. The source for this information is the paper which she submitted to the prioress on this issue.

The difficulties of papal enclosure

Having accepted the conditions of papal enclosure, the nuns also represented to Rome, through Archbishop Kelly, the difficulty and expense of erecting a wall 'entirely around our present property, some 140 acres or more'.[22] On 4 July 1921 Archbishop Kelly walked the grounds of Subiaco with the prioress and senior nuns and suggested a semi-enclosure which might be observed for the present. In the meantime, the nuns considered the alternative of searching for another property, smaller in size, and more conducive to papal enclosure.

Several properties were visited and considered, mainly: Innisfail at Wahroonga, Mt Wilga at Hornsby, Curzon Hall at Eastwood, and Logan Brae at Bellevue Hill. The similarity and necessary feature of these four properties was a large house which could be adapted for monastic living, and added to in the future. This kind of real estate was sought after by many religious congregations making foundations throughout Australia. The home which had become Subiaco was a prime example: a large home, extensive gardens and grounds, the addition of cottages, and farm sheds. The community records show that thirty-one women were members of the Subiaco community at this time.[23]

Towards the end of the year, a letter was received from Archbishop Kelly telling the nuns that nothing may be done in this regard until permission comes from Rome. The next step for the nuns was to consider selling some of their land. On 12 June 1922 a document was signed between the Subiaco community and Mr Leonard Hooper for the sale of forty-six acres of land, referred to as in the Field of Mars, County Cumberland.[24] A second setback came when Mr d'Apice, the Archbishop's lawyer, visited the nuns. He conveyed to them that ecclesiastical powers disputed whether Subiaco was the property of the Benedictine nuns.[25] This matter was settled in favour of the nuns,

---

22 Community Chronicles, April 1920.
23 Community Ledger, begun in 1856 by Sr Mary Scholastica McCarthy.
24 Community Chronicles, 12 June 1922.
25 Two similar cases are documented by Ganley, in *The Long Road*. (1) The Presentation Sisters of Wagga Wagga, New South Wales, were denied ownership (by the Diocesan Bishop) of their convent, which had been built for them by wealthy laity in and around Wagga Wagga, c. 1874, (p.17). (2) In 1938, the Bishop of Rockhampton refused to return to the Queensland Presentation Institute the title deeds of their own property at Yeppoon, until the Mother General pursued the issue through legal channels (p.45).

and their difficulties were further settled by a 'letter from the Delegate saying that Rome granted leave for us to continue at Subiaco under present conditions until a more suitable property could be secured and Subiaco satisfactorily disposed of'.[26]

Subiaco Community, c. 1923

Episcopal and papal enclosure

It needs to be understood that the 1917 Code explicitly describes the difference between papal enclosure and episcopal enclosure. A milder form introduced in the sixteenth century, episcopal enclosure 'had the sanction of episcopal not of papal censures'.[27] 'Imposed on Institutes whose members take solemn vows, especially the female orders',[28] papal enclosure required that:

> within the enclosure of nuns or Religious with solemn vows, no one, of whatever class, condition, sex or age, shall be admitted without the permission of the Holy See except the following persons:

26 Community Chronicles, 24 December, 1921.
27 Ayrinhac, *Penal Legislation*, V.264 (section 280).
28 Augustine, *A Commentary*, Vol. III, 310.

The Ordinary or regular superior to make the canonical visitation; the confessor to administer the sacraments to the sick or attend the dying; Cardinals and rulers of nations with their wives and retinue; doctors, surgeons, and other persons whose assistance is needed. (Can. 600)[29]

With regard to papal enclosure, the Code specifically names the areas of the house affected: 'the orchards and gardens reserved to the religious, but not the public Church with its Sacristy, or guest-house [...] and the parlour, which should, where possible, be placed near the entrance to the house'.[30] Norm 3 states that once the boundaries of enclosure are established, they 'must be clearly indicated, not only to the regulars [nuns] themselves, but also to outsiders [...] by a sign inscribed "Private Entrance" or "Positively No Admittance"'.[31]

The Benedictines of Subiaco had observed enclosure from the time they were founded in Australia, as did all Benedictine women. It was part of their tradition. In accordance with the Rule of Benedict, enclosure was understood as stability of place and stability of heart—living and working within the boundaries of the monastery property and journeying with a particular community of like-minded, dedicated, faith-filled women or men. St Benedict wrote, in his Rule for Monasteries: 'The workshop where we toil faithfully [...] is the enclosure of the Monastery and stability in the community' (RB80 4:78).

The effects of papal enclosure

What took place, with the introduction of papal enclosure, was part of an overall shift of focus which effected changes in the identity of this one Benedictine community, without their school as a main means of income. They had come to Australia in 1848, opened a school in 1851, and kept it functioning until 1921. Now they had only a small income, from the sale of their handmade and embroidered liturgical garments.

---

29   Ayrinhac, *Penal Legislation*, V.264–65 (section 281c).
30   Canon 597:1.
31   Augustine, *Commentary* Vol. III, 313.

They had a property proving impractical to enclose according to the laws of the 1917 Code, with the possibility of moving from what Polding always foretold would be a temporary home. What did become clear with the 1917 Code was the equation: Papal Enclosure = Solemn Vows = Divine Office. As the nuns sought to move forward in the tradition of Benedictine monasticism and to live out the many charisms of the Benedictine life, the focus was primarily on the divine office (Liturgy of the Hours), and on manual work. A word from Casey at this point serves as a reminder:

> Tradition is not an archive. Tradition is not a school of thought or a series of rituals. It is more like the human memory which continually reshapes its contents according to present interests and concerns.[32]

This is also the *obsculta* of the Benedictine Rule which has become a way of life.

With the Liturgy of the Hours giving first place to the definition of their identity, there is evidence of literature on liturgical prayer and a theology of the Liturgy of the Hours—a seeking to understand their vocation within the wider Catholic Church. A theology of the Liturgy was given importance beside ritual and ceremonial. A monastic vocation to a life of prayer and work from the heart of the Church became the objective description for this kind of Benedictine community. This monastic community would remain the only Benedictine women's community on the vast continent of Australia. They would be erroneously described as 'enclosed' nuns or 'contemplative' nuns. In truth, they were and still are, monastic women.

To the Liturgy of the Hours, the nuns added the prayer of 'watching'. This meant perpetual adoration of the Blessed Sacrament. The night watching was added on 13 August 1922. Before that, 'day' watching was practised. During the night, the nuns relieved each other hour by hour. Perpetual Adoration had been desired by the community since the 1870s, and has been noted earlier in this book

---

32 Casey, 'Tradition, Interpretation, Reform', 400.

(p. 194).³³ Every year from this time onwards, on 26 January, a day of reparation (in addition to the Liturgy of the Hours) was held—the anniversary of the 'foundation of the colony' as it is referred to in the community chronicles. It was not named Australia Day until 1935, and not celebrated in its present form until 1994. In 1922, for the nuns of Subiaco this day was characterised by a more concentrated prayer of 'reparation' for the atrocities of the British penal system which dominated the historical and social beginnings of the colony of New South Wales.

Post-World War I

While the effects of papal enclosure were being encountered and the search for a suitable property continued, vocations also continued to grow. The first vocation after World War I was Elsie Enge, whose father was German and whose mother was Australian. She won a scholarship at Lewisham Parochial School, which paid her way to St Vincent's College, Potts Point.³⁴ She then earned a scholarship to the University of Sydney and was enrolled in the Faculty of Arts (1913–1915). Her degree was obtained with second class honours in Latin. She was the last link with the Benedictine Academy of Lyndhurst, in that she studied under Professor Thomas John Butler, who in turn had been tutored at Lyndhurst by the Rev. Norbert Quirk, OSB.³⁵ Her freedom to accomplish a Bachelor of Arts degree during the Great War is not surprising, since Australian women were in active service on the battlefield as nurses, as volunteers in the Red Cross, and as the strength behind the various fund-raising war projects at home. In post-war Australia, wives and mothers went back to being 'home-makers', even

---

33 Exposition (Adoration of the Blessed Sacrament) was reduced somewhat after the community relocated to a new monastery in Pennant Hills, West of Sydney. One of the reasons for this decision was the absence of a resident chaplain.
34 St Vincent's College was founded by the Sisters of Charity, the first religious congregation of women who came to Australia (1838).
35 Thomas Butler was the first graduate of the University of Sydney to hold a Chair therein. In 1890, the Department of Classics had been divided. Butler then held the Chair of Latin. Elsie Enge was one of his students. (Dunstan, 'Thomas John Butler, 1857–1937'.

if they had been in the foreground of battle. Following her graduation from the University of Sydney, she became a secondary school teacher, before entering Subiaco on 6 January 1919. Although embracing the monastic life estranged her from her family and affected her emotionally, she brought with her many gifts which could enrich the Benedictine community as it discerned its future.

Sr Mary Gabriel Enge OSB, c. 1923

Positions assigned to Elsie Enge during her years as a Benedictine nun were: Zelatrix,[36] Choir Director, Mistress of Ceremonies, Subprioress,[37] Superior at the Lawson Monastery,[38] and then in her final years both Cellarer and Bursar. She also worked at translation when called for—both from Latin and French into English. It was Elsie Enge who assisted Prioress Brady with the translation of letters from the Abbot Primate, or the Sacred Congregation for Religious. Such letters were always written in Latin, even up to the end of the Twentieth Century.

When she and others entered the community in the post-World War I era, the *labora* (work) of the Benedictine tradition was the

---

36   Assistant to the Novice Mistress, but not an Assistant Novice Mistress.
37   At this time in the Community's history there was only a prioress and a subprioress. The superior of the Lawson monastery was delegated by the prioress of Subiaco.
38   The Lawson monastery will be discussed further on in this chapter.

making and embroidering of vestments and all garments worn by deacons, priests, and bishops. In order to help the financial strain, much of the furniture of the school was sold, including pianos. It is noted that one piano remained in the monastery.[39] The selling of these items brought in a small income in the first half of the 1920s.

The fact that no parlour maids or domestic servants could remain at the monastery under the laws of papal enclosure worked in favour of the financial situation. On 25 July 1922 the last woman who had worked at Subiaco, and lived on the property (as a house-maid in the Guests' Cottage), had to return to her family at Cooma. She could no longer live at Subiaco with the restriction of papal enclosure.

The one other domestic servant of whom there is some personal background is Catherine Gogarty.[40] Her final days were spent in the employment of the nuns of Subiaco, where she died, aged 82, in 1871. She was buried with the nuns in the Subiaco cemetery. One may query why this servant wasn't buried with her family. The reason may have been that her children were emancipists and eager to rid themselves of the stain of convictism. There are many cases in Australia's history where this occurred, and many cases long after Federation, World War I, and World War II, and the financial depression of the 1930s. Fletcher presents an accurate summary of the resistance to penal beginnings and the convict stain. He notes that 'until after World War II, New South Wales remained sensitive to its penal beginnings. This was evident on several occasions, beginning with the 1888 centenary celebrations'.[41]

Mrs Gogarty (given her ticket of leave), Chloe Mary Hurley North (Aboriginal child), and a girl called Laura Edwards were all buried with the nuns within their own cemetery, prior to the acceptance by the nuns of papal enclosure. These burials would not have been permissible under papal enclosure.

---

39 This one piano was frequently used by Sr Dolores Haseldon, a concert pianist from the Royal London Conservatorium of Music, who entered the Subiaco community on 15 September 1919.
40 Catherine's details can be read in Voytas, *Elizabeth*. Catherine was a Catholic and mother of three children.
41 Fletcher, *Australian History*, 152.

Religious profession

One of the chapters of the 1917 Code of Canon Law dealt with religious profession: the laws governing the age of a candidate, suitability, consent of governing bodies, and—for the nuns of Subiaco, the most significant—that profession of solemn vows must be preceded by the profession of temporary vows. Canon 575 states that at the end of the first three years of temporary vows, 'a religious must either make his perpetual profession or return to the world'. There is the possibility of an exception, 'if the religious is not yet found worthy of being admitted to perpetual vows'. In this case, the religious may be given a second trial, but not a third. 'A third trial is not admitted by the law'.[42] Such a law went against the Benedictine Rule, Chapter 29, which states:

> If a brother, following his own evil ways, leaves the monastery but then wishes to return, he must first promise to make full amends for leaving. Let him be received back, but as a test of his humility he should be given the last place. If he leaves again, or even a third time, he should be readmitted under the same conditions.[43]

In this case, the law of the Church had to be obeyed. There was no option.

Decree of Pope Leo XIII

The Code also deals with the dismissal of a Religious (should the need arise) at the end of the period of temporary vows, and during the period of temporary vows. The law regarding the necessity of temporary profession was part of the 1902 Decree of Pope Leo XIII, but it was not known at Subiaco until after 1918. Forster asserts with accuracy that, between 1902 and 1918, nine women were admitted to solemn profession 'without making a previous profession'.[44] One of these women was Sr Ethelreda (Margaret) Searson, who maintained that the vows she had taken were not solemn but simple.

---

42 Papi, *Religious profession*, 26.
43 RB80 29:1–3.
44 Forster, 'Magdalen le Clerc', 331.

It is quite possible, but can't be proved, that with the death of Prioress Wallis, the years of trauma preceding this event—the preoccupation with the building of a monastery church, and inaugurating the Beuronese Constitutions—caused this oversight. Added to these suppositions was the possibility that literature was not readily available, or the cost of literature was an obstacle. Neither Cardinal Moran nor Archbishop Kelly alerted the prioress to this oversight. According to Papi,

> should anyone be admitted before the 19 May, 1918 (when the Law took effect), to perpetual vows without the three years of temporary profession required by the Code, his profession would not be made null and void by the new law.[45]

The nuns of Subiaco did not heed the decree of Pope Leo XIII, promulgated in 1902. This is one example where the teaching of the Church was not obeyed. It was surely not disobedience, just a lack of communication between the hierarchy of Sydney and the nuns about the existing decree.

The second textbook on the 1917 Code, used by the prioress from 1920 onwards, was the Rev. Chas Augustine's *Commentary on Canon Law*. The Introduction, written by Cardinal Gasquet, states that

> the most important change which has been introduced—at least so far as the older Orders are concerned—is the law which imposes a period of three years of 'temporary simple vows after the noviciate, before perpetual vows, simple or solemn'. Benedictines are numbered among the 'older orders'.[46]

The need to purchase new property and to belong to a larger congregation

Following the acceptance of the revised Constitutions at the end of 1922, there were two issues at work in the lives of the Subiaco community: one was the need to purchase a smaller property; the second

---

45   Papi, *Religious profession*, x.
46   Augustine, *Commentary*, 3.

to 'belong' to a more extensive Benedictine congregation. The resolution of the first issue began with a permission granted by Dr Cattaneo for the selling of several acres of the Subiaco Estate, the money from the sale helping to pay for the erection of an enclosure wall. The wall, it is explained in the prioress' letter of 25 January 1925, 'will be of galvanised iron, so that if, eventually, the monastery and remaining acres are also disposed of, profitably, we shall be able to remove the iron to the new site'.[47] She mentions that this matter was under discussion when Abbot Gariador, Abbot President of the Subiaco Congregation (1920–28), an international congregation of Benedictine monks and nuns,[48] was there in 1924, during his tour of the monasteries of the province,[49] but is diplomatic in reassuring the Apostolic Delegate that Gariador had nothing to do with it.

Broader horizons

With the second end in sight, Prioress Brady sought, and was given permission by Archbishop Kelly through Dr Norman Thomas Gilroy (later Cardinal Gilroy), to undertake a visit of England and Europe with a companion, to gain experience and to view the wider Benedictine scene. One of her advisors in this regard was the same Abbot Benedict Gariador.

---

47 Prioress Brady, 'Letter to His Excellency, the Most Rev. B. Cattaneo D.D., Apostolic Delegate, North Sydney, 25 January 1925'. The residence of the Apostolic Delegate (i.e. the Pope's representative in Australia), today is in Canberra, Australia's national capital.
48 Benedictine women's communities can only be affiliated to the Subiaco Congregation. They do not have voting rights.
49 *Advocate* (Melbourne), 15 January 1925.

Abbot Benoît Gariador, Abbot President of the Subiaco Cassinese Congregation, 1920–1928

When Abbot Gariador was in Australia and visited Subiaco in 1924, he had asked the prioress what the community intended doing if an offer was made for the purchase of the monastery buildings, and what plans they had made for the building of a new monastery which would conform to the conditions of papal enclosure. Since the prioress, an Australian, had never seen a monastic house with the physical signs of enclosure: grilles, enclosure walls, or been exposed to the 'Regular Observance' of other monastic communities, the Abbot advised her to put the matter before the Archbishop of Sydney, as her Superior, and ask permission to travel to England and Europe to see first-hand what the 'Regular Observance' for enclosed Benedictine nuns involved. Her aim was to experience monastic discipline in the regular observance of a monastery: Liturgy of the Hours, times for meals, the formal living of communal life, the work schedule, and the nature of the work, ceremonies, and the use of plain chant, physical structures of enclosure, and plans, if possible, for a new monastery.

Prioress Brady's Pilgrimage

Her pilgrimage took her to many monastic communities of England and Europe, where she imbibed the wisdom of other leaders, and gained the tools for the renewal of her Australian Community. As

Prioress Wallis had done, so Prioress Brady did: listened as a disciple. Her companion was Mary Editha Thompson who had made solemn profession in 1916, and was one of the nine women who had done so without first making temporary profession. Her family were wealthy and had given an outdoor 'Calvary Setting', in life-size statues for her profession. The setting was made in Verdun in 1914/1915, shipped to Australia during World War I, and installed at the monastery in 1916—always a poignant reminder of the sufferings of the Australian Imperial Forces on the Western Front, and those who had lost lives at Gallipoli.

Sr Mary Editha Thompson OSB, c. 1923

Although her aim was to visit as many Benedictine houses as possible, Prioress Brady's journey was not restricted to Benedictine houses. In order to help her community in Australia, she set out to gather a fair assessment of ceremonial, music, and the daily *horarium* observed by Benedictine women and men. Twelve Benedictine houses in the British Isles were visited, and information recorded for the purpose of enriching the Subiaco community at Rydalmere, NSW. Of the houses visited, Prioress Brady rates them according to Liturgy and ceremonial. In her own words,[50] they were

50 Prioress Mary Joseph Brady to the Subiaco community, 7 December, 1925 (JAA, Transcribed letters of Prioress Brady: Letter no. 23). The letter was written from Teignmouth Abbey, Devon, England.

grand and entirely liturgical: (i) Stanbrook, East Bergholt, Oulton, Teignmouth, Holme Eden, and Talacre; (ii) Dumfries in Scotland—not so liturgical. Dumfries was given to Perpetual Adoration, and was a Benedictine Convent, rather than a grand Abbey;[51] (iii) Colwich and Atherstone—not so liturgical but devoted to Perpetual Adoration;[52] (iv) Teignmouth—the only Abbey where the nuns rise at midnight to pray Matins. They are called at 1.30 a.m. for Matins which begins at 1.45 a.m., and on big feasts, Matins ends at 2.45 a.m. The nuns rise again at 5.45 a.m. for meditation at 6.15 a.m. The nuns did not eat meat, in accordance with the Rule of Benedict:

> to regain their strength, the sick who are very weak may eat meat, but when their health improves, they should all abstain from meat as usual.[53]

On the Continent

On the Continent, a visit was made to Solesmes, the home of the Nineteenth Century neo-monastic revival; to Abbeville, Wisque, Brussels (Maredsous), and Maredret in Belgium, a monastery *sui juris*, immediately subject to the authority of the Local Ordinary.[54] Visits were also made to the abbeys of Notre Dame de Jouarre, a member community of the Federation of the Immaculate Heart of Mary, and to Pradines in Lyon. A visit was organised for what was then considered the greatest Benedictine Abbey of monastic women (*moniales*) in the world: the Abbey of Ste Cécile on the Isle of Wight. This was a daughter house of Solesmes.

---

51 The Benedictine Convent at Dumfries was founded by Macia, Lady Herries, who brought the first nuns from Arras. It was founded specifically for Perpetual Adoration of the Blessed Sacrament. In 1993, the Convent was marketed for sale. (This information was gained from Stanbrook Abbey, Wass, Yorkshire).
52 Colwich and Atherstone were sister houses. One was founded from the other. Both were noted to be financially poor.
53 Rule of St Benedict, 36:9.
54 This was a similar situation for the community of Subiaco Rydalmere, the Local Ordinary being the Archbishop, and the monastery being a monastery *sui juris*.

The Abbey of Notre Dame du Pré in Lisieux,[55] with its school for girls, was the educational institution of Therese of Lisieux for four and a half years of her life. It was to this school and community that Prioress Mary Brady and Sr Editha Thompson made a visit in November 1925. This kind of visit was in the spirit of 'pilgrimage', as was the visit to Lourdes, and to some of the traditional Catholic shrines in Rome.[56] When in Rome, Prioress Mary Joseph Brady and her companion had an audience with Pope Pius XI, and were introduced to the Pope by Abbot Benedict Gariador as nuns from Australia who 'were going to build a new Monastery'.[57]

Prioress Mary Joseph Brady, Abbess Cecilia Heywood (Abbess of Stanbrook Abbey), Sr Mary Editha Thompson, Dame Laurentia McLachlan

---

55   Thérèse of Lisieux was canonised by Pope Pius XI on 17 May 1925. She was canonised under the title 'St. Thérèse of the Child Jesus of the Holy Face'. Her canonisation sent a wave of new devotion through the Catholic Church, as people took on her spirituality and the devotions she practised. A shrine to the holy face was set up in the monastery of Subiaco, Rydalmere, based on the legend of the woman stepping from the crowd on the *Via Crucis*, using her head-cloth to soak up the blood and sweat on the face of Jesus. Images of the holy face were set up as shrines in monasteries, religious houses and in some parishes. The incident between the woman (Veronica—'true image'), and Christ became part of the Stations of the Cross and was popular in Catholic piety from the 14th Century onwards. The devotion was once more popularised because of a prayer written by St Thérèse of Lisieux: Cross, 'Teresa of Lisieux'; Hollings, *By Love Alone*; Lafrance, *My Vocation is Love*.
56   The tomb of Pius X was one such 'holy' place.
57   Prioress Mary Joseph Brady, 'Letter to her community at Subiaco, 9 August 1925'. (JAA, Transcribed letters, Vol. 2).

Stability of income

One of the gains from this journey abroad was to establish on a more sound foundation the main work of the community—ecclesiastical embroidery, and the making of all ecclesiastical liturgical garments. Mary Editha Thompson was the force behind this business project, which saw more use made of the Singer sewing machines,[58] and a more economical use of work time, apart from the principal work: The Liturgy of the Hours. The community still struggled financially, even though benefactors were plentiful. Prior to this, all sewing was done by hand, and therefore poor eyesight was considered a valid reason for a novice not being admitted to profession. In spite of these machines being in use, it is recorded in the chronicles of the community that one nun, who entered Subiaco in 1908, made (in a very short time), eleven monastic habits, eleven veils, and three cowls—all sewn by hand.[59] The year was 1929. This leads perhaps to the conclusion that the machines were restricted to the Vestment Department which was the official earning department. In 1929, the sale of work brought in £326.17.0. The cost of materials was £372.00.[60]

---

58 The first sewing machine, most probably used for the making of monastic garments and liturgical vestments, is dated 1903. A second machine was either purchased or given to the community in 1907, and the 1924 model with the oscillating hook for wider use was similarly bought or given (Community Chronicles).

59 The nun was Sr Mary Bede Muschialli, from Queensland. The veil of a nun is the sign of consecration to God. The cowl is the official monastic garment for a monk or nun, and is worn at the Hours of Lauds and Vespers daily, and at Mass depending on the availability of a priest. Priests were more plentiful at this time in the community's history.

60 Community Ledger, begun in 1856 by Sr Scholastica McCarthy, of Princethorpe Priory. In use until 1945.

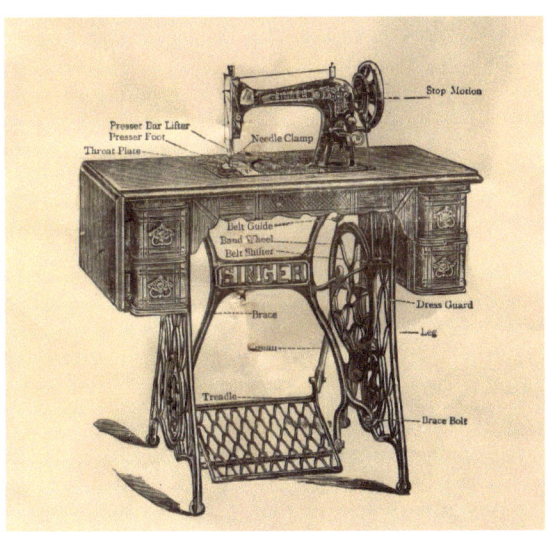

1903 Singer Sewing Machine

Having gained from the experience of her visitation of other Benedictine Abbeys of Regular Observance, Prioress Mary Joseph Brady returned to Australia with the desire that her community of Subiaco be affiliated to a larger Benedictine Congregation. She had listened as a disciple to the wisdom figures she met on this pilgrimage. In a letter of 18 March 1927 to Archbishop Kelly, she explains her reasons for wanting to join a larger Congregation—not the Subiaco Congregation as thought, but rather the Cassinese Congregation. She explains to Archbishop Kelly that the Benedictine Order throughout the world is divided into fourteen Congregations,[61] and that it is the aim of each Benedictine community to be associated or received into one or other of these. Her further reasons are the 'isolation' of Australia from Europe, the fact that both the monks of New Norcia, Western Australia, and of St Bede's in the Philippines belong to the Cassinese

---

61 The Congregation of Santa Cruz del Cono Sur; Congregation of Solesmes, the heart of the neo-monastic revival of the 19th Century; Congregation of Perpetual Adoration (France); Congregation of Perpetual Adoration of the Blessed Sacrament; Congregation of St Bathilde; Congregation of the Annunciation; Congregation of the Benedictines of the Eucharistic King; Congregation of the Holy Spirit; Congregation of the Netherlands; Congregation of the Pure Heart of Mary; English Benedictine Congregation; the Olivetan Congregation, founded in the 14th Century; the Cassinese Congregation; the Subiaco Congregation.

Congregation, and that these two communities are the closest geographically to Sydney.

Belonging

Prioress Mary Joseph Brady also mentioned the fact that she met the Abbot General of the Cassinese Congregation when she was in Rome, and that she had already put the matter before him. He had organised a meeting with Cardinal Laurenti, who 'seemed to consider the request as quite a natural one'.[62] He did mention one 'condition'—that if the nuns left their present monastery to build a new monastery, they should settle near an abbey of Benedictine monks. At this time in history, New Norcia was the only abbey of Benedictine monks in Australia. It appears from various letters and papers filed in the community archives that this was not a preferred option—the foundation of the community was bound up with Polding's mission to the penal colony of New South Wales, not the Spanish Benedictine mission to Western Australia. This conclusion speaks of discussion, listening, and discernment, in the spirit of Casey's words, that 'an honest conversation needs to take place between received tradition and the ambient culture so that monasticism is truly a response to the world in which it lives and not merely a reaction'.[63]

However, was it possible at this time in the history of the community of Subiaco to have an honest conversation between received tradition and the ambient culture of the times, when the Church of Rome was so heavily chained to the minutiae of Canon Law? An honest conversation of this nature was not the way forward for the women of Subiaco or for religious in general. After the Second Vatican Council, it slowly emerged as a positive method for a new era in the Catholic Church. Congregations everywhere gathered for discernment days, and conversed over the most fruitful ways to walk with the people of God on their earthly pilgrimage. Was monasticism, as lived in the community

---

62 Prioress Mary Joseph Brady, 'Letter to her community at Subiaco, 25 February 1926'. (JAA, Transcribed letters, Vol. 2)
63 Casey, 'Tradition, Interpretation, Reform', 427.

of Subiaco, a response to the world or a reaction to the world? At this time, it may have been both. Certainly, a reaction to the world and worldly influences was uppermost in many religious congregations in any period of history, prior to the Second Vatican Council.

The Subiaco community of this time consisted of nineteen nuns in solemn vows, and eight lay sisters. Of the eight lay sisters, only one was born in Australia. Of the nuns in solemn vows, all nineteen were born in Australia.[64] The nature of the community was changing, as was the ambient culture. The law however, was not changing.

> The enclosure prescribed by the Church for all monasteries under solemn vows is papal. Its special object is retirement and seclusion from worldly influences. Let all strive to keep these [worldly influences] out of the House of God. The prescriptions laid down by the Sacred Canons regarding papal enclosure are to be observed with the greatest exactitude.[65]

Even more heavily weighted is Declaration 1, of Chapter 49, on the observance of Lent:

> Having forsaken all things to follow her Divine Spouse, the nun should be holy in body and in soul, leading a most pure angelic life. This purity is, as it were, the ground-work of the whole monastic system, whose discipline has been formed to preserve it; a religious must do violence to nature, kill the works of the flesh by the spirit, become crucified to herself and to the world [...] the sisters should love and appreciate monastic discipline, completing thereby their Conversion of Manners and martyrdom of love.[66]

All of this formed the monastic milieu of Subiaco and of so many monastic communities of women worldwide. In contrast to this more rigorous tone, the language of Chapter 64, declaration 2, on the abbess, or mother of the house, states:

---

64 These figures do not include those in initial formation.
65 Chapter 66, Declaration 1, Revised Constitutions, 1922.
66 This is one of the Benedictine vows, the other two being stability, and obedience.

As Mother of the House, the Abbess is to govern her family with a watchful eye and heart, wisely ordering, arranging and deciding everything in the House of God [...] Above all, she will help the souls of the sisters, when necessary, with advice, consolation and support [...] she will endeavour to keep on the Mountain of Prayer and in the Divine Presence, thus becoming a model for her flock.[67]

The Lawson Monastery

As time moved towards the Great Depression, the nuns became accustomed to their revised constitutions and the demands upon them—both spiritual and temporal.

In 1930, the Lang Government wanted to buy Subiaco, and gave the nuns a week to find another place. At the time, a suitable property for a new monastery, which would meet the demands of papal enclosure, had come onto the real estate market. This was Cadia Park, in Lawson. Dr Reginald Brady, the brother of the prioress and also a Macquarie Street specialist who was the community's doctor, noticed the property and suggested its suitability for the community of Subiaco. The asking price for Cadia Park was £13,240.[68]

Cadia Park, Lawson, c. 1930s

---

67 Chapter 4, Declaration 2. Revised Constitutions, 1922.
68 This figure is stated in business letters in archival storage: Monastery of the Holy Spirit, Lawson.

In 1921, the nuns had sold land on the north side of Victoria Road (approximately fifty-six acres) to Mr Hooper, for £8,000.[69] All business concerning this sale was in the hands of A. W. d'Apice, solicitor. The price was to be paid in instalments, according to the contract which was held in d'Apice's office. In 1924, Lionel Bridge, of Brodie & Bridge (Land Developers), bought the rest of the land, less seven acres which was reserved for the monastery grounds. The payment for this land was £12,000. All this was done with Archbishop Kelly's approval, having insisted that all business be placed in the hands of d'Apice. The nuns objected. It being the eve of the prioress' departure for Europe, there was no option but to appoint d'Apice as attorney during her absence. In the meantime, Lionel Bridge paid the amount in full, rather than in instalments. This was never relayed to the prioress.

When the prioress returned to Australia in 1926 she continued pursuing the financial situation. In 1927 she was introduced to Mr E. J. McCarthy, a friend of some of the younger nuns of the community. She asked him to look into the business matters, which were troubling her. When McCarthy did so, he uncovered the fraud that had been happening at the expense of the Benedictine nuns. One instance was a property at Dural, the dowry of one choir nun, Sr Gertrude Hishon. From 1915 (her election) until 1937, the prioress was aware that rates were being paid on this property. One elderly workman/handyman at Subiaco offered to go and see the Dural property. His findings were summed up accurately: a good block of land, and a man named Reid had bought part of it. The man was working with Neil Collins, who was using the nuns for his own financial 'nest'. Prioress Harnett (d.1915) had entrusted Collins with most of the community's finances. When she needed cash, he gave her £2.00 at a time. At the same time, she was wary of him. Prioress Wallis (d.1902) and the older nuns of her time had also trusted him absolutely, and he said 'she gave him permission to take everything into his hands, and

---

69   There was no Torrens Title over the land at that time, but before the sale, this land and the adjoining land was placed under that title.

anything he did was to be as if with his own property and management'.⁷⁰ Prioress Brady asked him for financial statements and, at first, they were a mixture of business and private family news. She insisted on 'business' only.

Business only

Prioress Brady knew there were properties pertaining to the dowries of the earlier nuns, because the statements that Collins did send mentioned rates that had been paid. However, she did not know where the properties were located, and she never saw the deeds. Up until 1943 the community continued to pay rates on the Dural property until they finally refused, unless the deeds were handed over to them. Thus, a good thirty years of Prioress Brady's term of office was plagued by financial stress, lies, and fraud on the part of those who were supposedly trusted: the same names appearing as valuers and owners, solicitors and owners, or solicitors who were working for the Archdiocese against the nuns. McCarthy took over the supervision of business in regard to the nuns, and finally the financial mess was sorted. McCarthy recommended E. Wolfenden, Public Government Auditor, to look after all financial interests, under the supervision of McCarthy.⁷¹

As the Great Depression of the 1930s took hold on the world financial markets, the Government of New South Wales became bankrupt, and thus could not go ahead with the purchase of Subiaco. In the meantime, the community had purchased Cadia Park at Lawson, with the intention of making the necessary adaptations for monastic living.⁷² The fact that this private residence, on fifty-one acres and well-known throughout the Blue Mountains, was sold three times in the 1920s, was

---

70 This information was located in a paper written by the third elected prioress, Hilda Brady, about the financial troubles of her term in office. It is possible that it was presented to the nuns in solemn vows at Chapter. There is no date. If it was post-1931, Sr Mildred Potts would have assisted in unravelling the financial mess.
71 The chronicles state that McCarthy was known to some of the younger nuns and recommended to the Prioress. Wolfenden was recommended by McCarthy. All payments to McCarthy are recorded in folders and loose pages kept in JAA, Mother Mary Joseph Brady, Papers.
72 The property is described in detail in Kullas, *Sixtieth Anniversary*.

indicative of the forthcoming financial depression. The price, already noted, was also an indication of the future. There are two prices recorded in two different documents in the Abbey archives. The document written by the prioress of the time states the cost as £13,240, which should probably be taken as the more accurate figure.[73]

The Depression of the 1930s

With two monasteries and a divided community (some at Lawson, some at Subiaco), the Benedictine nuns faced both spiritual and temporal challenges. The Depression of the 1930s, triggered by the crash of Wall Street in October 1929, resulted in overwork, and a meagre income.[74] At the Lawson monastery the diet was inadequate, and the 'cold' of the lower Blue Mountains defied the greatest of ascetical spirits.[75] Despite these rigours, charity was always available for the homeless and unemployed who would come to the back door of Subiaco, asking for food. Lived Christology was in operation here, on the part of those who had listened and interiorised RB80 72:11—'Let them prefer nothing whatever to Christ'. The homeless persons who slept under the Clyde railway bridge at night and who came down during the day were given food by a devoted lay sister, Nora Mary (Sr Mary Anthony) O'Connor, born in Toowoomba in 1869. She was known to give food and money to the unemployed and homeless. It is also written into the community's history that a young Queensland priest sent an occasional £1 note for her 'tramps'.[76] Food for the community was shared between Lawson and Subiaco during these years. Women who entered during the Depression—that is, those for the

---

73   The alternate price, £5,500, is noted by Kullas, who has used the information in Malone, 'Obit List', (28), 31–86; (30), 74–75. The contribution of £5000, by the mother of the prioress may be accurate. Whatever the price was, the nuns did purchase the property.

74   In 1930, the nuns earned £371.9.7 from the sale of work. By 1935, this dropped to just £19.10.4. It improved very slowly, and by 1939 the income from the sale of work was £86.2.6. (Community Ledger, introduced by Sr Scholastica McCarthy in 1856.)

75   The nuns I lived with in the 1980s and 1990s, now deceased, who had been at Lawson (Cadia Park), remembered hunger and cold. There was not enough money to pay the electricity bills, even though Cadia Park was fitted out with heating, even in the bathrooms.

76   Malone, 'Obit List', 65.

choir, had their dowries adjusted. A small table brought by a woman in 1935 survives today and is a reminder of the frugal years of the 1930s. One could bring what one could afford or had, in the way of finance or furniture. The dowry of £500 was waived.

The Great Depression was not the kind of event that gave one a choice. It was forced upon everyone—the nuns of Subiaco were not an exception. It enforced upon them an identification with the poor, and a listening to the hungry, the homeless and the jobless. The spirit of the community at this time appears to have been one of unity and generosity. Vestments made were often given at a reduced price to a priest who was also struggling with the financial downfall.

In 1922 Archbishop Michael Kelly granted the following dispensations from papal enclosure, upon the request of the prioress:

1. That Superiors and others be dispensed from papal enclosure when necessity requires.
2. That priests, doctors, dentists, nurses, workmen and others be permitted to enter the enclosure when the duties of their office require.
3. That postulants (new-comers to the monastic life) be permitted to see friends and relations outside the grille for the first month after their entrance and on the day they receive the Religious Habit.
4. In case of danger, fire, accident, serious illness, surgical operations, insanity, or other necessary cause, dispensations be granted to leave the enclosure.
5. That the chaplain or any priest be permitted to enter the enclosure for the performance of an office in accordance with the priestly ministry. (This would include the ministering of the Last Rites to the dying).
6. That sacristans have permission to go beyond the sanctuary grille to attend to necessary duties—adornment of the altar, sweeping, dusting, renovations, lighting and extinguishing of candles.
7. That lay sisters be permitted to act as 'out sisters' for necessary duties as that of portress, and attendance on the chaplain's quarters, when appointed by Superiors.

8. If at any time there is a piece of land suitable for a garden which we cannot at present afford to fence off—if later we are able to do so—can this be included in the enclosure?[77]

Permissions continued

In 1927, the prioress wrote to Archbishop Kelly, asking for permission for one nun to leave the enclosure of the monastery. A Parramatta doctor had already seen the nun. He was concerned and recommended a Macquarie Street specialist as the next step. Later, in February 1939, an elderly nun fell and broke her hip.

> The doctor came and said she must go to hospital at once (4.30 p.m. on a Sunday). We phoned Archbishop Gilroy—he was away—then the Apostolic Delegate—he was in New Zealand —then the old Archbishop (Michael Kelly)—and were told he was not attending to business, so we had to presume permission, and send her by ambulance to the Mater Hospital.[78]

On 18 March 1927 the prioress wrote to the Archbishop of Sydney, Michael Kelly—a letter already referred to, in which is mentioned the matter of joining the Cassinese Congregation. Another significant issue in this letter is the title of 'abbess'. The prioress states that,

> according to our Constitutions, the superior is always referred to as Abbess, but we did not think it necessary to assume this title until we were privileged to call our Monastery an Abbey.[79]

The problem at this particular point in time was that the next election of a prioress was due to take place on or near 21 May 1927. Before that time, as Prioress Brady explained to the Chapter, 'it will be necessary to insert a phrase in the Constitutions which was omitted; otherwise, we should be taking a precedent which is quite contrary

---

77 This list of dispensations is part of the Archdiocesan and legal papers in the file of Prioress Mary Joseph (Hilda) Brady. (JAA, Mother Mary Joseph Brady, Papers).
78 Paper written by Prioress Brady in 1940, summarising the difficulties of papal enclosure. (JAA)
79 In the history of the community, this did not take place until 1982.

to Benedictine tradition'.[80] She strengthens her case by referring to the fact that it was the Abbot Primate of the Benedictine Confederation who mentioned the matter to her when she was in Rome (1926). He was the one who noticed the omission in Chapter 64, Declaration 1 of the revised Constitutions. It was an omission which made the declaration incomplete. The Declaration read 'the abbess is elected for a term of six years'. He explained that the clause should be 'The abbess is elected for a term of six years, with right of re-election'. This is the tradition of the Benedictine Order.

The nuns did not know, when the Constitutions were being revised and translated in accordance with the 1917 Code of Canon Law, that they could claim exemption from the Law on this point. Only when in Europe did the prioress find out that this was so, and therefore, she explained to Kelly, it was a 'matter of duty for me to put the question before the Community on my return, and then forward the result to the Sacred Congregation for Religious to consider without delay'.[81] Since the issue affected her personally, she refrained from carrying out this duty immediately. When she did deal with the matter, the community voted to petition 'that the abbess should be elected for life'.[82] She then proposed that it would be giving special honour to the Mother of God, if they elected her as their Perpetual Abbess, so as to permit the Superior of the community to retain the title of prioress—with right of re-election. A majority of votes were in favour of the Mother of God, with the proviso that the prioress in such a case should be elected for life. The notion of the Mother of God as a Perpetual Abbess was not unheard of. One of the founding communities, Princethorpe Priory, Warwickshire, had the same custom.

Other requests which had been forwarded to the Abbot Primate and shared with Archbishop Kelly were: one change in the time of the 'hour' of Lauds; a request if the monastery will be raised to the status of an abbey; the possibility of their being received into the Cassinese Congregation without having to leave New South Wales. Finally, that

---

80   Prioress Brady, Talk given to the Chapter nuns. (JAA, Mother Mary Joseph Brady, Papers).
81   Prioress Brady, 'Letter to Archbishop Michael Kelly', [n.d.].
82   Prioress Brady to His Excellency, Most Rev. John Panico D.D. Jud., Apostolic Delegate, 24 July 1940 (JAA, Mother Mary Joseph Brady, Papers).

the election of the prioress be delayed because of the community's difficult circumstances—being divided in numbers and in two houses.

A letter from the Abbot Primate of the Benedictine Confederation, Fr Fidelis Stotzingen, written in October 1939 in response to all the requests, is to say simply that such petitions cannot be settled quickly, and to allow months to receive a decision. The only petition granted immediately is for the election of the prioress 'not to take place in your Monastery at present, but be postponed until after the final decision of the Sacred Congregation […] you are confirmed in your Office until that decision arrives'. Stotzingen is not in favour of the Mother of God being a Spiritual Abbess. He points out that 'it is altogether contrary to the best tradition of our Order, which demands that an Abbey should be governed by an earthly Abbess'.[83]

The Cassinese Congregation

The possibility of being incorporated into the Cassinese Congregation was addressed in 1934 by the Abbot General of that Congregation. He reminded the nuns that they were under the jurisdiction of the Archbishop of Sydney, that he was their Superior and they must submit to his rule in conformity with Canon Law and their own constitutions. He suggested that a change in their situation might be brought about in three ways: they might be incorporated into the Congregation of the Primitive Observance (Cassinese), and then they would be under the jurisdiction of the respective Superiors who would take the place of the Bishop of their Diocese. He added that this would be very difficult because only the Holy See can grant it, and the Holy See would certainly want the consent of the bishop, and he foresaw that the bishop would object.[84]

He then presented the second difficulty: they would require the consent of the Cassinese Congregation's General Chapter. This he foresaw would 'probably encounter great objections, especially on account of the great distance which separates you from us'.[85] He sug-

---

83 Abbot Primate Fidelis Stotzingen, 'Letter to Prioress Brady', 18 October 1939.
84 Abbot General, Cassinese Congregation, 'Letter to Prioress Brady, 12 November 1934'.
85 Abbot General, Cassinese Congregation, 'Letter to Prioress Brady, 12 November 1934'.

gested affiliation to the Subiaco Congregation with the advantages of being able to use the *Ordo Divini Officii*[86] (with the permission of the Holy See). The Superior of the 'Subiaco Congregation' might be delegated by the bishop to hold the Canonical Visitation. This, it is noted, could be done without the affiliation.

The Subiaco Congregation

The affiliation might be granted but not without difficulty, because of the great distance. The third option was to remain under the jurisdiction of the local bishop, with the 'dominative power' being conferred 'definitively' on the Abbot of New Norcia (Western Australia). This is put forward as the best option, and the one to which the bishop may more easily consent. But it could not be done without the intervention of the Holy See.

Finally, the great obstacle of distance is raised again, both distance from Rome, where the Abbot President of the Subiaco Congregation resides, and also the distance between Sydney and New Norcia. The Chapter which was to take place in 1936 at Easter would discuss the situation and the request of the nuns. When Archbishop Kelly visited Subiaco, the community sensed that he was not happy about them being under someone else's jurisdiction. Perceiving that their present Archbishop would not agree to their being withdrawn from his jurisdiction, the matter was finally settled by the nuns themselves. The prioress states that their present situation of being associated with the English Benedictine Congregation is satisfactory. They also use the *Ordo Divini Officii* of that Congregation, with the permission of the Holy See.[87]

---

86 The *Ordo* of the Subiaco Congregation. This would have its own difficulties in an Australian community, when feasts of Australia, such as 'Our Lady Help of Christians', Australia Day, and Anzac Day, were part of the National Australian *Ordo*. An *Ordo* is an abbreviation for the Order of the Mass according to Sundays, First and Second Class Feasts, Ordinary time, and the Seasonal days such as Lent, and Advent. Every Benedictine Congregation had an *Ordo*. The English *Ordo* was heavily weighted with Saints of the Benedictine Order. The German *Ordo* favoured German Benedictine Saints.

87 Quotations have been taken from two letters: Prioress Brady to Abbot Mauro Etcheverry, Abbot General of the Cassinese Congregation, 26 June, 1934; Dom Mauro Etcheverry, OSB, Abbot General of the Cassinese Congregation to Prioress Brady, 12 November, 1934.

Obsculta within the law of the Catholic Church

There had been ongoing contact with New Norcia, because of the translation work Romanus Rios had done in 1919 in relation to the Constitutions of 1921–22. From their previous experience of him, the nuns had come to trust this monk and he had become a reference person for them when it came to monastic matters and matters that affected their Constitutions. In 1937 several queries were raised with the Abbot Primate of the Benedictine Confederation, and the same queries were sent to Romanus Rios who, at this time, was living at St Augustine's Abbey, Ramsgate, England. They ask that Romanus Rios translate their requests from English into either Latin or French for the benefit of the Cassinese Abbot.[88] The interaction between Prioress Brady and Fr Etcheverry about these requests illustrates a Benedictine *obsculta*—listening to the minutiae of law, in order to do justice to the Rule of Benedict and the laws of the Catholic Church.

The first issue concerned Chapter 39 of the Benedictine Rule. Declaration I refers to 'two dishes of meat'. Chapter 39, as set out in the Constitutions of 1922 is headed: 'Of the measure or quantity of meat'. Declaration 1 states:

> At dinner, besides soup, the Sisters shall have two dishes of meat, or on abstinence days, of fish, eggs etc., with the customary cold or warm vegetables—also fruit if there be any […] meat is only allowed once a day, except on Sundays, the principal recreations [Solemnities] of the year and whenever the Abbess may judge it expedient.[89]

---

88   Latin was the language of the Catholic Church, and used for all official correspondence with the hierarchy of the Catholic Church in Rome, or the Abbot Primate of the Benedictine Confederation (at this time, Fidelis Stotzingen). The French language would have been known in the Vatican, along with Spanish and Italian. It was a language familiar to the Subiaco community because of the origin of the Community, with one foundress from St Mary's Priory Princethorpe, originally founded from Montargis in France. French as a language was taught in the Subiaco School until its closure at the end of 1921 and in Catholic Secondary Schools well into the 1980s.

89   Subiaco Constitutions 1922, Declaration 1.

This is how it reads in the Constitutions of 1922. In the Rule of St. Benedict it is '*cocta duo pulmentaria*'—two dishes of cooked food. The financial rigours of the 1930s most probably led the prioress to ask if she could be permitted to use her own discretion about food. She also asks this permission for those who will rule after her. In the 1930s, it is recorded that gifts of food were given to the nuns from time to time. With no refrigeration, food had to be consumed. The prioress is requesting that this Declaration be altered accordingly.

The prioress was concerned about the issue of 'Out-Sisters and Oblates'. Can out-sisters have the same privileges and discipline as out-sisters at Stanbrook Abbey? The prioress adds that if there is any difficulty in the out-sisters having the same privileges and discipline as those at Stanbrook, would the Rules of the Beuronese out-sisters and oblates be attainable? She also asks if widows or elderly ladies, willing to give services, and follow the Rule of the Out-Sisters be permitted to come and live in the monastery as oblates, with the hope of making simple vows at the hour of death. She knows of many who would be glad of this privilege.

The third request was that she may visit the Lawson Community, with a nun as companion, or one from the noviceship, who could be better 'spared'. There is also the request that any of the nuns be permitted to visit doctors, hospitals, etc. with a companion when necessary. She also asks permission to change the *Ordo Divini Officii*, wondering if they could also include the feasts of St Alban, St Edmund, and St Thomas More, keeping them as duplex.[90] In addition, she presented their problem with the Rule of St Benedict concerning the Guest House. The Guest House at this time was the chaplain's

---

90 In the Monastic office, this was the highest grade of a feast on which all the antiphons of Vigils, Lauds and Vespers I and II are doubled. This means that an antiphon comes before a psalm and the same antiphon after a psalm. So, for example, such an office has three nocturns at Vigils, each following the pattern: Antiphon, Psalm, Antiphon repeated. As Feasts went, there were *Duplicia Primae Classis* and *Duplicia Second Classis*. (see Figure 6, pp. 166–167) The latter included the Most Holy Trinity, the Circumcision of the Lord, the Annunciation of the Lord, the Immaculate Conception of the Mother of God, the Visitation of Mary to Elizabeth—to name just a few. I believe that what the prioress is asking for is that Sts Alban, Edmund, and Thomas More be celebrated also, probably as *Memorias*. This is the term used in the *Ordo* since the Second Vatican Council.

residence. Yet, Chapter 58 of the Rule states that a postulant must be tried in the Guest House—for a few days—before entering the novitiate. They want to know if they are allowed to let such women enter the novitiate without this period of trial.

Finally, the prioress, on behalf of the nuns in solemn vows, asked if they are to wear cowls always in the choir. This may mean that cowls were being worn for every 'hour' and for Mass. If so, this was not the Benedictine custom. The cowl is the official monastic garment, and is worn for the major Hours and for the daily Mass. This issue may have arisen from the harsh conditions of the Australian summer. A cowl worn over a monastic habit in a church without any system of cooling could quite easily result in illness. This may be yet another change necessary for monastic living in Australia.

A woman skilled in business affairs

In 1931 a woman skilled in business affairs entered the monastery at Subiaco. Gladys Potts had been educated by the Sisters of Mercy, at Our Lady of Mercy College, Parramatta. A brilliant student, she had won third place in the state for her Leaving Certificate. She was offered a position in the Department of the Postmaster General (1906–1907).[91] Unlike women who graduated from the University of Sydney as lawyers or doctors, and who were kept from practising by men who wouldn't accept them as equals, women like Gladys Potts and others who were skilled as typists and stenographers could become telegraphists and postmistresses.[92] When Gladys Potts entered the Benedictine Community of Subiaco in 1931 at the age of forty-one, she was one of the highest paid women in the Public Service.[93] She became an assistant to the prioress, using her secretarial skills and business acumen.

---

91 This is noted in her references.
92 Macintyre, *The Oxford Dictionary of Australia*, 58.
93 This was noted in the references which she brought to the monastery from her employer and her parish priest.

By 1940, there was a movement towards having 'exits' from the enclosure catered for and covered by law. This meant asking for a series of permissions which would be granted by the proper authority for a period of one calendar year, and would have to be sought for the next year.[94]

Gilroy, Kelly, D'Apice, and the Benedictine nuns

A letter of a different nature (marked 'confidential') to Archbishop Gilroy in June 1940, addresses a number of difficulties being experienced. First, it presents the strained relationship between the nuns of Subiaco and Mr d'Apice, the Archdiocesan Solicitor. The prioress begs Gilroy:

> Please do not put too much reliance upon any statements made about our business matters by Mr. W. A. d'Apice. For many years, he has not been a true friend of ours, and has misrepresented many things to the old Archbishop—seeming to have him completely under his sway.[95]

From the point of view of the nuns, d'Apice had persuaded 'the old Archbishop' (Kelly) to regard the nuns as 'tenants or usufructs, with no right to claim the capital from the sale of their land or to receive any interest therefrom'—in relation to land sold in 1921 and in 1924. When the prioress asked him (Kelly): 'What shall we live on? We only sold the land to get an income',[96] he displayed anger which they had not experienced to this point in time. They had only known his kindness and paternal care. After this episode, he did sign documents which left the nuns with their land and in peace.

94　The abbess is still obliged to do this annually, by way of a formal letter to the Bishop of Wollongong, in whose Diocese the abbey is today. Such a letter requests a series of permissions each year. One such permission is that the abbess may grant six months leave of absence to a sister who is pursuing academic studies, or who needs help from a psychiatrist, or specialist doctor. Even so, the abbess is unable to proceed without the support of the Diocesan Bishop.
95　Brady to Archbishop Gilroy, 17 June, 1940. (JAA, Mother Mary Joseph Brady, Papers)
96　Brady to Archbishop Gilroy, 17 June, 1940.

The prioress did not have any communication with d'Apice from 1928 until 1940. After the death of Michael Kelly on 8 March 1940, d'Apice phoned and wrote to say that he had asked Norman Thomas Gilroy (Kelly's successor) to act as Trustee in Kelly's place. In a letter to Gilroy, the prioress states that her secretary, Sr Mildred Potts, 'has been through the archives and finally typed many pages to explain some matters. To send them, just as they were, would be like presenting a pistol at your head, defying you to be a trustee for us'.[97]

As the letter progresses, it is stated clearly that all the matters with which she needed help had been deferred because of the ageing Archbishop Kelly, who referred her to Mr d'Apice for all her permissions. When they were looking for a suitable property to replace Subiaco, the old Archbishop said: 'When you have to go out to visit places, ask Mr. d'Apice'.[98] And so, in a list of six permissions, the prioress asks Gilroy in this letter that 'for safety's sake in these days of war, we would be pleased if you would consent to act as Trustee for our Estate—although in ordinary times we have had the right to appoint trustees, only from the community'.[99] She states that d'Apice 'has been able to give clear statements of our business matters since the death of Archbishop Kelly, but it was not always so'.[100]

Prioress Brady also includes a new request in this list, concerning the cemetery:

> Our cemetery is outside the enclosure: about 100 yards outside. I should like to check the numbers of the graves—to compare with a chart we have and to note spaces for future interments.[101]

Further issues with papal enclosure

The Second World War, the nuns foresaw, would affect them financially and spiritually. The need to bring the two houses together and

---

97 Brady to Archbishop Gilroy, 17 June, 1940.
98 Brady to Archbishop Gilroy, 17 June, 1940.
99 Brady to Archbishop Gilroy, 17 June, 1940.
100 Brady to Archbishop Gilroy, 17 June, 1940.
101 This original chart is held in the JAA.

live as one community had become more urgent. The prioress was faced at this time with disposing of one of the houses. She proposed to Gilroy that the Ladies of the Grail 'may be allowed to inspect the place at Lawson' and that 'it would be found most suitable'.[102] She also proposes that if they [the Ladies of the Grail] could not purchase it, they 'may find it possible to take it for a term—paying rent with right of purchase'.[103] This would allow the nuns to pay the taxes[104] and keep the place in repair. She is aware, at the same time, that the beginning of the Second World War is not an appropriate time for this proposal, as the Subiaco monastery may be needed to house Australian armed forces. She sought the Archbishop's advice in all of this.

Then, in this same document, there are the usual permissions for exits from the enclosure. These are similar to those granted by Michael Kelly in 1922, and renewed through the years: permission to go to hospital, specialist doctors, for X-rays (a new addition),[105] to visit the Lawson Monastery, to take care of the altar and vestments and associated tasks. This was significant financially. The work was being done by extern sisters—those who were not bound by the laws of enclosure that applied to nuns in solemn vows. It was extremely difficult to find

> young people to come as externs—it is too lonely—and where one succeeds in employing two [extern sisters], they disagree. We have to pay 1 pound to each and another to the extern at Lawson. Then: two chaplains, two confessors, two extraordinary confessors, two retreats. The expense for everything is very great—also

---

102 Brady to Archbishop Gilroy, 17 June, 1940. The Ladies of the Grail came to Sydney in 1836, from the Netherlands. This Christ-centred organisation was, and still is, a group of women who meet the needs of the times. Today they are to be found in a number of countries world-wide. In each country, their faith and prayer reflect their cultures. Respect for the 'other' is one of the foundations of their lives.
103 Brady to Archbishop Gilroy, 17 June, 1940.
104 Since no religious group or church group has paid taxes since Federation, this probably refers to various local payments, such as those listed in n.106.
105 While the X-ray was invented by Wilhelm Roentgen in 1895, and used for the wounded in both the Boer War and World War I, it was not freely used in Australia until the late 1920s, and into the 1930s. There was still a question over the damage it caused to both doctors and patients.

the expense of paying workmen here and at Lawson.[106]

Gilroy replies favourably in July 1940 and the nuns are granted permissions accordingly. That same month the prioress also wrote a letter to the Most Rev. John Panico, D.D., the Apostolic Delegate.[107] This letter asks for permission to leave the enclosure when circumstances render it necessary. It is a long letter with extensive background information about the situation both at Subiaco and at Lawson. However, the first matter of uncertainty was: 'To whom we were to apply for permission to leave the Enclosure?' The prioress states that Archbishop Kelly, after one of his visits to Rome, gave 'us to understand […] that he had complete authority over us, as our Ordinary […] it was not wise, therefore, to incur the displeasure of His Grace by asking for further information'.

It is at this point that Fr McCabe comes into the picture—the extraordinary confessor to Subiaco. The prioress asks him to discuss this with the Delegate and give definite information about the matter.[108] He makes it clear for the nuns that such permissions are a matter for the Holy See, to be given by the Apostolic Delegate—the Pope's representative in Australia. The arrival of McCabe's letter coincided with a visit of Archbishop Gilroy to Subiaco. As a result of discussion on the matter, the Archbishop promised to explain to the Delegate the difficult circumstances which militated against strict papal enclosure. The monastery at Subiaco was not built for enclosure—almost everything militated against it.

The prioress explains in her letter to the Delegate that the orchard, gardens, and paths are within the enclosure, whereas a properly planned monastery would have a farm attached—but outside the enclosure—the products of which would be brought to the entrance by the workman appointed for that purpose—they would never need

---

106 From January 1925 they were also paying one pound per annum to the Sydney Harbour Trust Office for the lease of one and three fifths perches of land and the sites of 'five piles beyond high water mark at Subiaco, Parramatta River'. This was the area around the Jetty. Many visitors still came by boat.
107 Prioress Brady to His Excellency, Most Rev. John Panico D.D. Jud., Apostolic Delegate, 24 July 1940 (JAA, Prioress Mary Joseph Brady, all letters and documents.).
108 Fr. McCabe to Prioress Mary Joseph Brady, 8 August, 1940. (JAA Box labelled Prioress Mary Joseph Hilda Brady, all letters and documents).

to enter the enclosure. She had witnessed this, in her experience of other monasteries in England and Europe in 1925–26.[109]

At Subiaco, however, the reverse was the case. The workman must come into the enclosure to do the necessary work which cannot be carried out by the nuns. This situation caused distress within the community, and an endeavour was made to carry out the requirements of Canon Law by having two sisters always available to open the gate for the workman to enter, and then to let him out again when necessary. In practice, it was found that this was quite unworkable, because from 6.00 a.m. when he came in to milk the cow, until he finished his work in the evening, he was in and out of the enclosure, attending to work elsewhere, having meals etc. It was considered to be the task of the lay sisters to hold the gate, but two of them were too old, and a third was infirm. The two able-bodied were involved in work that could not be left. The attempt, therefore, to meet the demands of Canon Law, in this matter, had to be abandoned.[110]

In order to cover the situation of visiting Lawson, which Gilroy had suggested should occur at least four times annually, and in the permission for the nuns to work in the side chapel and priest's sacristy and sanctuary, the prioress suggested to the Delegate that, instead of the nuns having to wait for twelve months to renew their permissions, he give a certain number of permissions which could be renewed even before they had availed themselves of the previous list. Or in the case of the work in the sacristy and adjacent areas, he give a general permission, since this is a daily commitment.

In the case of meeting of emergencies in the form of illness and hospital, the Delegate recommended that these be dealt with as they arise. The last two permissions are for a visit to the cemetery, and for the prioress to go outside of the immediate enclosure to check on alterations which will be taking place in the monastery grounds. Although these permissions were all granted, that they had to be

---

109 One of the reasons for making the journey to England and the Continent was to see monasteries and abbeys. She entered Subiaco monastery, her own monastery in Australia, having never seen monasteries of the old world. It was Abbot Gariador, on his visit to Australia, who persuaded her to travel and see other abbeys and monasteries.

110 Community Chronicles (JAA).

requested shows how the strong arm of the Catholic Church's legal systems reached into the lives of the women of Subiaco, to the point of oppression.

World War II

While these issues were being addressed, the Second World War was gaining momentum, and the nuns of Subiaco were continually exhorted by the prioress to pray more earnestly, not just for Australian troops but for the armed forces of every country involved in war. Although *The Sydney Morning Herald* came daily to the monastery, it was available only to the prioress. However, she read the war news to the nuns in solemn vows each day.

Within twenty-four hours of the Japanese surprise attack on Pearl Harbour on 7 December 1941, the news had reached Subiaco. The nuns were aware of the seriousness of the Pearl Harbour attack, and that America had entered the war. Precautions were taken at Christmas. Midnight Mass was forbidden by Archbishop Gilroy, because the Government had ordered 'black-outs'. Air raid shelters were being built throughout Sydney. On the 11, 12 and 13 January, the cellars of the Macarthur house were prepared by the nuns for a possible air raid. They were cleared and limed, and non-perishable food was stored. A temporary chapel was arranged in the Chapter Room (the old Macarthur ballroom). Permission had to be obtained from the Apostolic Delegate to have the Blessed Sacrament moved to this location in a different but secure Tabernacle. All this was set in place ahead of a possible air raid by the Japanese.[111]

On 15 January 1941 the prioress addressed the community again, concerning their obligation to pray for those at war, especially those in the Australian forces 'sacrificing their lives for us'.[112] On 21 January 1942 Archbishop Gilroy, who had himself served as a wireless operator at Gallipoli in 1915, ordered two nuns or sisters from every convent in Sydney to attend lectures at St Mary's, in order to prepare

---

111 Community Chronicles, 11, 12, 13 January 1941 (JAA).
112 Community Chronicles, 15 January 1942 (JAA).

them for the procedure required in the event of an air raid. His aim was that they become registered Air Raid Wardens, to prevent outsiders coming into the convent precincts, and invading their privacy. The two nuns from Subiaco were Sr Mildred Potts and Sr Boniface McConnell. Through these lectures, they learned what was necessary in the way of directing arrangements should an air raid occur, which would endanger the lives and property of the community. Dealing with fire caused by bombing was just one aspect.

During this time, the 'Regular Observance' of the Benedictine life was adjusted to meet the situation of war. Just as Polding had made adjustments to the monastic life of the 1840s, '50s and '60s, so Prioress Mary Joseph Brady exercised freedom to meet the fear and anxiety of the nuns at this time. Monastic life was not so rigid that even the threat of war and invasion had to be kept at a distance, so that the nuns could get on with the monastic day. What had never characterised this community was an ossified rigidity.

The nuns of Subiaco took part in the 'trial' raids, along with the people of Sydney and surrounds. As with Pearl Harbour, when the war arrived in Australia with the Japanese attack on Darwin (10.00 a.m. on 19 February 1942), within twenty-four hours the prioress had informed the community. By August it is recorded in the community chronicles that Australia and America are at war with the Japanese in the Pacific. By November of the same year they are in touch with the sufferings of Australian troops in the jungles and swamplands of New Guinea. A poignant entry in the community chronicles on 9 November 1942 cries out and prays:

> Oh, for peace! So many brave men are falling, on all sides—men for whom Christ's Precious Blood has been shed—men of every nation. May they rest in peace.

The American forces give the Benedictine nuns a steady income

Despite its suffering caused to the Benedictine nuns of Subiaco along with the rest of the world, it was the Second World War which changed the course of their history by giving them a new work with a solid and steady income. On 4 May 1944 there was a telephone call from St Mary's Cathedral in Sydney. The priest, a Fr Toohey, asked to speak to the prioress. A request had come from the Senior Catholic Chaplain with the American forces based in Brisbane.[113] It was a request for altar breads for the American troops, at the rate of several thousand per week. The community saw this as a noble work for the war effort, and a work which would enhance the fruits of their Liturgical life as Benedictines. They were living the Benedictine *obsculta*, assuring that their monastic life was truly a response to the world in which they lived—a world at war. Meeting one of the needs of the world at war was for them the work of the Holy Spirit calling them to new depths of their Benedictine *obsculta*.

Laurence Schneider, Chaplain to US Navy, USS Pensacola, 1941

---

113 An inaccurate entry in the Community Chronicles. There was one chaplain for the Navy, one for the Air Force, and one for the Army. The Chaplain to the Navy in 1941 was Laurence R. Schnieder. His ship was Pensacola (a heavy cruiser), under command of Captain Norman Scott. The retired Archivist at St Stephen's Archdiocesan Archives in Brisbane was able to supply a Christmas card sent to Archbishop Sir James Duhig with the words: 'With every best wish to the world's most hospitable archbishop'. It was signed by Laurence R. Schnieder, chaplain to the U.S. Navy, and Captain Norman Scott, commanding officer of the U.S. Ship Pensacola.

Their initial help in this new work came from Fr McGovern, later Monsignor McGovern. He brought his own altar bread baking machine the next day, thus making two machines to begin the huge project.[114] The new work altered the interior of the monastery; a suitable venue had to be chosen and electricity installed. Fr McGovern, whose brother was fighting with the Australian Army, also brought the nuns a bread cutter and samples of altar breads made elsewhere. An urgent appeal for 30,000 small breads and 900 large breads were needed by 15 May. This request came from the American chaplain in Brisbane. The packaging and containers were supplied by the American Army. The Catholic chaplain in Sydney called at Subiaco to bring the necessary containers. By 15 June the order was ready. The first payment of £18 was forwarded to the prioress. The next order from the chaplain was for 42,000 breads. And so the making and cutting of altar breads became a community work, with a steady income.[115] This work went on beside the making and embroidering of liturgical garments until the 1980s.

Monsignor Joseph J. McGovern, c. 1940s

114 It was of interest to the nuns of Subiaco to see that the driver of the army jeep was a woman in uniform. The officer with her was a passenger—a witness to changing times.
115 A short prayer ritual was adopted before the making of altar breads, and a prayer that no one who partook of Holy Communion with the altar breads made at Subiaco would make a bad communion (partaking of the Lord's Body and Blood while living a non-Christian life, or even a sinful life).

Prioress Brady Resigns

On 22 November 1945, Prioress Brady resigned after thirty-one years in office. She had led the community of Subiaco through the years post-World War I, the 1920s, the Great Depression, and then another World War. In all this, the Benedictine charisms of Christian love, reverence, liturgical prayer, *Lectio Divina*, silence, community bonding, and hospitality were adhered to faithfully, within the spirit of the Benedictine Rule. Prioress Brady died four years after her resignation, on 30 December 1949.[116]

The next chapter will detail post-war society, then the rise of industry, ongoing 'listening', resulting in the necessity of relocating a monastic community to a property away from industrial noise and poor air quality.

---

116 *Peterborough Times* (South Australia) 20/1/1950: The death occurred last month of Rev. Mother Mary Joseph, Mother Prioress of the Benedictine Monastery, Subiaco, NSW. Rev. Mother Joseph was the only daughter of the late Mr. and Dr. Brady. She was educated at the Peterborough Catholic School and left from here about 46 years ago to enter the Convent.

CHAPTER TEN

Prioress Mildred (Gladys) Potts 1945-1968: Leaving Subiaco

Prioress Mildred Potts

Prioress Mary Joseph Brady was succeeded by her secretary and faithful advisor on many business matters. Mildred Potts became the fourth elected prioress of the Subiaco community. Prior to her election, the work to which she was appointed by Prioress Brady had always carried serious responsibility. Bursar was one of these appointments and it was in this capacity that she was able to investigate thoroughly the interest owed to the community on certain dowries of nuns both living and dead. As prioress, she began to face the challenge of post-war Australia.

Work

It was Prioress Mildred Potts who set the Altar Bread Department on a secure footing, as a business with steady income—and one that didn't depend on the American forces. Once this work was established she also purchased more light machinery to help in the work of the monastery. The result of this was that the nuns were less fatigued and more able to sustain the Liturgy of the Hours and communal gatherings, formal and informal. Prioress Potts brought a fresh look to the Lawson/Subiaco situation. She saw within a short time that the solution to the situation was to sell Lawson and to bring the nuns back to Subiaco. It was easier to sell the Lawson property than the Subiaco property and buildings. In 1949, she closed the Lawson house as a Benedictine monastery and sold it to the Sisters of St Joseph. This decision cut out much extra expense and enabled the community to be as 'one' again. It increased the numbers of those who could work in both the Altar Bread Department and the Vestment Department. It gave more strength of voice and depth of prayer to the Liturgy of the Hours, and to the Mass.[1]

Mildred Potts, Prioress 1945–1957

Devotional Practices

Prioress Mary Joseph Brady had entered the monastery in 1904 at the age of twenty-six, at the dawn of the twentieth century, and had been a gifted spiritual director and counsellor, especially to the pupils in the school. Mildred Potts was forty-one years of age when she entered the monastery, coming from a background of skilled business management, and so, perhaps inevitably, her care of the community was

---

1   Community Chronicles, 1945–1947.

of a very practical nature. Prioress Brady's care of the community was weighted more heavily on the spiritual side. It was Mildred Potts who removed the 'night watching' out of care for the nuns' spiritual health.[2] She had an ability to view situations with a reasonable and objective manner and, regardless of her late entry to the order, her understanding of the Rule of Benedict was detailed and true. Prioress Brady had arrived in the community when the Beuronese Constitutions were still awaiting approval. These constitutions leaned heavily on 'ardent devotion', first to the Sacred Heart of Jesus, which was linked to two Benedictine female saints: Gertrude of Helfta, and Mechtild von Hackeborn. The nuns were to foster a 'tender love for the Immaculate Virgin Mary', and confidently place themselves under her protection.[3]

More evidence of devotional practices is found in Declaration 1, where the traditional devotions of the Catholic Church are listed: The Rosary, the Way of the Cross, and other spiritual exercises which holy Church had enriched with Indulgences. Indulgences were the key that Catholics once turned to open the door to heaven with the utmost speed, or to gain freedom from purgatory for themselves or relatives and friends who had died. In addition to these devotions, the nuns were to 'pray for the triumph of the Church, the propagation of the faith, the extirpation of heresy and schism, the conversion of heathens, infidels and sinners, the perseverance of the just and the deliverance of the souls in Purgatory'.[4] Norms written into the community's Constitutions and Declarations are not optional.

The Benedictine Rule has no teaching on the Eucharist or the Catholic Mass. The editors of RB80 agree that the Eucharist is summed up in the word *communio*, which occurs three times, 'but never in the

---

2   Night watching was adoration of the Blessed Sacrament, hour by hour. The nuns were rostered, and therefore lived with interrupted sleep.
3   Beuronese Constitutions, Chapter 20, Declaration 1.
4   In Addis, et al., *Catholic Dictionary*, 483, heresy is described under several headings: heresy in the Scriptures, heresy according to the *Summa* of Thomas Aquinas, and formal heresy. This last is 'a most grievous sin, for it involves rebellion against God, who requires us to submit our understandings to the doctrine of His church. This guilt, if externally manifested, is visited by the Church with the greater excommunication, absolution from which, except in the articles of death, can only be given by the Pope'.

Liturgical Code'.⁵ In RB80, the

> monks are directed to approach the 'kiss of peace' and the 'communion' according to their rank in the community. Almost certainly this is a reference to the reception of the Eucharist. But it does not necessarily refer to the celebration of Mass.⁶

The devotion towards the Eucharist, a devotion which the nuns of Subiaco were to willingly cultivate, had its own history originating in the Seventeenth Century. Books of devotions to the Blessed Sacrament were used across the Catholic world. One book, printed in 1910 and used by members of the Subiaco community, is a compilation of prayers from the Liturgy, the writings of the saints, and the *Paradisus Animae*. The *Paradisus Animae* contains three pages on the Scriptural texts referring to the Eucharist and ten pages on the Eucharistic teachings of the Popes and Church Councils, beginning with the Council of Trent and the Decree of 1679. Such devotion was world-wide, and not the priority of Benedictine nuns or any other religious congregation. The difference between the Subiaco community's participation in this devotion, and that of an ordinary Catholic in a parish, is that for the nuns the espousal concept was the driving force of their prayer. It is also stated in Chapter 63:1 of the community constitutions, that 'On days when the Blessed Sacrament is exposed for adoration they will offer their homage to the King and *Bridegroom of their hearts* with the greatest devotion and zeal'.⁷ This was the spirituality of the thirty-year term of Prioress Mary Joseph Brady.

Lawson as a foundation house of Subiaco

Prior to the selling of the monastery at Lawson in 1949, a situation arose which was in conflict with the precepts of the Benedictine Rule and the tradition of Benedictine life. Since 1930, when Cadia Park was

---

5   Fry, *RB 1980*, Liturgical Code in the Rule of Benedict, Appendix 3, 170.
6   RB80, Chapter 63, v. 4.
7   Italics added. Jesus Christ was the Spouse of each nun. Written inside the ring given to a nun on her solemn monastic profession day are the words: 'I am espoused to Him whom angels serve'.

purchased, several nuns had suggested to Prioress Brady that Lawson become a foundation monastery separate from Subiaco. After thoroughly discussing the pros and cons of such a suggestion the Chapter (the body of solemnly professed nuns) determined that the suggestion was not a wise one. Listening, discernment, and discussion had led to the decision.[8]

However, Sr Mary Editha Thompson, appointed Lawson superior by the prioress at Subiaco, continued to hold a strong desire for Lawson to be made a foundation house of Subiaco with its own prioress, completely separate from Subiaco. The superior was in a friendship with a lay woman in the Lawson parish, a woman who was wealthy and could help the Lawson house with whatever was needed in the way of maintenance. In return, the superior promised to provide permanent accommodation for the lay woman in the front of the Lawson house (the original house built in 1913). The superior wrote to Cardinal Gilroy to the effect that the prioress at Subiaco was in the wrong for not agreeing to make Lawson a foundation monastery.[9] The Cardinal then wrote to Prioress Potts asking her for her reasons for objecting to this proposal. Not having any previous information about the proposal, she made the journey to Lawson to discuss how this matter had reached the point it had.

The monastic theology and spirituality of Columba Marmion, OSB.

Prioress Potts found stability of spirituality in the books of Columba Marmion. His writings reflected the neo-monastic revival of the Nineteenth Century. In 1909 Marmion was elected Abbot of Maredsous in Belgium. The abbey of Maredsous was founded from Beuron, which was in turn founded from Solesmes, the very heart of the revival. Subiaco had already been influenced by the revival movement of Beuron and Solesmes, after Prioress Wallis had encountered Placid and Maurus Wolter during her trip to Europe in 1876–77 (p. 148). Columba

---

8   Community Chronicles, 21 January 1946.
9   A copy of this letter has not been found in the Jamberoo Abbey Archives, but a reference to it is found in the Community Chronicles, 21 January 1946.

Marmion brought together the teaching of the decades of renewal in three books. It was Marmion's book, *Christ The Ideal of the Monk*, that spoke most powerfully to Prioress Potts and to the community of that time. The book was a combination of monastic spirituality, monastic theology, and Christology. It was written by a Benedictine for Benedictines.[10] *Christ the Ideal of the Monk* is exhortative, comparative, and practical. In his chapter on the Liturgy of the Hours (the work of God for Benedictines), he draws a comparison between the monk, or nun, at prayer, and the religious woman, or man, at work on the mission field. Monks and nuns at prayer, like the missionaries, should work without counting the cost: 'God loves generosity in His service, but, according to the energetic expression of Scripture, He vomits the tepid, those who are indifferent to the interests of His glory and those of souls'.[11]

Marmion begins this work with a chapter on seeking God, before moving on to the Christology of the Benedictine rule, and then a chapter on faith, as the necessary condition of all life and all spiritual progress. On this occasion, his comparison is with the root of a majestic tree:

> Look at a majestic tree, with mighty trunk, vigorous branches and abundant foliage. Whence comes to it this strength and beauty? From something unseen: the roots. These are plunged in the soil there to take a firm hold and draw the nourishing sap necessary to the life of this giant. Should the roots dry up, the tree will decay.[12]

Marmion also teaches the Benedictine vows in the same style: their meaning, their application, what is acceptable and what is not. His work was formative for the nuns of Subiaco through the Chapter talks of their prioress—yet another example of their readiness to listen to the teaching of the Holy Spirit at work in their midst.

---

10   Marmion's other popular work, *Union with God*, was a collection of his letters to Benedictine and Carmelite nuns, and lay women.
11   Marmion, *Christ*, 333, alluding to Christ's words to the church of Laodicea (Rev. 3:16).
12   Marmion, *Christ,* 95.

Post-World War II novitiate

The post-war novitiate began on 11 July 1946. There is no record of a woman entering the community during the Second World War. The first vocation after the war was Patricia O'Shea (Sr Mary Cecilia), who entered officially after First Vespers of the Solemnity of St Benedict (July 11th).[13] She was born in Australia, of Australian parents who lived in the New England district of New South Wales. Her education was with the Ursuline Nuns[14] in Armidale, until the Depression of the 1930s began to take its toll on the O'Shea family and caused a move to Arncliffe in Sydney, where there were more possibilities for work. Patricia had to forfeit higher education, and take employment to help support her family and extended family, who had come together in the one house in order to survive the rigours of the time.[15] Her work was with the Gestetner Company of Sydney. Impressed with her ability, they trained her as an accountant, which skill was of great use later in monastic life.[16]

Sr Patricia O'Shea OSB, **Sr Marie Gregory Forster** OSB, **and Sr Elizabeth Funder** OSB, **c. 1949**

13 Canonical records for Sr Mary Cecilia O'Shea.
14 The Ursulines were founded in Italy in 1535, and came to Australia in 1882. Armidale was their first foundation; cf. MacGinley, *A Dynamic of Hope,* Table 1, 343.
15 Information given to the then prioress of Subiaco, Mildred Potts.
16 In 1973, she was appointed Cellarer. In a Benedictine community, there is a Cellarer and a Bursar. The Cellarer deals directly with the members of the community and their needs. The Bursar pays the invoices and deals with pension money, investments and interest.

Sr Marie Margaret Forster, who became Sr Marie Gregory, was the second vocation immediately after World War II. She entered on 14 September (the Exaltation of the Holy Cross) 1946. Marie Forster was awarded her Bachelor of Arts degree at the University of Sydney on 17 June 1944, majoring in History. This was her passion and over many years of monastic life her writings expressed the fruits of her research. Prior to her entering the monastery, she had done extensive research on the history of Lyndhurst Academy and its students.

The third woman to enter the monastery after World War II was Australian-born Elizabeth Funder, also a graduate of the University of Sydney. Her introduction to the Benedictines of Subiaco was through Fr John McCrystal, who took Catholic university students who were members of the Newman Society on the occasional pilgrimage to the monastery after the war years.[17] Sr Elizabeth Funder entered the monastery in 1947.

Prioress Mildred Potts and the Community with Cardinal Norman Gilroy celebrating the centenary, 1949.

17 The first record of these pilgrimages with names of students is for 26 October 1946. The Newman Society organised this pilgrimage to honour Archbishop Vaughan, whose body had been recently brought from England to be re-interred in the crypt at St Mary's Cathedral (23 October 1946).

All three women gave themselves to the sincere living of monastic life. For all the embrace of modernity, Sr Elizabeth Funder recalled that Prioress Potts had a strong grasp on the Benedictine tradition and on monastic theology, grounded in the books of Columba Marmion.

Post-war industrial development

By the 1930s the area around the Subiaco monastery had begun to attract heavy industry. After demobilisation, the post-war era saw a significant increase in manufacturing, building materials, and equipment. Of all the industrial companies in the area, it was Rheem, manufacturers of hot water heaters, which most effected dramatic changes in the monastic life of the nuns of Subiaco. In the early 1950s, Rheem sought a site with a rail siding, water, good transport, and located near a housing area, suitable for factory workers. The land at Rydalmere met all of these requirements and in 1953 the company moved to their new site at Rydalmere.[18] Rheem also purchased the Subiaco cemetery, which meant that fifty-four graves had to be disinterred and re-interred at the North Rocks Catholic Cemetery.[19] Before this event, and attuned to the pace of industrial development, Prioress Brady bought a burial plot for the nuns at The Field of Mars Cemetery.[20]

With the arrival of Rheem and other companies, the continuity of tradition and charism was affected negatively by the close proximity of industrial noise. The Liturgy of the Hours, work, and a spirit of silence were punctuated with the noise of machinery. The metal dust settling on furniture daily provided all the evidence of a health hazard for the Subiaco community. Sleep was disturbed by machinery through the night and 'the whistle of the good train'.[21] It appears that legislation governing industrial noise was not an issue in the 1950s. Noise however was a growing public concern. The *Daily Telegraph* of 21 May 1950 carried the following:

18 Rheem Australia Limited, *The History*.
19 The nuns agreed to this, so that the graves would not be built over by industrial factories.
20 The Benedictine community has four places of burial: North Rocks Catholic Cemetery, Field of Mars Cemetery, Castle Hill Lawn Cemetery, and Jamberoo Abbey Cemetery.
21 Elizabeth Funder, 'Memoirs', 58. This is an unpublished document.

Our health experts declare war on noise! The Federal Health Department is about to make an exhaustive survey of the effects of industrial noises on individuals. A State Health Dept. film aims to develop communal concern about noise.[22]

Noise was one of the major factors in the consideration of a relocation. The prioress worked closely with a local real estate agent who had a knowledge of available and suitable land away from encroaching industry, or at that time, suburbia. The property settled on was 'Hillcrest' in West Pennant Hills. It consisted of forty-five acres, giving the community a healthy alternative to Rydalmere. Prioress Potts, always aware of the Benedictine *labora*, saw that this property was in an area where it was convenient for priests or parish workers to collect and deliver altar breads. This had become the main work and income of the community. The sewing and embroidering of liturgical vestments continued, as did the making of altar breads for many of the parishes of Sydney.

Benedictine Abbey, West Pennant Hills

22 'Our Health Experts Declare War on Noise', *The Daily Telegraph*, 21 May 1950, 9.

Relocation

Subiaco was sold to the Sylvestrine Benedictine Monks, who also established a school as a means of earning a living. The nuns relocated to 'Hillcrest', in Franklin Road West Pennant Hills in 1957. The property was owned by the Hughes family for generations and sold in 1950 to Dr Darcy Williams. Prioress Potts, acting for the Subiaco community, purchased the property on 16 August 1954. In preparation for the move, from 1954 until 1957 some of the nuns took garden cuttings and trees in an attempt at continuity. Vegetable and flower gardens were established. Overall, the garden was a 'European' garden, with many exotic trees. When purchased it was a citrus orchard of forty-five acres. Gradually the orchard was reduced in size until in the end only a few stone fruit and citrus trees were kept for the use of the community.[23] The relocation day for the community came on 19 December, 1957. Faithful to the Benedictine liturgical tradition, the 'Hour' of *None*[24] (mid-afternoon) was prayed at Subiaco, and the 'Hour' of Vespers[25] was celebrated at the new Benedictine monastery in West Pennant Hills.[26]

Prioress Mildred Potts died in office in 1968. Towards the end of her life, a group of nuns wrote to Cardinal Gilroy, complaining that she was holding back the changes of the Second Vatican Council. Only one nun showed her the letter she was sending. Gilroy ordered a Canonical Visitation to address the contents of the letters. During this visitation, the prioress had a stroke and died, and therefore did not have to face the Canonical visitors. Cancer was also a factor in her death. Prioress Placid (Edna) Wilson was elected in her place.[27]

---

23   Community Chronicles 1954–1957.
24   '*None*' is the traditional monastic name for the Liturgical prayer at the ninth hour of daylight.
25   Evening Prayer.
26   After Rheem's demolition of Subiaco in 1961, the columns of the house were relocated to adorn the entrance walkway to the University of New South Wales. https://mhnsw.au/stories/general/architectural-remnants-vineyard-subiaco/; https://digitalcollections.library.unsw.edu.au.
27   Record of canonical elections.

CONCLUSION

This story began in the 6th Century with Benedict of Nursia, his Rule for Monasteries and the first word of that Rule: *obsculta* (listen carefully). Writing for monastics of the 21st century, Chittister says: '...listening is a spiritual discipline, a step toward full moral maturity, a parallel path to the demands of tradition tried and true. To listen and be listened to, the Rule of Benedict assures us, is an invitation to rethink what we have always thought to be absolute but now know, thanks to the experience and honesty of others, must be rethought'.[1] The continuity of charism and tradition in Benedictine history is able to live and flow only in a listening heart and a listening community. Aquinata Böckman says that 'for Benedict, listening is the fundamental attitude from which all other attitudes flow'.[2] Chittister takes her readers to a challenging depth when she says:

> Life is a teacher of universal truths. That may be the reason why the religious readings of so many nations speak of the same situations and fasten on the same insights. The Rule of Benedict… deals with answers to the great questions of the human condition: the presence of God, the foundation of relationships, the nature of self-development and the place of purpose. To the wise, it seems, life is not a series of events to be controlled. Life is a way of walking through the universe whole and holy.[3]

---

1 Chittister, *Monastic Heart*, 144.
2 Böckmann, *Listening Community*, 6.
3 Chittister, *Rule of Benedict*, 19.

Walking through the universe whole and holy is walking as a listener, attentive and aware that one is walking in a procession of continuity. The first women who began Benedictine life in a Colonial house on the bend of the Parramatta river in 1849, brought their *obsculta* to an ancient land, whose Indigenous people knew inner deep listening, an awareness of nature:

> a mode of contemplation that is turned outwards… turned outwards to the land and the things about [them], but deeply conscious of the living springs within.
>
> *Dadirri.*
> Inner deep listening and quiet awareness. Waiting patiently for what is surely coming. There may be sounds,. There may be silence.
>
> *Dadirri.*
> Listen. The world is full of words. Wait patiently. The sunrise is coming.
> A deep theme is unfolding.[4]

Senior Australian of the Year 2021, Dr. Miriam Rose Ungenmerr-Baumann teaches that *dadirri* recognizes the deep spring that is inside us, and taps into that deep spring. She adds: 'This is the gift that Australia is thirsting for. It is something like what we call "contemplation"'.[5] Coming from a teacher, an artist, and respected elder, this shouldn't be taken lightly. This thirst that Dr. Ungenmerr-Baumann refers to is expressed by the Australian religious poet, James Macauley, in his Letter to John Dryden: 'Incarnate Word in whom all nature lives, cast flame upon the earth. Raise up contemplatives among us, those who walk within the fire of ceaseless prayer, impetuous desire. Set pools of silence in this thirsty land'.[6]

For 175 years in Australia, the Benedictine nuns have lived in a spirit of inner deep listening and awareness, in the spirit of *obsculta*,

---

4   Cameron, *Alcheringa*, 24.
5   https:llwww.miriam rosefoundation.org.au.
6   Murray, *Anthology*, 166–174.

'within the fire of ceaseless prayer, impetuous desire'. They have embraced the ancient land that embraced them and have trodden lightly upon that land, first populated by the Burramatagal Nation, (Rydalmere), the Dharug Nation (West Pennant Hills), and today at Jamberoo on the land of the Dharawal Nation. The monastic women of today continue the journey begun on February 2, 1849—the procession of continuity—'whole and holy'.[7]

7   Chittister, *Rule of Benedict*, 19.

BIBLIOGRAPHY

PRIMARY SOURCES

ARCHIVES

JAA	Jamberoo Abbey Archives: Jamberoo, N.S.W.
Moore	Moore College Library
MSA	Archives of the Sisters of St Joseph North Sydney
PPA	Princethorpe Priory Archives: now kept at Douai Abbey, Upper Woolhampton, Reading, Berkshire,, England.
SAA	Sydney Catholic Archdiocesan Archives: Sydney, N.S.W.
StAA	Stanbrook Abbey Archives: Yorkshire, England.

DOCUMENT COLLECTIONS

Archbishop of Sydney and the Hierarchy of New South Wales
    Decrees of the Fourth Plenary Council, concerning Religious Sisters and Brothers and Catholic Schools of the Archdiocese of Sydney. JAA

Pope Pius X *1917 Codex Iuris Canonici*. JAA

NEWSPAPERS

https://trove.nla.gov.au

PRIVATE DOCUMENTS IN THE CUSTODY OF THE ABBESS OF JAMBEROO ABBEY, NSW

Copies of all Vow Papers of nuns in solemn vows from the foundation of the community in 1849 until the present. JAA

Rules, Rituals, Customs and Constitutions of Benedictine Nuns

Ceremonial Monastique pour Les Religieuses de Notre-Dame Des Anges De Montargis, Ordre De S. Benoit. 1706. JAA

Baker, Augustine, OSB	*Commentary on the Rule of Benedict.* Manuscript. JAA
Subiaco Monastery	*Book of Customs.* JAA
Subiaco Monastery	*Constitutions of St. Mary's Priory*, Princethorpe. JAA
Subiaco Monastery	Copy of *Beuronese Constitutions.* JAA
Subiaco Monastery	*Declarationes et Constitutiones Monialium* OSB. 1922. JAA

St Mary's (Sydney) Rules

Declarations of St. Mary's, 1855 (Liverpool: Rockliff and Sons, 1855). JAA

Kavenagh, Terence	'The 1855 Monastic Declarations of St. Mary's Sydney: Adapting RB to Colonial Australia? Part 1: The history', *Tjurunga* 34 (1988), 65–74.
Kavenagh, Terence	'The 1855 Monastic Declarations of St. Mary's Sydney: Adapting RB to Colonial Australia? Part 3', *Tjurunga* 36 (1989), 73–80.
Kavenagh, Terence	'The 1855 Monastic Declarations of St. Mary's Sydney: Adapting RB to Colonial Australia? Part 4', *Tjurunga* 38 (1990), 88–96.
Kavenagh, Terence	'The 1855 Monastic Declarations of St. Mary's Sydney: Adapting RB to Colonial Australia? Part 5: The history', *Tjurunga* 39 (1990), 114–126.
Walker, Graeme, and Terence Kavenagh	'The 1855 Monastic Declarations of St. Mary's Sydney: Adapting RB to Colonial Australia? Part 2', *Tjurunga* 35 (1988), 44–80.

TRANSLATION OF BENEDICTINE RULE

Fry, Timothy (ed.) — *RB 1980: The Rule of Benedict in Latin and English with Notes* (Collegeville, MN: Liturgical Press, 1981).

UNPUBLISHED COLLECTIONS, PAPERS

Brady, Prioress Mary Joseph — Transcribed copies of letters written from Europe and England to the Subiaco Community. 15 April, 1925–15 June, 1926. JAA. Brady, Prioress Mary Joseph Papers

[Christesen, Clem] — 'The Family of Hugh and Sarah Byrne'. Unpublished manuscript in the possession of Dr Clem Christesen.

Christensen, Joseph — 'The Romantic Figure of Jose Guillermo Hay, an Early Western Australian Conservationist.' Unpublished paper presented to the Royal Western Australian Historical Society on 20 April, 2005. JAA.

Community Chronicles — 1849–1925 (unpaginated). JAA

Congress of Benedictine Abbots — A Statement on Benedictine Life, adopted by the Congress of Benedictine Abbots, held in Rome, September 1967. Translated into English by the monks and nuns of the English Benedictine Congregation, 1967.

Forster, Marie, OSB — 'Compilation of extracts from the *St. Mary's Monastic Journal*, concerning the Benedictine Nuns of *Subiaco*: 1848–1856'. JAA

Forster, Marie, OSB — *Subiaco Resource Book*, Volume 1, 2 and 3. Printed at the Benedictine Abbey, Jamberoo. JAA

Forster, Marie, OSB, and Ann Prendergast — 'Alumnae Subiaco' (compiled in the 1990s). JAA (Box: 'Subiaco School').

Funder, Elizabeth — 'Memoirs'. Unpublished manuscript, JAA.

Gregory, Scholastica (Jane), OSB Small collection of transcribed letters written from *Subiaco* to Princethorpe Priory, Warwickshire, England. 1848–1850. PPA and JAA

Le Clerc, Magdalen (Constantia) Transcribed copies of original letters written from *Subiaco* to Stanbrook Abbey, England. 1848–1878. StAA and JAA (Box marked: 'Magdalen le Clerc. LETTERS').

Jamberoo Abbey *Pax. With the Gospel for our Guide*

Advent/Christmastide (2021–2022), and Ordinary Time Through To Ash Wednesday, 2 March, 2022. https://www.jamberooabbey.org.au/wp-content/uploads/2021/12/PAX-Advent-Christmas-to-Ash-Wed.pdf

Post-Pentecost 1 2022. https://www.jamberooabbey.org.au/wp-content/uploads/2022/07/pxpent1.pdf.

Moran Letters Sydney Catholic Archdiocesan Archives.

Nunan, Terry and Wendy Dame Mary Clare (Florence Eugenie) Gabriel. Her Ancestry and Family Tree. Compiled: 2007–2008. JAA

Smythe Chronicles Community Chronicles kept by Sr Mildred Smythe, 1903–1931. JAA

Stanbrook Abbey Stanbrook Abbey Chronicles. StAA

See also Records of Stanbrook Abbey. https://nla.gov.au/nla.obj-1127486185/findingaid

Wallis, Prioress Walburge (Ruth Woods) Transcribed copies of original letters written from Europe and England, to the community at *Subiaco* during two absences: 1876–1877 and 1888–1889. JAA

Waterhouse papers Documents related to 'The Vineyard' 1790 to 1820, from the papers of Thomas Moore. Moore College Library, Sydney. Collection 084/1 - Papers of Captain Henry Waterhouse.

	http://atom.library.moore.edu.au/index.php/papers-of-captain-henry-waterhouse, for index, originals, and transcriptions.
Whelan, Basil, OSB	*Annals of the English Congregation of Black Monks of the Order of St. Benedict 1850–1900* (unpublished typescript, 1932; slightly augmented in 1942, and re-issued in 1971). Although the publisher is not noted, it could have been printed by any of the Benedictine houses of England, perhaps Ampleforth, Whelan's own Abbey.

SECONDARY SOURCES

[*ADB*]	'Grey, Sir George (1812–1898)', Australian Dictionary of Biography, National Centre of Biography, Australian National University, https://adb.anu.edu.au/biography/grey-sir-george-2125/text2691, published first in hardcopy 1966 (Volume 1).
Addis, William, and Thomas Arnold	*A Catholic Dictionary* (London: Paul Kegan, Trench, Trübner & Co. Ltd., 1909).
Andrews, Brian	*Creating a Gothic Paradise, Pugin in the Antipodes* (Hobart: Museum and Art Gallery, 2002).
Augustine, P. Chas, OSB	*A Commentary on the New Canon Law* (London: B. Herder Book Co., 1919).
Austen, Jane	*Pride and Prejudice* (Middlesex: Penguin, 1972).
Ayrinhac, Henry Amans	*Penal Legislation in the New Code of Canon Law* (Liber V) (New York: Benziger brothers, 1920). Archive.org.
Barcan, Alan	'Education for a Liberal Democracy, 1856–1866: The Hunter Valley', *Journal of the Royal Australia Historical Society* 97 (2011), 66–83.

Barth, Karl	'Fearless', in E. Busch (selector), *Insights. Karl Barth's Reflections on the Life of Faith* (O.C. Dean, jnr., transl. Louisville, KY: Westminster, 2009 [German: 2001]), 12, from *Der Götze wackelt. Zeitkritische Aufsätze, Reden und Briefe von 1930 bis 1960* (Berlin: Vogt, 1961), 159–61.
Bartley, Nehemiah	*Australian Pioneers and Reminiscences, 1849–1894* (Sydney: John Ferguson, in association with the Royal Australian Historical Society, 1978).
Beaumont, Joan (ed.)	*Australia's War, 1914–1918* (St Leonards, NSW: Allen & Unwin, 1996).
Bede	*A History of the English Church and People* (Leo Sherley-Price, trans. and introduction; London: Penguin, 1990).
Bellinger, Dom Aidan	'The English Benedictines: The Search for a Monastic Identity, 1880–1920', in Judith Loades (ed.), *Monastic Studies, the Continuity of Tradition* (Bangor: Headstart History, 1990), 299–321.
Birt, Henry Norbert	*Benedictine Pioneers in Australia, Volumes 1 and 2* (London: Herbert and Daniel, 1911).
Birt, Henry Norbert	*History of Downside School* (London: Paul Kegan, Trench, Trübner & Co. Ltd, 1902).
Blainey, Geoffrey	*A Land Half Won* (Melbourne: Sun Books, 1983).
Böckmann, Aquinata, OSB	*A Listening Community. A Commentary on the Prologue and Chapters 1–3 of Benedict's Rule* (Matilda Handl, OSB, and Marianne Burkhard, OSB, transls.; Marianne Burkhard, OSB, ed.; Collegeville, MN: Liturgical Press, 2015 [German: 2011]).

Böckmann, Aquinata, OSB *Perspectives on the Rule of Benedict. Expanding our Hearts in Christ* (Matilda Handl, OSB, and Marianne Burkhard, OSB, transls.; Marianne Burkhard, OSB, ed.; Collegeville, MN: Liturgical Press, 2005 [German: 1986]).

Böckmann, Aquinata, OSB *Around the Monastic Table. Growing in Mutual Service and Love* (Matilda Handl, OSB, and Marianne Burkhard, OSB, transls.; Marianne Burkhard, OSB, ed.; Collegeville, MN: Liturgical Press, 2009).

Boland, Thomas Patrick *James Duhig* (Brisbane: Queensland University Press, 1986).

Bolt, Peter G. 'Moore and the Merino', *Thomas Moore of Liverpool: One of our Oldest Colonists. Essays & Addresses to Celebrate 150 Years of Moore College* (Studies in Australian Colonial History, No. 1; Camperdown, NSW: Bolt Publishing Services, 2007), 43–59.

Bolton, G. C. 'Stokes, John Lort (1812–1885)', Australian Dictionary of Biography, National Centre of Biography, Australian National University, https://adb.anu.edu.au/biography/stokes-john-lort-2703/text3793, published first in hardcopy 1967 (Volume 2).

Botsman, Peter *The Great Constitutional Swindle: A Citizen's View of the Australian Constitution* (Sydney: Pluto Press, 2000).

Breward, Ian *A History of the Australian Churches* (Sydney: Allen & Unwin, 1993).

Brownrigg, Jeff 'Notes on Sir Richard Bourke in Australia', *Journal of the Royal Australian Historical Society*, 127 (2016), 2–4.

Burke, Janine *Australian Women Artists, 1840–1940* (Melbourne: Greenhouse Publications, 1975).

Butler, Cuthbert	*Benedictine Monachism: Studies in Benedictine Life and Rule* (London: Longmans, Green, 1919).
Butler, J. B.	'Jean Gourbeillon: A French Sculptor in Nineteenth-Century Sydney', *Tjurunga* 67 (2004), 35–47.
Bygott, U., and K. J. Cable	*Pioneer Women Graduates of the University of Sydney, 1881–1921* (Sydney: University of Sydney Press, 1985).
Byrne, John Henry	'Sacred or Profane, the influence of Vatican Legislation in the Catholic Archdiocese of Melbourne 1843–1938'. A thesis submitted in partial fulfilment of the requirements of the degree of Master of Music (Australian Catholic University, 2005).
Cahill, A. E.	'Archbishop Vaughan and St. John's College', *Australian Catholic Historical Society Journal* 14 (2015), 36–49.
Cahill, A. E.	'Cardinal Moran and Australian Federation', *The Australian Catholic Record* 78 (2001), 3–15.
Cameron, Rod	*Alcheringa: The Australian Experience of the Sacred* (Sydney: St Paul's, 1995).
Campbell, Craig, and Helen Proctor	*A History of Australian Schooling* (Sydney: Allen & Unwin, 2014).
Campion, Edmund	*Australian Catholics* (Sydney: Viking, 1987).
Campion, Edmund	*Rockchoppers: Growing up Catholic in Australia* (Ringwood: Penguin Books, 1982).
Cannon, Mary	*Chronicles of Australian Contemporary History* (Melbourne: Addison Wesley Longman, 1996).
Cannon, Michael	*Australia in the Victorian Age, Volume Three — Life in the Cities* (Sydney: Thomas Nelson, 1975).

Casey, Michael, OSCO	'Community and Tradition', *Tjurunga* 4 (1973), 45–58.
Casey, Michael, OSCO	'The Dynamic Unfolding of the Benedictine Charism', *American Benedictine Review* 51 (2000), 149–167.
Casey, Michael, OSCO	'The Hermeneutics of Tradition', *Tjurunga* 5 (1973), 39–50.
Casey, Michael, OSCO	'Leadership in a Benedictine Context: An Interrogation of Tradition', *Tjurunga* 22 (1982), 5–103.
Casey, Michael, OSCO	'The Rule of Benedict and Inculturation: A formation perspective', *Tjurunga* 62 (2002), 445–490.
Casey, Michael, OSCO	'Tradition, Interpretation, Reform. The Western Monastic Experience', *American Benedictine Review* 69.4 (2018), 400–428.
Chapman, Fr. John	*St. Benedict and the Sixth Century* (London: Longman, Green, 1929).
Chittister, Joan	*The Monastic Heart: 50 Simple Practices for a Contemplative and Fulfilling Life* (New York: Convergent, 2021).
Chittister, Joan	*The Rule of Benedict: Insights for the Ages* (New York: Crossroad, 1995).
Clark, Charles Manning Hope	*A History of Australia. IV. The Earth Abideth For Ever. 1851–1888* (Melbourne: Melbourne University Press, 1978).
Clear, Catriona	*Nuns in Nineteenth-Century Ireland* (Dublin: Gill and Macmillan; Washington, D.C.: The Catholic University Press, 1987).
Cleary, P. S.	*Australia's Debt to Irish Nation-Builders* (Sydney: Angus & Robertson, 1933).
Connolly, George	'Catherine Heydon, 1858–1868. From Subiaco to Carcoar', *Journal of the Australian Catholic Historical Society* 25 (2004), 19–47.

Cross, F.L. (ed.) *Oxford Dictionary of the Christian Church* (London; New York, NY: Oxford University Press, 1958). Articles cited: 'Benediction of the Blessed Sacrament', 156; 'Candelmas', 226; 'Connolly, Richard Hugh (1873–1948)', 330–331; 'Litany of Loreto', 813; 'Oratorians', 985–986; 'Teresa of Lisieux, St. (1873–1897)', 1332–1333.

Cross, F.L., and E.A. Livingstone (eds.) *Oxford Dictionary of the Christian Church, 3rd edition* (Oxford: Oxford University Press, 2005; Online: 2009).

Cruesen, J. *Religious Men and Women in Church Law* (Milwaukee, WI: Bruce Publishing Company, 1958).

Curtin, J. C., P. W. Joyce, P. D. Nunan, J. T. Ryan, and N. M. O'Donnell *Irish Heraldry, Topography and Modern History, Parts I and II* (Dublin; New York, NY: Murphy and McCarthy, 1904).

D'Arcy, Anthony 'O'Haran, Denis Francis (1854–1931)', Australian Dictionary of Biography, National Centre of Biography, Australian National University, https://adb.anu.edu.au/biography/oharan-denis-francis-7894/text13727, published first in hardcopy in 1988 (Volume 11).

Daly, R.A. 'Makinson, Thomas Cooper (1809–1893)'. Australian Dictionary of Biography, National Centre of Biography, Australian National University, https://adb.anu.edu.au/biography/makinson-thomas-cooper-2423/text3219. Published first in hardcopy in 1967 (Volume 2).

Davies, J. G. (ed.) *Dictionary of Liturgy and Worship* (London: SCM Press, 1972).

Delatte, Dom Paul, OSB	*The Rule of Benedict, A Commentary* (London: Burns, Oates and Washbourne, 1921).
Dictionary of Sydney	'Rydalmere'. https://dictionaryofsydney.org/place/rydalmere.
Donnelly, D.	'Listening and the Rule of St. Benedict', *American Benedictine Review* 46 (1995), 169–182.
Dowd, Christopher, OP	*Rome in Australia. The Papacy and Conflict in the Australian Catholic Missions, 1834–1884* (Boston/Leiden: Brill, 2008).
Duffy, C. J.	'O'Mahony, Timothy (1825–1892)', Australian Dictionary of Biography, National Centre of Biography, Australian National University, https://adb.anu.edu.au/biography/omahony-timothy-4332/text7031, published first in hardcopy 1974 (Volume 5).
Dunn, Judith, OAM, FRDHS, and Rosemarie Morris FRDHS	*The Parramatta Cemeteries. Saint Paul's, Carlingford, including Private and Demolished Cemeteries of the Parramatta Area* (Parramatta District Historical Society Inc. Sydney: Inscope Books, 2017).
Dunstan, A. J.	'Thomas John Butler, 1857–1937', Australian Dictionary of Biography, National Centre of Biography, Australian National University, https://adb.anu.edu.au/biography/butler-thomas-john-5450/text9255, published first in hardcopy 1979 (Volume 7).
Dutton, Geoffrey	*Queen Emma of the South Seas: A Novel* (New York: St. Martin's Press, 1977).
Earls, Tony	*Plunkett's Legacy. An Irishman's contribution to the Rule of Law in New South Wales* (Melbourne: Australian Scholarly Publishing, 2009).

Engwerda, Robert	*Conscription: Australia during World War I* (Melbourne: Education Centre, State Library of Victoria, 1993).
Evangelista, Amber Graciana	'"… From squalor and vice to virtue and knowledge …": the rise of Melbourne's Ragged School system', *Provenance: The Journal of Public Record Office Victoria*, issue no. 14, 2015. https://prov.vic.gov.au/explore-collection/provenance-journal/provenance-2015/squalor-and-vice-virtue-and-knowledge.
Farmer, David Hugh (ed.)	*Benedict's Disciples* (Herefordshire: Fowler Wright Books, 1980).
Farrell, John Joseph	'Archbishop Vaughan and the Resignation of Bishop O'Mahony, First Bishop of Armidale', *Journal of the Australian Catholic Historical Society* 15 (1993), 7–23.
Feiss, Hugh	*Essential Monastic Wisdom: Writings on the Contemplative Life* (New York, NY: Harper Collins, 1999).
Fitzwalter, Pauline, SGS	'Archbishop Polding and Mary: An Attempt to Ascertain the Archbishop's Awareness of Mary', *The Australasian Catholic Record*, 54 (1977), 32–42.
Fletcher, Brian H.	*Australian History in New South Wales, 1888–1988* (Sydney: UNSW Press, 1993).
Fletcher, J. J.	*Clean, Clad and Courteous: A History of Aboriginal Education in New South Wales* (Sydney: J. J. Fletcher, 1989).
Fogarty, F. M. S.	*Catholic Education in Australia, 1806–1950* (Vol. I. Melbourne: Melbourne University Press, 1959).

Forster, Marie	'Fragment of a Diary kept by Sr. Mary Scholastica Gregory, on her Voyage from Liverpool England, to Sydney, Australia: 1847–1848', *Tjurunga* 26 (1984), 52–72.
Forster, Marie	'Lyndhurst and Benedictine Education', *The Australasian Catholic Record* 23 (October 1946), 67–71.
Forster, Marie	'Magdalen le Clerc', *Tjurunga* 8 (1974), 259–337.
Forster, Marie	'Monks-Missionaries-Mission in 19th Century Australia', *Tjurunga* 14 (1977), 39–74.
Fortescue, A.	'Some Notes on Fasting', *The Tablet* (21 September, 1918), 206–207.
Foucault, Michael	*Archaeology of Knowledge* (Routledge Classics; London: Taylor and Francis, 2002 [French: 1969]).
Foulcher, Jane	*Reclaiming Humility: Four Studies in the Monastic Tradition* (Collegeville, MN: Liturgical Press, 2015).
Fowler C. F. (ed.)	*At Sea with Bishop John Bede Polding. The Journals of Lewis Harding. 1835 (Liverpool to Sydney); 1846 (Sydney to London)* (transcribed and edited with an introduction by C. F. Fowler; Adelaide: ATF Publishing, 2019).
Fox, Brian	'Joseph Hay, One of Lawson's Pioneers', *Blue Mountains History Journal* 1 (2010), 16–25.
Freeman, James.	'Two Hundred Years of Devotion to Our Lady Help of Christians in Australia', *Journal of the Catholic Historical Society* 10 (1988), 43–46.
Fremantle, Anne (ed.)	*The Papal Encyclicals in their Historical Context. The Teaching of the Popes from Peter to John XXIII* (New York, NY: Mentor-Omega, 1956, 1963).

Ganley, Maree — *The Long Road to School. Sea Pictures of a Convent Boarding School: St. Ursula's Yeppoon, founded in 1917* (Northgate, QLD: Maree Ganley, 2020).

Godden, Judith — 'Hospitals', Dictionary of Sydney, 2008. http://dictionaryofsydney.org/entry/hospitals.

Green, Bernard OSB — *The English Benedictine Congregation* (London: Catholic Truth Society, 1979).

Gregory the Great — *Life and Miracles of St. Benedict, Book Two of the Dialogues* (translated by O. J. Zimmerman, OSB., and B. R. Avery, OSB; Collegeville, MN: Liturgical Press, 1949).

Grimshaw, Patricia, Marilyn Lake, Ann McGrath, and Marian Quartly — *Creating A Nation, 1788–1990* (London: Penguin Books, 1994).

Grocott, Allan M. — *Convicts, Clergymen and Churches: Attitudes of Convicts towards the Churches and Clergy in New South Wales from 1788–1851* (Sydney: University of Sydney Press, 1980).

Haines, Gregory — 'The Traditions of Australian Catholics', *Tjurunga* 18 (1979), 113–126.

Haines, Gregory, Mary Gregory Forster, and Frank Brophy (eds.) *T h e Eye of Faith. The Pastoral Letters of John Bede Polding* (Melbourne: Lowden Publishing Company, 1978).

Hales, Edward Elton Young — *The Catholic Church in the Modern World. A Survey from the French Revolution to the Present* (Garden City, NY: Image Books, 1960).

Hawke, Shé M. — 'Seeking Matrology: A Reconsideration of the Under/mis representation of Early Church Women', *Studies in Spirituality*, 30 (2020), 229–251.

Heydon, Peter	'Heydon, Jabez King (1815–1885)', Australian Dictionary of Biography, National Centre of Biography, Australian National University, https://adb.anu.edu.au/biography/heydon-jabez-king-2180/text2765, published first in hardcopy in 1966 (Volume 1).
Higginbotham, George	'Science and Religion, or The Relations of Modern Science with the Christian Church, A Lecture' (Melbourne: Samuel Mueller, [1883?]).
Higgins, Rory, FSC	*The Woman of Many Names. Jane Hawthornthwaite (1805–1882)* (De La Salle Brothers, District of Australia, 2021).
Hilpisch, Stephanus, OSB	*History of Benedictine Nuns* (Collegeville, MN: St. John's Abbey Press, 1958).
Hitchcock, David	'Why History from below matters more than ever'. Online symposium, July 22, 2013. https://manyheadedmonster.com/2013/07/
Hollerman, Ephrem	'Where there was Need: Evangelization and North American Benedictines', *American Benedictine Review*, 63 (2012), 303–320.
Hollings, Michael (ed.)	*By Love Alone, Daily Readings with St. Therese of Lisieux* (London: Darton, Longman & Tod, 1986).
Hosie, John	'1859, Year of Crisis in the Australia Catholic Church', *Journal of Religious History* 7 (1973), 342–361.
Hosie, John	*A Lonely Road: Fr. Ted McGrath MSC* (Adelaide: ATF Press, 2010).
Hughes, Kathryn	*The Victorian Governess* (London and New York, NY: Hambledon, 1993).
Hughes, Robert	*The Fatal Shore. A History of the Transportation of Convicts to Australia, 1787–1868* (London: Collins Harville, 1987).

Hyland, William Patrick 'Missionary Nuns and the Monastic Vocation in Anglo-Saxon England', *American Benedictine Review* 47 (1996), 141–174.

Jenkins, Keith *Re-Thinking History* (London; New York, NY: Routledge, 1991).

Johnston, Elizabeth 'Francis Timoney: the Bushmen's Priest', *Journal of the Australian Catholic Historical Society* 16 (1994–1995), 39–53.

Judd, Stephen, and Kenneth J. Cable *Sydney Anglicans. A History of the Diocese* (Sydney: Anglican Information Office, 1987).

Kavenagh, Terence, OSB 'The End of the Sydney Benedictines: Some Further Documents', *Tjurunga* 8 (1974), 195–216.

Kavenagh, Terence, OSB 'Vaughan and the Monks of Sydney, Benedictine Tradition and Australia: Some Observations', *Tjurunga* 25 (1983) 147–233.

Knowles, David *Bare Ruined Choirs. The Dissolution of the English Monasteries* (Cambridge: Cambridge University Press, 1963).

Kullas, Henry *Sixtieth Anniversary of the Lawson Parish—an Insight into the History of the Lawson Parish* (Lawson, NSW: H. & A. Kullas, 1989).

Lafrance, Jean *My Vocation is Love* (Paris; Montreal: Éditions Paulines, 1994).

Latta, David *A Memorial to Forgotten Australian Buildings* (Sydney: Angus & Robertson, 1986).

Lawrence, Clifford Hugh *Medieval Monasticism: Forms of Religious Life in Western Europe in the Middle Ages* (London: Longman, 1984).

Leclercq, Jean 'Monasticism in the Church of Christ according to the Thought of Paul VI', *Cistercian Studies* 20 (1984), 204–214.

Lewis, Brian	*Our War: Australia during World War 1* (Melbourne: Melbourne University Press, 1980).
Lewis, Gertrud Jaron, and Jack Lewis	*Gertrud the Great of Helfta, Spiritual Exercises. Translation, Introduction Notes and Indexes* (Kalamazoo, MI: Cistercian Publications, 1989).
Linane, T. J.	*From Abel to Zundolovich Vol. 1: Contribution of Religious Orders Australian Priesthood Vocations up to 1900* (compiled by Fr. T. J. Linane. Melbourne: MDHC Catholic Archdiocese of Melbourne, 1979).
Livingston, Kevin	'Anselm Curtis', *Tjurunga* 8 (1974), 195–216.
Loades, Judith (ed.)	*Monastic Studies. The Continuity of Tradition* (Bangor: Headstart History, 1990).
Lotz, Ezekiel, OSB	'Quicquid Agunt Homines: "The Benedictine Cultural Mission to a Postmodern World"', *American Benedictine Review* 63 (2012), 75–92.
Lowrie, J. Daly, SJ	*Benedictine Monasticism: Its Formation and Development through the 12th Century* (New York, NY: Sheed and Ward, 1965).
Luttrell, John.	*Norman Thomas Gilroy. An Obedient Life* (Sydney: St. Paul's Publications, 2017).
McCusker, John, OSB	'Implementing a Program of Spiritual Direction at a Benedictine Monastery', *American Benedictine Review* 66 (2015), 20–29.
McDonough, J. C. D., OP	'Cloister for Nuns: from the Early Centuries to the 1917 Code', *Review for Religious* 54 (1995), 615–621.
MacDougall, Garry	*Belonging: A Photo Novel* (Belmont [N.S.W.]: Hightor Trading, 2007).
MacGinley, M. R.	*A Dynamic of Hope: Institutes of Women Religious in Australia* (Sydney: Crossing Press, 1996, corrected edition 2002).

MacGinley, M. R.	*A Lamp Lit. History of the Poor Clares, Waverley Australia, 1883–2004* (Sydney: St Paul's, 2005).
MacGinley, M. R.	*Ancient Tradition, New World — Dominican Sisters in Eastern Australia, 1867–1958* (Sydney: St Paul's, 2009).
MacGinley, M. R.	'Irish Women Religious and Australian Social History', *Journal of the Australian Catholic Historical Society* 17 (1996), 56–66.
Macintyre, Stuart	*Australia's Boldest Experiment—War and Reconstruction in the 1940s* (Sydney: UNSW Press, 2015).
Macintyre, Stuart	*The Oxford History of Australia.* Vol. 4: *The Succeeding Age, 1901–1942* (Melbourne: Oxford University Press, 1993).
Macintyre, Stuart, and Julian Thomas (eds.)	*The Discovery of Australian History 1890–1939* (Melbourne: Melbourne University Press, 1995).
Macmillan, David S. (ed.)	*Two Years in New South Wales, by Peter Cunningham, Surgeon, R.N.* (Sydney, Melbourne and London: Angus and Robertson, 1966).
Malone, Marie Therese	'Cardinal Moran and the Subiaco Constitutions', *Tjurunga* 32 (1987), 62–71.
Malone, Marie Therese	'An Obit List and Brief History of the Nuns of Subiaco, Rydalmere, and the Benedictine Abbey, Pennant Hills', *Tjurunga* 28 (1985), 35–80; 29 (1985), 47–71; 30 (1986), 74–80; 31 (1986), 58–78.
Marmion, Columba	*Christ The Ideal of the Monk: Spiritual Conferences on the Monastic and Religious life* (London: Sands, 1926).
Marmion, Columba	*Union with God: Letters of Spiritual direction* (Bethesda, MD: Zaccheus Press, 2006).

Matthews, Brian	*Federation* (Melbourne: Text Publishing, 1999).
Matthews, Jill Julius	*Good & Mad Women: The Historical Construction of Femininity in Twentieth Century Australia* (Sydney: Allen & Unwin, 1984).
Mitchell, Bruce	'Hargraves, Edward Hammond (1816–1891)', Australian Dictionary of Biography, National Centre of Biography, Australian National University, https://adb.anu.edu.au/biography/hargraves-edward-hammond-3719/text5837, published first in hardcopy 1972 (Volume 4).
Mohler, James A., SJ	*The Heresy of Monasticism* (New York, NY: Society of St. Paul, 1971).
Molony, John N.	*The Penguin Bicentennial History of Australia. The Story of 200 Years* (Ringwood: Paul Hamlyn, 1987).
Molony, John N.	*The Roman Mould of the Catholic Church* (Melbourne: Melbourne University Press, 1969).
Morrall, J. A.	*Saints of the Benedictine Order* (London: John Hodges, 1896).
Morrall, J. A. (ed.)	*The Benedictine Calendar, January, February and March* (London: John Hodges, 1896).
Morrissey, Jane	'Scholastica and Benedict: A Picnic, a Paradigm', in Julia B. Holloway, Constance S. Wright, and John Bechtold (eds.), *Equally in God's Image: Women in the Middle Ages* (New York, NY: Peter Lang, 1990), 251–260.
Mowle, L. M.	*A Genealogical History of Pioneer Families of Australia* (Adelaide: Rigby, 1978).
Murray, Les A. (selector)	*Anthology of Australian Religious Poetry* (Blackburn, Vic.: Collins Dove, 1986).

Murray, P.L.	*Official Records of the Australian Military Contingents to the War in South Africa* (Melbourne: A.J. Mullett, 1911). Archive.org.
Nairn, Bede	'Coningham, Arthur (1863–1939)', Australian Dictionary of Biography, National Centre of Biography, Australian National University, https://adb.anu.edu.au/biography/coningham-arthur-5749/text9737, published first in hardcopy in 1981 (Volume 8).
Nairn, Bede	'Macarthur, Hannibal Hawkins (1788–1861)', Australian Dictionary of Biography, National Centre of Biography, Australian National University, https://adb.anu.edu.au/biography/macarthur-hannibal-hawkins-2388/text3149. Published first in hardcopy in 1967 (Volume 2).
O'Connell, Mary	*Eileen O'Connor and the Founding of Sydney's Brown Nurses* (Sydney: Crossing Press, 2009).
O'Donoghue, Frances	*The Bishop of Botany Bay. The Life of John Bede Polding, Australia's First Catholic Archbishop* (Sydney: Angus & Robertson, 1982).
O'Farrell, Patrick	*The Catholic Church and Community in Australia* (Melbourne: Thomas Nelson, 1977).
O'Farrell, Patrick	*Documents in Australian Catholic History, Volumes 1 and 2* (London; Melbourne: Geoffrey Chapman, 1969).
O'Farrell, Patrick	*The Irish In Australia* (Sydney: UNSW Press, 1986).
O'Neill, George, SJ	*Life of the Reverend Julian Edmund Tenison-Woods (1832–1889)* (Sydney: Pellegrini, 1929).
O'Neill, Rose	*A Rich Inheritance: Galway Dominican Nuns* (Galway: Dominican Sisters, 1994).

Oppenheimer, Melanie	'Australian Women at War' (July 2008). https://anzacportal.dva.gov.au/resources/media/file/australian-women-and-war.
Orth, Clement R.	*The Approbation of Religious Institutes* (Canon Law Studies, No. 71; Washington, D.C.: Catholic University of America, 1931).
Papi, Hector	*Religious Profession: A Commentary on a Chapter of the New Code of Canon Law* (New York, NY: Kennedy and Sons, 1918).
Parkes, Henry	'The Crimson Thread of Kinship' (1890). http://foundation1901.org.au/the-crimson-thread-speech/.
Pearson, Charles Henry	*National Life and Character: A Forecast* (London: Macmillan, 1893).
Pender, Graeme	The Life and Contribution of Bishop Charles Henry Davis, OSB (1815–1854) to the Catholic Church in Australia (ThD thesis, University of Divinity, 2016). https://repository.divinity.edu.au/divinityserver/api/core/bitstreams/d69ea7b1-9289-4488-a8e2-11bdfd305fe1/content.
Phegley, Jennifer	*Courtship and Marriage in Victorian England* (Santa Barbara, Colorado and Oxford: Praeger, 2012).
Phillips, V., S. Drury, D. Latta, and R. Gurnani-Smith	*New Ways in an Ancient Land: Australia from Penal Colony to Prosperous Nation, 1778 to 1900* (Sydney: Bay Books, 1986).
Player, Anne V.	'Julian Tenison Woods 1832–1889: The Interaction of Science and Religion', Unpublished MA Thesis, Australian National University 1990.

Polding, John Bede	*Letters of John Bede Polding, Volumes 1, 2 and 3* (M. Xavier Compton, ed.; Glebe Point, New South Wales: Sisters of the Good Samaritan, 1996).
Port, Andrew I.	'History from Below, the History of Everyday Life, and Microhistory', *International Encyclopedia of the Social and Behavioral Sciences, 2nd edn.* (James D. Wright, ed.; Amsterdam: Elsevier, 2015 [1st: 2001]), 11: 108–113.
Potter, Lesley	'Independent Women: Midwives of two Cities, Sydney and Edinburgh in the mid-19th century', *Journal of the Australian Royal Historical Society* 101 (2015), 79–92.
Prendergast, Ann	'The Benedictine Schools and Students of Colonial Sydney', *Journal of the Australian Catholic Historical Society* 21 (2000), 67–79.
Press, Margaret	*John Henry Norton, Bishop of Railways* (Kent Town, South Australia: Wakefield Press, 1993).
[Princethorpe]	*A Short History of the Benedictines of Princethorpe* (Ditchling: Ditchling Press, 1945). This 40 page pamphlet is based upon Frideswide Stapleton, *The History of the Benedictines of St Mary's Priory Princethorpe* (Hinckley: Samuel Walker, 1930).
Principe, Walter H. CSB	'Western Medieval Spirituality', *The New Dictionary of Catholic Spirituality* (Michael Downey, ed.; Collegeville, MN: Liturgical Press, 1993), 1027–1039. Archive.org.
Rediker, Marcus	*The Slave Ship: A Human History* (New York, NY: Viking-Penguin, 2007).
Rees, Daniel	'The Benedictine Revival in the Nineteenth Century', in D.H. Farmer (ed.), *Benedict's Disciples* (Leominster: Fowler Wright, 2002 [1980]), 324–349.

Rheem Australia Limited	*The History of Rheem at Rydalmere* (Sydney: Rheem Australia Limited — Water Heater Division, 1992).
Risse, Guenter B.	*Mending Bodies, Saving Souls, A History of Hospitals* (Oxford: Oxford University Press, 1999).
Robson, R.W.	*Queen Emma: The Samoan-American Girl who Founded a Commercial Empire in 19th Century New Guinea* (Sydney: Pacific Publications, 1973).
Rudder, Lionel, J. V.	*Magnificent Failure: The Life and Times of Enoch William Rudder, 1801–1888 — founder of Kempsey* (Kempsey: Kempsey Shire Council, 1986).
Saunders, Kay, and Raymond Evans	*Gender Relations in Australia: Domination and Negotiation* (Sydney: Harcourt Brace Jovanovich, 1992).
Scheiba, Manuela, OSB	'Explanation of the Rule of Benedict, as a Sign of the Times. Rule Commentaries of the Twentieth Century', *American Benedictine Review* 61 (2010), 138–149.
Shanahan, Mary	*Out of Time, Out of Place, Henry Gregory and the Benedictine Order in Colonial Australia* (Canberra: Australian National University Press, 1970).
Sheldrake, Philip, SJ	*Spirituality and History* (London: SPCK, 1991).
Sherington, Geoffrey, and Craig Campbell	'The History of Education. The Possibility of Survival', *Change* 5 (2002), 46–64.
Shutz, Alfred	'The Dimensions of the Social World', in Arviel Broderson (ed.), *Collected Papers 11: Studies in Social Thought* (The Hague: Martinus Nijhof, 1964), 58–59.

Smith, C. E.   'Merewether, Francis Lewis Shaw (1811–1899)', Australian Dictionary of Biography, National Centre of Biography, Australian National University. https://adb.anu.edu.au/biography/merewether-francis-lewis-shaw-4189/text6737, published first in hardcopy 1974 (Volume 5).

Smith, C. E.   'F. L. S. Merewether', *Journal of the Royal Australian Historical Society* 59.1 (March 1973), 1–15.

Southerwood, W. T.   *A Time-Line of Catholic Australia* (Sandy Bay, Tasmania: Stella Maris Books, 1993).

Stanbrook Abbey   *Stanbrook Abbey Press: Ninety-two Years of its History* (Worcester: Stanbrook Abbey, 1970).

Stanbrook, Benedictines of   *In a Great Tradition, Tribute to Dame Laurentia McLachlan, Abbess of Stanbrook* (London: John Murray, 1956).

[Stinson],   *Subiaco Rydalmere, N.S.W.* (Sydney: Atkins, McQuitty, Limited, 1910), acknowledging W. Stinson, Photographer, West Maitland.

Stokes, J. Lort.   *Discoveries in Australia; With An Account of the Coasts and Rivers Explored and Surveyed During the Voyage Of H.M.S. Beagle, in the Years 1837-38-39-40-41-42-43, by Command of the Lords Commissioners of the Admiralty* (2 vols.; T. & W. Boone, 1846). Archive.org.

Sutera, Judith   *True Daughters: Monastic Identity and American Benedictine Women's History* (Atchison, KS: Mt. St. Scholastica, 1987).

Suttor, T. L.   'Polding's Intellectual Formation', *Tjurunga* 16 (1978), 15–28.

Therry, Sir Roger, Esq.   *Thirty Years Residence in New South Wales and Victoria, with a Supplementary Chapter on the Ticket of Leave System* (London: Sampson Low, Son and Co., 1863).

Thornton, Francis B.	*Cross Upon Cross: The Life of Pope Pius IX* (New York, NY: Benziger Brothers, 1955).
Thorpe, Osmund	'MacKillop, Mary Helen (1842–1909)', Australian Dictionary of Biography, National Centre of Biography, Australian National University, https://adb.anu.edu.au/biography/mackillop-mary-helen-4112/text6575, published first in hardcopy 1974 (Volume 5).
Totah, Mary David, OSB (ed.)	*The Spirit of Solesmes* (London: Burns & Oates, 1997).
Ullathorne, William	*The Catholic Mission in Australasia* (Adelaide: Libraries Board of South Australia, 1837).
Ullathorne, William	*The Horrors of Transportation Briefly Unfolded to the People* (Birmingham: R.P. Stone, 1838).
Ungunmerr Baumann, Miriam Rose	https:llwww.miriam rose-foundation.org.au.
University of Virginia	'Early Research and Treatment of Tuberculosis in the 19th Century [2007]', http://exhibits.hsl.virginia.edu/alav/tuberculosis/.
University of Western Sydney	'Female Orphan School', https://www.westernsydney.edu.au/femaleorphanschool/home.
Upton, Julia, RSM	'Thomas à Kempis', *The New Dictionary of Catholic Spirituality* (Michael Downey, ed.; Collegeville, MN: Liturgical Press, 1993), 832.
Van Zellar, Hubert	*Downside By And Large, A Double Fugue in Praise of Things Lasting and Gregorian* (London: Sheed & Ward, 1953).
Vermeersch, Arthur	'Religious Profession'. In *The Catholic Encyclopedia* (New York: Robert Appleton Company, 1911). http://www.newadvent.org/cathen/12451b.htm

Vogüé, Adalbert de	'Benoit, modèle de vie spirituelle d'après le Deuxième Livre des Dialogues de Saint Grégoire', *CollCist* 38 (1976), 158–173.
Voytas, Suzanne	*Elizabeth 1828: The Worst and Most Turbulent: From Celtic Cross to Southern Cross* (Springwood, NSW: Suzanne Voytas, 2010).
Waldersee, James	*Catholic Society in New South Wales, 1788–1860* (Sydney: University of Sydney Press, 1974).
Walker, Eliza	'Old Sydney in the Forties: Recollections of Lower George Street and "The Rocks"', dictated by Mrs Eliza Walker, *Journal of the Royal Australian Historical Society* 16/4 (1930), 292–320.
Walker, Graeme, and Terence Kavenagh	'The 1855 Monastic Declarations of St. Mary's Sydney: Adapting "RB" to Colonial Australia?', *Tjurunga* 35 (1988), 229–233.
Walsh, K. J.	*Yesterday's Seminary: A History of St. Patrick's Manly* (Sydney: Allen & Unwin, 1998).
Walsh, Margaret	*The Good Sams. Sisters of the Good Samaritan, 1857–1969* (Mulgrave, Victoria: John Garrett Publishing, 2001).
Wark, Anne	*Journal of a Voyage to Australia 1855–56: Myles Athy, a Recruit for St. Mary's monastery, Sydney* (Hindmarsh, SA: ATF Publishing, 2017).
Waterworth, J.	*Canons and Decrees of the Council of Trent* (London: C. Dolman, 1848).
Watson, Frederick	*History of the Sydney Hospital from 1811–1911* (Sydney: Government Printer, 1911).
Wolter, Maurus, OSB	*The Principles of Monasticism* (London and St. Louis, MO: Herder Book Co, 1962).
Wynne, John, SJ	*The Great Encyclicals and Letters of Leo XIII* (New York: Benziger Brothers, 1903).

ACKNOWLEDGEMENTS

PAGE	DESCRIPTION	SOURCE (AND PERMISSION)
Front Cover	*Subiaco* front drive, c. 1910	Photograph: W. Stinson. [no author], *Subiaco Rydalmere NSW* (Sydney: Attkins, McQuitty, Limited, 1910), probably from the Prospectus 1911 (no longer in JAA); see Prendergast, 'Benedictine Schools'.
Back Cover	View of *Vineyard*, Parramatta, ca. 1851–1858.	Pencil and wash watercolour. Artist: unknown. Mitchell Library, State Library of New South Wales (SV/95; a128373). https://collection.sl.nsw.gov.au/digital/QVbdlyg8rL8Dd Out of copyright.
ii–iii	Driveway into Jamberoo Abbey	Courtesy: Jamberoo Abbey
xii	Two nuns in Jamberoo Valley	Courtesy: Jamberoo Abbey
4	Sr Hildegard Mary Ryan, OSB	Courtesy: Jamberoo Abbey
10	Downside Abbey, Bath, England	Courtesy: Jamberoo Abbey
31	Entrance to Jamberoo Abbey	Courtesy: Jamberoo Abbey
34	Nun at well, Jamberoo Abbey	Courtesy: Jamberoo Abbey
36	Heraclitus	https://commons.wikimedia.org/wiki/File:Filosofo_detto_eraclito,_da_villa_dei_papiri,_peristilio_quadrato.jpg
38	Archbishop John Bede Polding (1794–1877), c. 1840s.	Courtesy: Jamberoo Abbey
40	Dame Magdalen le Clerc (1798–1878), c. 1848.	Stanbrook Abbey Archives, England. Courtesy: Jamberoo Abbey
42	Dame Gertrude More (1606–1633).	Stanbrook Abbey Archives, England. Courtesy: Jamberoo Abbey. https://www.flickr.com/photos/60861613@N00/4014963259/in/set-72157620725122065

48	Dom Henry Gregory OSB (1813–1877), c. 1840s.	Courtesy: Jamberoo Abbey.
53	Roman Catholic Church, Hyde Park [St Mary's, Sydney]	Mitchell Library, State Library of New South Wales (PX*D 123, item 2c; a623009) https://collection.sl.nsw.gov.au/record/YK5Qwl8n Drawings in Sydney [ca. 1840–1850] Watercolour drawing. Artist: unknown Out of copyright.
58	Cover for the Rule of St Benedict Hand tooled by the Benedictine Nuns, Jamberoo. Circa 1990s	Courtesy: Jamberoo Abbey.
61?	Philip Schäffer's land grant (top right corner)	Reuss and Browne's map of the subdivisions of Parramatta and environs [cartographic material] / compiled and drawn by F. H. Reuss & J. L. Browne. 1859. State Library of NSW: 74Vv7bxgZZJd; SLNSW_FL8772531
62	Samuel Marsden and Rowland Hassall to Thomas Moore Esqu, 17/3/1813	Moore College: Waterhouse Papers: 7c–7d Valuation of Waterhouse Farm at Parramatta 1813.
62	The Vineyard, c. 1830s	Mitchell Library, State Library of New South Wales (SV/95; 9arp6XXn) Pencil and wash drawing. Artist: unknown [c. 1851–1858] https://collection.sl.nsw.gov.au/record/9arp6XXn Out of Copyright.
65	Monastic Ceremonial	Courtesy: Jamberoo Abbey.
66	Legal Document signed by those entering the community	Courtesy: Jamberoo Abbey.
70	Princethorpe Monastic Ceremonial, c. 1600s	Courtesy: Jamberoo Abbey.
79	Lyndhurst College near Sydney	Mitchell Library, State Library of New South Wales (PXA 1988) William Leigh – Sketches in New South Wales, 1853. (No. 29). SLNSW_FL1149176. https://collection.sl.nsw.gov.au/record/1l4d8xq1 Out of copyright.
86	The Ascended Christ with Illawarra flame tree behind, Jamberoo Abbey Church	Courtesy: Jamberoo Abbey.
91	M. Magdalen Le Clerc (top centre) with Dom Bede Sumner and Angelo Ambrosoli, c. 1860s.	Courtesy: Jamberoo Abbey.

94	Subiaco, Rydalmere, c. 1850s.	Painting. Courtesy: Jamberoo Abbey.
100	Freeman's Journal Masthead, 2/1/1851	Trove, https://trove.nla.gov.au.
106	Prioress Walburge (Ruth Woods) Wallis, c. 1870s	Courtesy: Jamberoo Abbey.
108	Cloister window at night, Jamberoo Abbey	Courtesy: Jamberoo Abbey.
112	Bishop Charles Henry Davis OSB (1815–1854), c. 1850	Courtesy: Jamberoo Abbey.
117	Subiaco School, c. 1910	Photograph: W. Stinson. [no author], *Subiaco Rydalmere NSW* (Sydney: Attkins, McQuitty, Limited, 1910), probably from the Prospectus 1911 (no longer in JAA); see Prendergast, 'Benedictine Schools'.
120–121	Letter written by a pupil of Subiaco School to her father	Emily Heydon to Jabez King Heydon, 25/7/1852. Jamberoo Abbey Archives
124	Girls down by the Parramatta River, c. 1910	Photograph: W. Stinson. [no author], *Subiaco Rydalmere NSW* (Sydney: Attkins, McQuitty, Limited, 1910), probably from the Prospectus 1911 (no longer in JAA).
125	Emma Coe (1850–1913) as a schoolgirl in the United States	From the 'Sydney *Daily Mirror* 1970s', posted on https://pngaa.org/emma-coe-known-as-queen-emma-and-phoebe-coe-papua-new-guinea-1878-1944/
126	Down by the Parramatta River, c. 1910	Photograph: W. Stinson. [no author], *Subiaco Rydalmere NSW* (Sydney: Attkins, McQuitty, Limited, 1910), probably from the Prospectus 1911 (no longer in JAA).
127	Girls in drama class, c. 1910	Photograph: W. Stinson. [no author], *Subiaco Rydalmere NSW* (Sydney: Attkins, McQuitty, Limited, 1910), probably from the Prospectus 1911 (no longer in JAA).
128	View of Subiaco from Parramatta River, c. 1910	Photograph: W. Stinson. [no author], *Subiaco Rydalmere NSW* (Sydney: Attkins, McQuitty, Limited, 1910), probably from the Prospectus 1911 (no longer in JAA).
130	Archbishop John Bede Polding OSB, c. 1870	Courtesy: Jamberoo Abbey.

132	Sketch of Parramatta River, showing location of Subiaco (=McArthur house), 1853	State Library of New South Wales (A 331A) Illustrations from Progress in Public Works & Roads in NSW, 1827–1855/ Sir Thomas Mitchell. Sketch of Parramatta River (opp. p.304) NZ5Moq6dejkx7; FL3311251/FL3311595 (Web) https://collection.sl.nsw.gov.au/record/92eVDzPY/NZ5Moq6dejkx7. SLNSW_FL3311251 Out of copyright.
134	Archbishop Roger Bede Vaughan OSB (1834–1883), c. 1873	Courtesy: Jamberoo Abbey.
136	Sr Mary MacKillop (1842–1909) and Fr Julian Tenison Woods (1832–1889)	Painting for the Sisters of St Joseph of the Sacred Heart, Perthville, for their 125th Anniversary in 1997. Artist: Reg Campbell Courtesy: Jamberoo Abbey.
138	Dom Bede Sumner OSB, c. 1860s	Courtesy: Jamberoo Abbey.
140–141	A Postulant's List: what to bring when Entering the Monastery, 1871.	Jamberoo Abbey Archives
143	Dame Gertrude d'Aurillac Dubois OSB Abbess of Stanbrook Abbey 1872–1897	Stanbrook Abbey, England, Archives. Courtesy: Jamberoo Abbey.
151	Obituary: Magdalen (Constantia) le Clerc	*Cumberland Mercury,* 30 March 1878. Trove. https://trove.nla.gov.au/newspaper/article/248613659
156	Archbishop Patrick Francis Moran, c. 1880s	Courtesy: Jamberoo Abbey.
159	Map of Dundas - Ermington and Rydalmere. Parish of Field of Mars (1885–1890)	City of Sydney Archives. A-00530164 Atlas of the suburbs of Sydney, 1885–1890 (Higinbotham & Robinson) https://archives.cityofsydney.nsw.gov.au No copyright
163	Mother Justina (Eliza) Merewether, c. 1910	Courtesy: Jamberoo Abbey.
176	Mt St Margaret's Hospital, Ryde. Founded by the Little Company of Mary sisters, specializing in psychiatric nursing	State Library of New South Wales (PXA 635 item 777; 823353) Broadhurst collection of postcards of New South Wales scenes, ca. 1900-1927; Buildings of Ryde https://collection.sl.nsw.gov.au/record/Y0KBV6P1/2p4do43y5qpoN Out of copyright

184	Hildebrand de Hemptinne (1849–1913), first Abbot Primate of the Benedictine Confederation, c. 1890s	Courtesy: Jamberoo Abbey.
187	Death Certificate of Chloe North	Transcription from Registry of Births, Deaths and Marriages, requested by Kiama Family History Centre, 8 November 2023. Courtesy: Jamberoo Abbey.
193	Nuns during Adoration	Courtesy: Jamberoo Abbey.
195	W. Ullathorne, *The Horrors of Transportation* (1838)	National Library of Australia. Trove. https://nla.gov.au/nla.obj-448164941 Out of Copyright
197	Pictorial Souvenir of the Federation of Australia, 1 January 1901	National Library of Australia. Trove. http://nla.gov.au/nla.obj-90660157 Out of Copyright
200–201	Obituary: Prioress Walburge (Ruth Woods) Wallis	Philip Anderson, *The Tablet* 13 December, 1902 Trove, https://trove.nla.gov.au.
201	Death Certificate. Ruth Woods Wallis	New South Wales Registry of Births Deaths & Marriages. Death Certificate 15736/1902
204	Louisa Harnett (nee Murray), c. 1870s Mother of Prioress Ignatius Harnett OSB	Courtesy: Jamberoo Abbey.
208	St Mary's Cathedral today	Photograph: Peter Miller. Courtesy: Jamberoo Abbey.
212	The Plans for the Monastic Church	Courtesy: Jamberoo Abbey.
212	The Monastic Church, opened 1910	Courtesy: Jamberoo Abbey.
213	Archbishop Michael Kelly, early 1900s	Official Portrait Of Monsignor Michael Kelly (1850 - 1940), Former Archbishop Of The Metropolitan See Of Sydney, Australia. Courtesy: Jamberoo Abbey.
215	1915 Buick C Series hearse	Photographer unknown. Source: Grave Limos. https://www.pinterest.com.au/pin/725994402406016336/
218	Prioress Mary Joseph (Hilda May Brady), c 1915	Courtesy: Jamberoo Abbey.
225	Subiaco Community, c. 1923	Courtesy: Jamberoo Abbey.
229	Sr Mary Gabriel Enge OSB, c. 1923	Courtesy: Jamberoo Abbey.

234	Abbot Benoît Gariador, Abbot President of the Subiaco Cassinese Congregation, 1920–1928	The Subiaco Cassinese Congregation. The History of the Congregation https://www.benedettinisublacensicassinesi.org/the-congregation/the-history
235	Sr Mary Editha Thompson OSB, c. 1923	Courtesy: Jamberoo Abbey.
237	Prioress Mary Joseph Brady, Abbess Cecilia Heywood (Abbess of Stanbrook Abbey), Sr Mary Editha Thompson, Dame Laurentia McLachlan	Stanbrook Abbey Archives. Courtesy: Jamberoo Abbey.
239	1903 Singer Sewing Machine	1903 Instruction 4 Style No. 11, No. 27 Singer Sewing Machine Form 7468 Manual. https://www.ebay.com.au/itm/234576856325
242	"Cadia Park", Lawson, NSW, c. 1930s. Photo: Prioress Brady.	Courtesy: Jamberoo Abbey.
261	Laurence Schneider, Chaplain to US Navy, USS Pensacola, 1941	Courtesy: Jamberoo Abbey.
262	Monsignor Joseph J. McGovern, c. 1940s	Granville Parish, Australia, Archives. Courtesy: Jamberoo Abbey.
264	Stained glass from church, Jamberoo Abbey. 'Our Lady's side' (above); 'Our Lord's side' (below)	Courtesy: Jamberoo Abbey.
266	Mildred Potts, Prioress 1945–1957	Courtesy: Jamberoo Abbey.
271	Sr Patricia O'Shea OSB, Sr Marie Gregory Forster OSB, and Sr Elizabeth Funder OSB, c. 1949	Courtesy: Jamberoo Abbey.
272	Prioress Mildred Potts and the Community with Cardinal Norman Gilroy celebrating the centenary, 1949.	Courtesy: Jamberoo Abbey.
274	Benedictine Abbey, West Pennant Hills	Hornsby Shire Recollects Photograph: Trevor Patrick hornsbyshire.recollect.net.au/nodes/view/3470. Used with permission.
276	Icons in Jamberoo Abbey Church: Our Lady (of Vladimir) and Our Lord (Christ Pantocrator).	Courtesy: Jamberoo Abbey.
279	Jamberoo Abbey cottages	Courtesy: Jamberoo Abbey.
280	Two nuns walking, Jamberoo Abbey	Courtesy: Jamberoo Abbey.

INDEX

(Note: *italics* for pictures)

A

Abbess, title of 247–248
Abbey of Beuron 147–148, 162–163, 269; *see also* Beuronese Constitutions
Abbey of Notre Dame du Pré, Liseaux 237
Act of Union (1800) 7
Ad Normam Canonis 220–221
Altar Bread Department 265–266
Amshurst, Sr Editha 89
Anderson, Elizabeth 199
Anderson, Philip 199
Anglican Church 110, 161
Athy, Edmund 87–88

B

'the ban' 174, 179, 183–185
Beuronese Constitutions 73, 164, 168–169, 172, 174, 202, 205–206, 220–221, 267
Bible, in English 75–76
Birt, Henry Norbert 21
Boer War 191–192
Bourke, Richard 9
Bradshaw, Elsie 210
Brady, Sr Mary Joseph (Hilda May) 217–264, *218*, *237*
   election to Prioress 215
   finance and property matters 244, 254–259, 273
   personal history and qualities 207–210, 266–267, 268
   pilgrimage to Europe 233–237, 239–240
   resignation and death 263
   wartime leadership 260
Bridge, Sr Evangelista (Elvina McIntyre) 175–181
Britain, monasticism in 235–236
Bryant, Mary Magdalene 210
Burrows, Sr Placida (Elizabeth/Eliza) 65–67, 82, 98, 122
Butler, Prof. Thomas John 228

C

Cadia Park *see* Lawson Monastery
Cambrai community 7, 41; *see also* Stanbrook community
Cambrai Constitutions 44, 46
Canonical Visitations 133–135, 140, 162, 172, 174, 178, 250, 275
Carroll, Margaret 144
Casey, Michael 36
Cassinese Congregation 239–240, 249–250
de Castella, Clotilde 210
Catechism 160
Catholic emancipation 6–7, 44, 122–123, 133
Catholic Emancipation Act (1829) 6–8
Catholic Relief Acts (1778, 1791) 6, 7
Catholicism; *see also* Catholic emancipation

in Australia 8–10, 12–13, 144, 155, 157, 161, 177, 211
in England 122
Chapter of Faults 170
charism 5–6, 35–37, 59, 69, 135–138, 263, 277
du Chastelet, Madame 89–90
Children of Mary 119–122
Chisholm, Caroline 56–57
Chivot, Sr des Anges 89, 97
choir nuns 83, 139, 206
le Clerc, Dame Magdalen 7, 35–58, *91*
death 150–151
finance and property matters 92–93, 123
personal history and qualities 40, 42, 51, 76, 85
relational tensions 45, 96–97, 100, 131–133
at St Mary's 52–54
at Subiaco 63–64, 75, 82, 90–92, 105–107, 111–113, 129, 131–133, 195
Code of Canon Law (1917) 217–218, 231, 240–242
Coe, Emma 124–125
coenobium (community) 14
Collins, Neil 243–244
Comyn, Catherine 105
Conditae a Christo 198
Connolly, Catherine 152
Connolly, Rev. Philip 8
Connolly, Richard Hugh 101
conscription 218–220
Constitutions 130, 141, 155, 162–165, 177, 221–222, 247–248, 251–252; *see also* Beuronese Constitutions; Cambrai Constitutions; Princethorpe Constitutions
continuity 14, 36–37, 71, 92, 105, 123, 273, 277–279
convict transportation 193–195
cowls 253

D
dadirri 278
d'Apice, W. A. 254–255

Davis, Bishop Charles Henry 111–114, *112*
Day, Ann 40
devotio moderna 72–73
devotional practices 72–73, 94, 266–268
Diamond, Margaret 66, 104, 105
Diamond, Susannah 66, 104, 105
Dill Macky, Rev. William 182–183
discernment 99, 152
discipline 125–128, 171
discourse analysis 18–19
Donovan, Sr Evangelista (Joanna) 98–99, 107, 152
Dowling, Christopher 9
Downside Abbey 9–10, *10*, 11
Doyle, John Benedict 208–209
Doyle, Mary Agnes 208–209
Dubois, Dame Gertrude D'Aurillac 142, *143*
Dwyer, John 98
Dwyer, Michael 98, 187
Dwyer, Rose 98
Dwyer, Sr Elizabeth (Mary Ann) 98

E
ecclesiastical embroidery 47, 230, 238
education 55–58, 60, 110–111, 144–147, 211; *see also* Subiaco school
Edwards, Laura 230
Egan, Agnes 152
Emblem, Sr Patrick (Sarah Catherine) 144
enclosure 143, 145; *see also* episcopal enclosure; papal enclosure
Enge, Sr Mary Gabriel (Elsie) 228–229, *229*
episcopal enclosure 225–226
Eucharist, the 6, 267–268
Europe, monasticism in 236–237
Exercises of St Gertrud the Great 74–75, 147
extern sisters 257

F

Faber, Fr Frederick 132–133
Fairland, Maria Rose 151
fasting 37, 221–222
feasts 165–167
Federation 191–192, 196–198
finance and property matters 92–93, 185–186, 214–215, 230, 238, 243–247, 273–275; *see also* Great Depression
Fitzpatrick, Sr Dominic (Margaret) 104, 195
Fitzpatrick, Thomas 104
food rules 251–252
Forster, Sr Marie Gregory (Marie Margaret) 21–22, *271*, 272
Freeman's Journal 100
Funder, Sr Elizabeth *271*, 272–273

G

Gabriel, Sr Mary Clare (Florence Eugenie) 151–152, 192
Gabriel family 124
Gallagher, Margaret 144
Gariador, Abbot Benedict 232–234, *234*
genealogy 15–16
Gilroy, Archbishop Norman Thomas 254–259
Gogarty, Catherine 230
Gold Rush 93, 123
Good Samaritan Sisters 207
Gothic Revival 47
Great Depression 244–247
Gregory, Henry 47, *48*, 52, 54–55, 80, 88, 106, 114, 122, 127
Gregory, Sr Scholastica (Jane) 7, 35–58, 63–64, 80, 82
Grey, Sir George 189
Guest House 252–253
Guilfoyle, Angela 66, 82

H

Harnett, John 204
Harnett, Margaret Louisa (née Murray) 203, *204*

Harnett, Patrick 203
Harnett, Sr Ignatius (Elizabeth Louisa) 203–216
Hawthornthwaite, Sr M. Bernard (Victorine) 98
Hay, Mary Anne 151
de Hemptinne, Hildebrand *184,* 184–185
Hennessy, Honora 183, 206
Heydon, Catherine 121
Heydon, Emily 121, 145
Heydon, Jabez King 121–122
Heydon, Sr Xaveria (Catherine) 100–101
Heywood, Abbess Cecilia 237
Higginbotham, George 156
Higgins, Dr Joseph 174, 178
'Hillcrest' 274–275
Hishon, Mary Ellen 151
Hogan, Mary 104
horarium 67–72
hospitality 135–139
Hunt, Fanny Elizabeth 160
Hurley, Margaret 186–187
hymns 49, 133

I

Imitation of Christ, The 74
immolation of self 71
indigenous people 114, 186–191
Indulgences 267
industrial development 273–275
Irish Christian Brothers 80, 146

K

Kelly, Archbishop Michael 202, 211, 213, *213,* 219, 224, 246–247
Kelly, Margaret 210

L

labora 77–85
L'année liturgique 76
Lawson Monastery *242,* 242–245, 256–257, 266, 268–269
lay sisters 168–169, 206
Lectio Divina 6, 51, 68–69, 72–73, 116–117, 263

Lett, Benedict (Alicia) 65–67, 98, 111
Lett, Helen Maria Magdaline 66
letters 171, 229
liturgy 165–167
Liturgy of the Hours 64, 75, 94, 116, 227, 238, 266, 270; *see also horarium*
Loughnan, Sr Placid (Isabella) 102, 131, 163
Loughnan family 131
Lyndhurst Academy 111, 146, 204, 228

M

Macarthur, Hannibal Hawkins 59–60, 158
MacKillop, Sr Mary 135–138, *136*, 177
Macklin, Margaret 170, 183
Macready, Agnes 192
Makinson, Edith 78
Makinson, Mr 53
Marmion, Columba 269–270
Marum, Julia 78, 119
Maurus (and Placid), Benedict disciples 67, 117, 147, 165, 167, 206
McCabe, Fr 257
McCarthy, E. J. 243, 244
McCarthy, Sr Scholastica 89, 92, 96–97
McConnell, Sr Boniface 260
McEnroe, Father John 8
McGovern, Monsignor Joseph 262, *262*
McLachlan, Dame Laurentia 237
McLachlan, Sr Gertrude (Teresa) 152–154
Merewether, Francis Lewis Shaw 103
Merewether, Sr Justina (Eliza) 103, 162, *163*, 175–181, 207–208
Montargis community 7
monuments 57–58
Moran, Archbishop Patrick Francis 155–202, *156*, 206
More, Dame Gertrude 41, 42
More, Thomas 41
Murray, Margaret Louisa *see* Harnett, Margaret Louisa
Murray, Sir Terence Aubrey 203
Muschialli, Agnes Ruby 210

N

Nagle, Sr M. Gertrude (Eliza) 101–102
New Norcia Abbey 221, 239–240, 250–251
North, Chloe Mary Hurley 186–191, 230
Norton, Rev. John Henry 207

O

oblates 252
obsculta 12, 78, 227, 251
O'Connor, Sr Mary Anthony (Nora Mary) 245
O'Grady, Margaret 151
Olier, Bishop 211
O'Mahony, Bishop 177
Order of St Benedict 32–33
O'Shea, Sr Mary Cecilia (Patricia) 271, *271*
O'Sullivan, Bridget 151
out-sisters 252

P

Panico, Most Rev. John 257
papal enclosure 223–228, 241, 246–247, 255–259
Parkes, Henry 147
Parkinson, Esther 151
Parkinson, Sara 144
Pechy, Frances 183, 206
'perfection' 50, 71
Perpetual Abbess 248, 249
Perpetual Adoration 193–194, 227–228
Placid (and Maurus), Benedict disciples 67, 117, 147, 165, 167, 206
plain chant 148–149, 209–210
Plunkett, John Herbert 8
Polding, John Bede *38*, 130
  authority and jurisdiction 64, 114–115
  consecration 11
  Constitutions 43–46, 95
  finance and property matters 78, 92, 130
  ministry to convicts 11, 152, 195
  mission to Australia 10, 11, 13, 37–40, 47–53, 87–90, 95–96
  pastoral practice 35, 95, 99, 134, 141, 152
  relational tensions 57, 98–99, 127, 172–173

at St Mary's 13
at Subiaco 63–64, 109, 127–128, 131–135
Pope Benedict XV 220
Pope Gregory the Great 15, 20
Pope Leo XIII 157, 198–199, 231–232
Pope Pius IX 194
Pope Pius XI 237
Postulant's List 139–141
Potts, Sr Mildred (Gladys) 253–254, 260, 265–275, *266*
Power, Rev. Daniel 9
prayer 72, 149, 192–194, 213–214, 219, 227, 259, 270, 278–279; *see also* Lectio Divina; Liturgy of the Hours
Prendergast, Ann 21–22
priests 37
Princethorpe Constitutions 43–46, 69–73, 89–90, 95, 103, 162–163
Princethorpe Priory 37–40, 41–43, 88–90, 248
probation 169–170

Q
Quirk, Rev. Norbert 228

R
rationalism 155–157
Regan, Sr Angela (Eliza) 98, 123
religious profession 231
reparation 192–194, 228
Rios, Romanus 221, 251
Rudder, Archibald 192
Rudder, Lindsay Ernest 192
Rudder, Wilfred 192
Rule of Benedict (RB80) 11–14, 20–21, 39, 73–75, 103–104
avarice 214
charity 245
discernment 99
humility 54
Lectio Divina 68–69
patience 172–173
religious profession 231
small faults 171
Rydalmere 158, *159*

S
Sacramental Test Act (1828) 7, 8
Schäffer, Philip 60
Schahill, Bridget 104
Schneider, Laurence *261*
Scholastica, Sr Mary 40
Sconce, Mr 53
Searson, Sr Mary Ethelreda (Margaret) 223, 231
Second Vatican Council 241–242
Sheehy, Fr Austin 131, 172–173, 202
Shortall, Bridget 104
sick, care of 81, 84–85
Sisters of Charity 80
Smythe, Lucy 183, 206
St Benedict 20, 116; *see also* Order of St Benedict; Rule of Benedict
St Cuthbert's College, Durham *121*, 122–123
St Mary's Cathedral, Sydney 208, *208*
St Mary's Church, Sydney 9, 52–55, *53*
St Mary's College, Sydney 13, 79, *79*, 111
St Scholastica 16
Stanbrook community 7, 40–41, 45, 97, 105–106, 115, 140, 142–143, 252
Stokes, John Lote 189–190
Stotzingen, Fr Fidelis 249
Subiaco church 210–214, *212*
Subiaco community 87–107, *94*, 149–152, 157–158, *225*
accessibility 149–150
Constitutions 69–71, 162–163
disease and deaths 82–84
estrangement from Archdiocese 172–174, 183
hospitality 135–139
jurisdiction 250
property matters 63, 130, 232–233, 250, 275; *see also* papal enclosure
tradition and ambient culture 240–242
Subiaco school 109–128, *117*, 144–146, 197–198, 222–223
suffering 54, 71–72
Sugrue, Honora 210
Sumner, Rev. Bede 129–130, *138*
Sydney Archdiocese 47

T

Therry, Jane 102
Therry, Rev. John Joseph 8–9
Therry, Roger 8, 102
Thompson, Sr Mary Editha 235, *235*, 237, 238, 269
Timoney, Fr Francis 191–192
Torreggiani, Bishop 153–154
tradition 36, 48, 227, 240–242
transport 149–150, 158
tuberculosis 82–84

U

Ullathorne, William 9–11, 194
Ungenmerr-Baumann, Dr Miriam Rose 278

V

Vaughan, Archbishop Roger Bede *134*, 134–135, 140–142, 146–147, 152–154, 162

Vestment Department 238, 266
'The Vineyard' 59–64, *62*
vows 223, 231–232

W

Waite, Dorothy 145
Wallington, Miss 209–210
Wallis, Walburge (Ruth Woods) 98, 105–107, *106*, 129–154, 162–164, 188, 199–202
Walsh, Mary 104, 210
Waterhouse, Henry 60
Wilson, Sr Placid (Edna) 275
wine 168
Wolter, Maurus and Placid 29, 147–148, 269
Woods, Fr Julian Tenison *136*, 136–137
World War I 215, 218–220
World War II 259–262

www.ingramcontent.com/pod-product-compliance
Lightning Source LLC
Chambersburg PA
CBHW041507010526
44118CB00006B/180